THE COMPOSER'S POINT OF VIEW

Essays on Twentieth-Century Choral Music

by Those Who Wrote It

THE COMPOSER'

Essays on Twentieth-Centur

Edited

OINT OF VIEW

horal Music by Those Who Wrote It

OBERT STEPHAN HINES

NORMAN · UNIVERSITY OF OKLAHOMA PRESS

THE PUBLICATION OF THIS VOLUME HAS BEEN AIDED
BY A GRANT FROM THE FORD FOUNDATION.

Library of Congress Catalog Card Number: 63–18073

*Copyright 1963 by the University of Oklahoma Press,
Publishing Division of the University.
Manufactured in the U.S.A. First edition.*

O sing unto the Lord a new song:
sing unto the Lord, all the earth.
Sing unto the Lord, bless his name;
show forth his salvation from day
to day.
Declare his glory among the heathen,
his wonders among all people.
For the Lord is great, and greatly
to be praised:
he is to be feared above all gods.
For all the gods of the nations are
idols:
but the Lord made the heavens.
Honor and majesty are before him:
strength and beauty are in his sanctuary.

PS. 96:1–6

INTRODUCTION

THIS BOOK is a collection of essays by twentieth-century composers in which each composer discusses a large choral work or works he has written, along with the principles that guided the composition. These essays were compiled and published because it was felt that the whole subject of contemporary choral literature had been neglected far too long. Regretfully, there is very little in print on this topic. Books simply do not exist, and the articles which are scattered throughout many domestic and foreign periodicals are, in most instances, not very definitive. Volume V, *Vocal Music,* in Sir Donald F. Tovey's collection, *Essays in Musical Analysis,*[1] long a standard reference for the choral musician and devotee, does not extend itself beyond the early years of our century. This is not a criticism. Tovey's objective was to compile a collection of his writings in which he had analyzed monumental choral works from the Renaissance through all periods of music history up to the early years of the twentieth century. His book remains to this day a useful and respected source of knowledge.

In all fairness, it must be acknowledged that the seed for *The Composer's Point of View* is a hybrid growing out of the Tovey collection. However, there are some significant factors that make this present volume quite different from the other. First of all, the essays are written by the composers themselves, the creators of the art, and are not the observations and opinions of a musicologist or critic. In this respect, *The Composer's Point of View* is unique in the history of music and publication. As far as I can discover, there has never been a similar volume— one in which the composers of a particular period have shared their views about their music and creative processes in a collection specifically

[1] Oxford University Press, 1937.

vii

devoted to this precept. These writings, consequently, may well become primary sources, a heritage of historical-musical documents, with universal appeal for succeeding generations of musicians and historians.

The performer has always found the written word a useful tool in his task as the re-creator of sound. The reason is basic: music's system of notation is and has been incapable of communicating subtle nuances of sound, style, and interpretation which characterize every artistic, aesthetically satisfying performance. Unfortunately, the performer's role of re-creating music exactly according to the composer's wishes is an ideal state which has rarely existed in the history of music. In the quest to be faithful to the composer's intentions, the performer has found it necessary to depend on other sources: the custom of passing musical tradition verbally from teacher to pupil; listening to performances— live or, more recently, on recordings; and the written word. Music, even in the twentieth century, is still a perishable art because of the weakness of its notational system. For this reason, the composers in this collection were asked to make suggestions concerning the "correct" interpretation of their music. Happily, most did.

The idea of gathering essays dealing with twentieth-century choral music germinated out of the inquiries of my students and myself into the problems just discussed. For when one stops to consider it, the entire study of music, be it theoretical, historical, or interpretational, is chiefly concerned with the study of the results of the creative process. In essence, this book explores this many-sided subject in the choral medium during the first six decades of the present century.

Although it would have been desirable, it was not possible for the editor to gather writings by all the leading twentieth-century composers. The reasons are easy to explain. Several composers who have made significant contributions are deceased. And there are several living composers who were unable to contribute because of previous commitments and commissions. Finally, there is a third group who prefer not to write about their music. It was interesting to note that the composers who were unable to participate expressed an intense concern in the project.

Even though the picture is incomplete, the reader will notice that the composers in this volume exemplify a vast majority of the styles of composition practiced in the first half of our century. When scanning the list of contributors, one cannot help being startled at the prodigious variety of individual musical expressions which the term "contemporary music" encompasses. Think of the stylistic differences between men like Howard Hanson, whose musical idiom is post-Romantic, and Ernst Krenck, who writes in a dodecaphonic idiom. These men and others make up this term "contemporary music" which is, in reality, so general. The standard joke that "all modern music sounds alike" certainly does not hold true.

When the format of *The Composer's Point of View* was drawn up, it was decided to invite the composers to write reflective, introspective articles describing musical as well as nonmusical factors that shaped their music. An insight into the creative act would be invaluable to the performer concerned with re-creating works by the composers, to the young musician learning and trying to understand the magnitude of the disciplines involved in music, and to the listener-reader seeking a wider knowledge of contemporary choral music and its new forms. To achieve the objective of the format, the composers were given every freedom to discuss their music in whatever manner they chose. An outline concerning the content of the essays was drawn up by myself, but the composers were informed that it was to serve only as a guide to the general information which readers might expect.

This liberal approach seemed imperative if the reader was to gain an insight into the composer as a man. It must be agreed: the composer as the creator of musical art and the composer as the man are inseparable. He is a part of society and a man with personal, philosophical, social, political, and religious beliefs which influence his life and art. These beliefs are impossible to trace in instrumental music, but in choral music the text invariably echoes the composer's inner convictions. It might be possible for a composer to set a text to music which is completely alien to his thinking, but it is quite unlikely. As will be seen in the essays that follow, composers have definite beliefs which guide and often dictate texts they choose to set for chorus.

Even though the composers had complete freedom in selecting the works which they would discuss, a majority of the existing choral forms developed in music's history are represented in this collection: Mass, secular and sacred oratorio, symphonic-choral tone poem, cantata, symphony with voices, a setting of the Lamentations of Jeremiah, and a collection of hymns and responses for the church year. This outcome is entirely accidental but a delightful surprise, for at no time did I hint, recommend, or cajole a composer into writing about a particular work.

An important fact which this collection demonstrates is that there is still an intense interest in choral composition, even though historians are inclined to label the twentieth century an instrumental age. The complexities of modern musical language can be and have been reconciled to choral music. Composers in our time, like those in every period of history, have built their personal expression upon the strong, natural qualities of human voices. These men have discovered anew the warm nuances and subtle beauties of choral singing that have always granted this kind of music a special place in the hearts of men.

This collection offers something to the music student, professional, musicologist, aesthetician, and layman. The reader expecting a note-by-note, chord-by-chord analysis of each choral work will probably be disappointed. The independence given the composers was not intended to accomplish this result. On the other hand, to the reader looking for a glimpse of the composer who expresses himself freely, and often in an outspoken manner, about his art, these essays will be more acceptable. Basically, the content of the articles should be evaluated in two respects: what each offers as a single essay reflecting a particular composer and his music, and what all the essays offer as a summary of twentieth-century musical thought and the problems of writing in the choral medium. In this light, the collection takes on new and more profound meanings with each successive reading. Whatever meanings the words and ideas expressed assume, it is frankly hoped that this publication will stimulate frequent performances and more recordings of contemporary choral literature. For this is music's sole function: to be heard!

A section of Musical Examples appears at the back of this book. In it are portions of the works of each artist except Lukas Foss, who prefers readers examine his complete scores. The other examples are, I believe, an invaluable adjunct to the essays, and I am grateful to the following music publishers who have allowed their reprinting: Summy-Birchard Publishing Company, Evanston, Illinois (Howard Hanson); Bärenreiter Music Publishers, Inc., New York and Kassel (Ernst Krenek); Carl Fischer, Inc., New York (Peter Mennin); Elkan-Vogel Co., Inc., Philadelphia (Vincent Persichetti and Bernard Rogers); H. W. Gray Co., Inc., New York (Leo Sowerby); Schott & Co., Ltd., London (Peter Racine Fricker, Michael Tippett, Conrad Beck, Karl-Birger Blomdahl, and Jean Françaix); Novello & Co., Ltd., London (Anthony Milner); Alfred Lengnick & Co., Ltd., London (Edmund Rubbra); Edizioni Suvini Zerboni, Milan (Luigi Dallapiccola); Éditions Costallat, Paris (Jean Langlais); Universal Edition, Vienna (Frank Martin); and B. Schott's Soehne, Mainz (Hermann Reutter). The Beck, Blomdahl, Françaix, Martin, and Reutter examples are used by permission of the original copyright owners and their United States representative, Associated Music Publishers, Inc., New York. The excerpt from the Gregorian *Salve Regina* is taken from the *Liber Usualis,* published by Desclée & Co., Tournai, Belgium, and is published by special permission.

Readers are encouraged to avail themselves also of the Catalogues of Composers' Works at the end of this volume. Most lists contain choral music of varying difficulty which can be performed in many situations. And, although these essays are devoted to the choral art, everyone should be acquainted with the composers' compositions in other media. The choral musician or instrumentalist who closets his mind with one phase exclusively is committing a serious sin of omission. In our age, really since the advent of music for voices and instruments, the interchange of ideas between the two areas has been so constant that any divorce of the two media is unthinkable.

These introductory remarks would be inconceivable without my expressing my deep, heartfelt thanks to the contributors. All these men gave freely of themselves despite heavy schedules as administrators, teachers, performers, and, most vital of all, composers. They gave freely of their most precious gift—time—simply because they believed in the necessity of a compendium of thought on twentieth-century music. I truly regret that it is impossible for each reader to share the pleasure which I experienced in corresponding with the composers during the months it took to gather the manuscripts. In essence, the letters revealed two basic traits which have characterized great men in every period of history: humility and devotion.

In closing, I also wish to thank the University of Oklahoma Press for its faith in this book.

ROBERT STEPHAN HINES

Wichita, Kansas
September 30, 1963

CONTENTS

PART ONE

United States Composers

1. *The Prairie, A Parable of Death,* and *Psalms*

LUKAS FOSS

Lukas Foss (born on August 15, 1922, in Berlin) showed unusual talent in piano and composition at an early age, having a piano work published when he was only fifteen. He came to the United States with his parents in 1937 and subsequently entered the Curtis Institute in Philadelphia. There he studied piano with Isabelle Vengerova, composition with Rosario Scalero and Randall Thompson, and conducting with Fritz Reiner. Several summers were spent in the conducting classes of Serge Koussevitzky at the Berkshire Music Center. Later at Yale, composition instruction was continued with Paul Hindemith. Foss was the youngest composer to be awarded a Guggenheim Fellowship (1945). He was pianist for the Boston Symphony Orchestra from 1944 to 1950, when he resigned to accept a two-year Fulbright Scholarship for study in Rome. In February, 1953, he became professor of composition and conductor of the university orchestra at the University of California in Los Angeles. A brilliant pianist and conductor, Foss frequently appears with major orchestras in the United States and abroad performing standard repertoire as well as his own compositions. In 1963, Foss became conductor of the Buffalo Philharmonic Orchestra.

I THINK of myself as a "vocal" composer. I have set words to music as long as I can remember. At the age of eight I composed a children's opera in German. At ten I wrote a French solo cantata. Though my chief instrument is the piano, the number of my vocal compositions far exceeds the number of my piano pieces.

Words help me; they suggest a meaning and a form, they set a task for me. They give me ideas, much in the way tone-rows sometimes give ideas to the dodecaphonic composer. There is scarcely a page in the dictionary that does not contain at least one word which I have set to music at one time or another. Yet, for all this, the number of songs that I have composed is small. I have not attempted a song cycle until

3

recently (though single songs occur in my larger works, cantatas, operas). On the other hand, there were but few years in my life when I did not write, or at least plan, a composition involving a chorus.

I like choruses. I like the idea of people singing. What attracted me to music in the first place was no mere fascination with sound, but rather people, playing and singing.

My choral music is not easy to master rhythmically. In my most recent work frequent atonal passages tend to create an added pitch-difficulty for the vocalist. Chances are that my next choral work will make extreme demands on the singers. New music, of course, has always been difficult music. I am very conscious of the difference between "difficulty" and "rewarding difficulty." The performer thrives on the latter. He wants to be challenged. He needs a music through which he may reveal *his* sound, *his* technique, *his* phrasing, a music in which he can function, live, and exercise his powers. To what extent I may have succeeded in creating such music, such vehicles for the performer, is not for me to say; nor is such assessment essential at a time when the bulk of my work lies, I hope, still before me.

Frankly, I consider all my music up to 1959 that of a young composer—in other words, early work. The pieces which I shall discuss here all belong to this early period and were written over a span of fifteen years. I shall cover three choral works: *The Prairie* (1941–42), *A Parable of Death* (1952), and *Psalms* (1955–56).

A few words about my approach to texts may be in order here. Once I choose a text I become extremely involved in it. The text must be just right for me, and right for me at that time in my life. I am reluctant to set to music a text chosen for me by others, commissioning parties, for instance. Even my finding a text beautiful is not enough. It has to be something I can live with, day in, day out. Nor do I seem able to set a text in a straight manner, the way the poet wrote it. I like to "play" with a text, combining, omitting, dividing into sections, exchanging the order of paragraphs or verses. This seemingly highhanded manner of dealing with the text has always been my way of working with words. Perhaps I am a frustrated poet at heart, or perhaps it is just the feeling that a composer does not merely add music to a text, he must "use" the text. He must have the courage to alter, even at the risk of spoiling. The poem will continue to exist in the form the poet gave it; in the new musical form it will serve a purpose—in short, it will *serve*.

No, I cannot believe in the perfect marriage of poetry and music. A marriage is based on a mutual need. Poetry does not need music. Rainer Maria Rilke has said: "I want to fill the whole room with my own voice. I do not want to be interpreted, expressed, labelled, illustrated." Most poets will subscribe to this. Poetry in need of music must be poor poetry. Empty moments in films are filled up, warmed up by music. Good poetry needs music as little as good music needs dance. Music can be made to serve dance, and poetry can be made to serve music. In either case, one art is in the background, the other in the foreground. This hardly implies a marriage. The Wagnerian ideal of the *Gesamt-Kunstwerk* has never been realized, even by Wagner.

But if this is so, what right do composers have to tackle poetry? My answer is: none whatsoever. Whenever I set poetry to music, I feel that I owe the poet an apology. I feel that I destroy his poem in the form in which I use it, I feel that I break its inner subtlety, but offer the subtlety of my notes in exchange, as an apology and as a token of my love for the violated poem. I seem to say, "Here, I used, I spoiled, but take my notes in return. They are (paradoxically enough) a homage to your poem." This attitude, seemingly arrogant at first sight, is on closer examination more modest and certainly more realistic than the common view that through music the composer improves, adorns, renders more complete and more beautiful that which has lived years or even centuries without his unsolicited musical addition.

But must we always spoil the poem when we set it to music? Need one always tamper with the poem? Perhaps not, yet even when the composer sets a text without changing, cutting, or repeating, music does have a way of destroying the poem, by the persistence of its moods, by the naïveté of musical declamation (infinitely less subtle than recited declamation), by its way of underlining, climax-building, emotional pinpointing: all this when, after all, the simple, sober word is what the poet intended, no more, no less.

And now for a brief discussion of the three choral works:

The Prairie was composed in the summers of 1941 and 1942 at Monterey, Massachusetts. The first performance took place in Town Hall,

New York, in 1943, with Robert Shaw conducting the Collegiate Chorale and an orchestra of thirty-five musicians. (This occasion, incidently, marked Robert Shaw's first venture with an orchestra.) Subsequent hearings included a performance with Arthur Rodzinsky, the New York Philharmonic Orchestra, and the Westminster Choir. The cantata can be done with either a chamber orchestra or a symphony orchestra.

Minimum orchestration:

    1 Flute (interchangeable with piccolo)
    1 Oboe (interchangeable with English Horn)
    1 Clarinet (interchangeable with Bass Clarinet)
    1 Bassoon (interchangeable with Contra Bassoon)
    1 Horn
    3 Trumpets
    1 Trombone
    1 Man for Timpani and Percussion
    1 Piano
      Strings

The duration is roughly fifty minutes. Besides the chorus and orchestra, *The Prairie* requires four soloists (soprano, alto, tenor, and bass).

Carl Sandburg's poem *Prairie* (from *Cornhuskers*) is young and enthusiastic. So was I. In *Prairie*, I recognized the oratorio potential (a certain flair for recognizing musical potential in a text is a valuable asset for the composer of vocal music).

True to the manner outlined above, I began to work on the text. I divided *Prairie* into seven sections:

    I. I Was Born on the Prairie
       Tenor Solo
   II. Dust of Men
       Chorus—Soloists
  III. They Are Mine
       Alto Solo—Chorus
       (Soprano Solo in the Introduction)
  IV. When the Red and the White Men Met
       Chorus

6

V. In the Dark of a Thousand Years
  Bass Solo—Male Chorus
VI. A. Cool Prayers
   Chorus
  B. O Prairie Girl
   Soprano Solo
  C. Songs Hidden in Eggs
   Soprano and Alto Duet
VII. To-morrow
  Chorus—Soloists

The order of these sections is not always true to the order of the poem. Add the many omissions and one will appreciate the hesitance, even fear, with which I approached the poet whose permission had to be secured. To my amazement, Carl Sandburg wrote: "You have revitalized the old poem." He wrote to his publishers: "Give the young man a break. It seems he has approached the music in the same sporting way in which I wrote the poem." Two or three years later I made Carl Sandburg's acquaintance. We met at Grand Central Station, New York, and proceeded to a political dinner where he introduced me as the "young demon welter-weight composer." In my many subsequent dealings with poets and librettists I have not always met with Sandburg's gallantry.

In *The Prairie* the solo tenor takes the part of the poet, speaking. The chorus is the Prairie, the earth, which buries the dead, which sees cities growing:

> *I am here when the cities are gone.*
> *I am here before the cities come.*
> *I nourished the lonely men on horses.*
> *I will keep the laughing men who ride iron.*
> *I am the Prairie, mother of men, waiting.*

Some of the sentences in *Prairie* are long and hard to set:

> *Listen to six mockingbirds flinging follies of O-be-joyful*
> *Over the marshes and uplands.*

It may be amusing to quote here the longest sentence I ever set to music. It occurs in a short choral piece, "Behold! I Build an House" (from Chronicles), for chorus and organ (or two pianos):

7

Behold, when they lifted up their voice, and praised the Lord,
With trumpets and cymbals and instruments of music, saying:
For He is good, for His mercy endureth forever, then the house
was filled with a cloud, for the glory of the Lord had filled
the house of God.

It is a challenge to overcome the difficulty which such a sentence presents. The only type of difficulty I avoid is that of setting words in a language I do not speak. I only did this once, with a Hebrew prayer, "Adon Olom," for chorus, tenor, and organ.

The Prairie contains passages which, taken by themselves, could be criticized on stylistic grounds. But they belong. I would not change a note now, except in the orchestration. It is its overall abundance which makes *The Prairie* peculiarly convincing. It is one of those terribly early works where the mature author looks almost with envy at the young author he no longer is, wondering why the work is so much better than "he knew how."

A Parable of Death was composed in Rome, Italy, in 1952. It was commissioned by the Louisville Philharmonic Society for Vera Zorina, Recitante. There is one superficial resemblance to *The Prairie:* this composition is also divided into seven parts.

 I. Prologue—O God, Give unto Every Man His Death
   Chorus
 II. Sing Now the Lovers
   Tenor Solo—Narrator—Chorus
 III. A. Who Built This House Where the Heart Has Led
   Chorus
   B. To Those Who Have Grace of Acceptance
    Recitative for Narrator
 IV. A. Listen! This Might Have Been Your Instant Innermost
   Chorus—Narrator
 V. Tears, Tears Rising to Drown Me
   Tenor Solo—Chorus
 VI. We Know Him Not
   Chorus
 VII. A Pale, Blue Flower
   Narrator—Tenor Solo—Chorus

The text of *A Parable of Death* is drawn from the complete works of Rainer Maria Rilke. I have loved the poetry of Rilke all my life. In 1951, I translated a book of Rilke's stories, *Geschichten vom lieben Gott*. I did this just for my own pleasure and that of my non–German-speaking friends, for the book could not be obtained in English. *A Parable of Death* is based on "Märchen vom Tod," which is part of the *Geschichten*.

However, I did not make use of my own translation. In order that the work might be sung in English as well as in the original German, a metrical translation was prepared for me by the American poet, Anthony Hecht. I had both the German and the English texts in front of me when I composed the music. I decided to have the narrator tell the story, and the chorus and tenor sing lines taken from other writings and poems of Rilke, which I chose carefully so that they would serve as a running commentary.

On January 23, 1919, Rilke wrote:

> If there is a task pure and independent that I may choose for myself, be it this one alone: to affirm an intimate trust towards Death out of the deepest joys and wonders of Life; that he, Death, who never was a stranger, emerge again, the silent knowing partner of the living.[1]

To Rilke, life is a series of transformations; the final transformation, Death, is the change from the world "without" to the world "within," "the nonilluminated side of life." He sees Death as the fruit or flower of Life.

In a letter to the Louisville Orchestra, I wrote of a problem confronting me when commissioned to write this work involving a speaker as soloist. I feared a kind of concerto for narrator and orchestra that would turn into "melodrama":

> Can the spoken word have a *raison d'être* in the concert hall? This was the problem confronting me when I set to work. I soon realized that my search for a text would take me far away from drama literature. A monologue surrounded with emotive, illustrative music would be in questionable taste; but a simple story, an old legend, could be "told." Such a story is not hard to find, but again what role would we assign to the music?

---

[1] I came across a letter by Mozart in which he described his attitude toward death in almost identical terms.—L. F.

9

At this stage of consideration, we must turn to the *Passions,* particularly the Bach *Passions,* and marvel at Bach's insight into the nature of story-telling in music, at his knowledge of what makes a text suitable for musical treatment. How well he knew that *drama* was subjected to laws other than *musical drama.* He avoids suffocating the story with an undue amount of music; he presents the story in the form of a simple and lucid recitative that weaves through the oratorio like a thread. The bulk of the musical substance he assigns to interruptions of the story, contemplations on the story, interpolations in the shape of arias, duets, chorales. Thus he discards drama on the theatre level and gives us drama in the realm of pure music.

My present work does not attempt grand oratorio. If Bach is mentioned here, it is because, once again, he provided the twentieth-century composer with a clue towards the solution of a problem, the narrative with music.

A Parable of Death was composed at the height of my involvement with neoclassic ideal and procedure. Therein lies its chief difference from *The Prairie,* which is American, almost popular at times. Needless to say, the choice of texts bears out this shift in orientation. The *Parable of Death's* duration is roughly thirty-two minutes. It is scored for chorus, narrator (I prefer a woman), tenor (a pure, Bach-type voice rather than the usual operatic-type tenor), and an orchestra of winds by twos (one trombone only, no tuba), piano, percussion, and strings. A chamber version in which the orchestra is replaced by an instrumental group of eight players (organ, piano, percussion, and string quintet) is available also. I recommend this version for use in small halls and for small choruses. But this version stands or falls with the virtuosity of each player, particularly of the organist. The orchestral version on the other hand is comparatively easy. One more hint: concerning the narrator, let the story be told in a simple and wise manner, much in the way that one would tell a fairy tale to children. Quietly and intimately the narrator tells about a man, a woman, and Death. The chorus and solo-tenor comment on the story.

Psalms was commissioned by the Stockbridge Bowl Association, Massachusetts, and composed in 1955–56, in Beverly Hills, California. The first performance took place in the spring of 1956. Dimitri Mitropoulos conducted the New York Philharmonic Orchestra and the Schola Cantorum. The duration of *Psalms* is approximately twelve minutes. The work is scored for chorus and orchestra (or two pianos).

The commission stipulated that the composition begin with the opening sentences of Psalm 121:

> *I will lift up mine eyes unto the hills, from whence cometh my help.*
> *My help cometh from the Lord who made Heaven and Earth.*

At this point my obsession for putting my own text together in my own way led me to continue with Psalm 95:4:

> *In His hands are the deep places of the earth: the strength of the*
> *hills is His also.*

Here I repeat the opening sentence. Together these lines form the invocation or prelude of the work.

At the very beginning is heard a solo-tenor voice (David accompanied by the harp). It is essential that this be a voice from the chorus and not a soloist placed next to the conductor. A little later a solo-soprano joins the tenor in octaves. The singing must have the quality of distance. The harmony has an open-air color which in a way harks back to *The Prairie*.

On the other end of the work is a prayer or epilogue, drawn from Psalm 23.

> *The Lord is my Shepherd; I shall not want.*
> *He maketh me to lie down in green pastures: He leadeth me beside*
> *the still waters.*
> *He restoreth my soul.*

This is *a cappella* music, choral seven-part writing.

Psalm 98:1, 4, 6 forms the main body of the work, occupying the place between invocation and epilogue. (*Psalms,* in spite of the division into three parts, is actually a one-movement composition framed by a prologue and an epilogue.)

> *O sing unto the Lord a new song; for He hath done marvelous things.*
> *Make a joyful noise unto the Lord, all the earth: make a loud noise,*
> *and rejoice and sing praise.*
> *With trumpets and sound of cornet make a joyful noise.*

The accompanying orchestra, which is used *in toto* only for this psalm, is divided into groups of four:

4 Wood Winds (or organ)

4 Brass Instruments

4 Percussion Players

2 Pianos and 2 Harps (one harp will suffice, if necessary)

Strings (Violin, Viola, Cello, Bass—in groups or singly)

The drastic reduction in the number of brass instruments (as compared to the normal orchestra) helps to assure supremacy of the choral element. The wood winds are equally reduced in numbers, and the particular choice of wood winds (piccolo, two clarinets, and contra bassoon) makes one think of a special organ mixture (hence the alternate possibility of an organ). The pianos, harps, and percussion, which should be placed in front (their parts being quasi-*concertante*), form the center of sound of this orchestra and carry the main burden.

Proper balance between chorus and accompaniment is not the only reason for the predominance of plucked and percussive sounds in the orchestration. The emphasis on these sounds was dictated by the texture of the music, which in turn is the result of the composer's feeling for the biblical text.

This setting of Psalm 98, the "joyful noise unto the Lord," is a special favorite of mine, with its extended fugal episodes, its many parallel fifths, its 3/2 dance rhythm, and its barbaric joyousness. Again, I recommend the orchestral accompaniment for large choirs (and large halls), the two-piano accompaniment for small choirs. Two genuine piano virtuosos are required for this version.

As for the orchestration, I like to refer to it as my "biblical band." In its nonsymphonic sound, it pointed the way for me toward a possible future approach. As far as instrumental accompaniment for chorus is concerned, a symphony orchestra has always been a problem. From the choice of instruments accompanying Stravinsky's choral works one may gather that he also wished to abandon the typical symphony sound in favor of a more special texture, and one varying with each choral piece.

Stravinsky once told me that he felt the symphony orchestra—as we have known it—was on its way out. There are a number of symptoms which tend to support this theory. Choral literature on the other hand shows a renewed vitality. Some of the most significant twentieth-century works are choral. It could well be that the era of the symphony, which gave us the Beethoven, Brahms, Bruckner, Mahler symphonies, is giving way to a choral era; that the dream "Music for the many and by the many" which, in the nineteenth century, found its natural expression in the symphony, has taken refuge in the choral music of the twentieth century.

2. *The Lament for Beowulf*

HOWARD HANSON

HOWARD HANSON (born at Wahoo, Nebraska, on October 28, 1896) studied at Luther Junior College, the Institute of Musical Art, and Northwestern University (M.A., 1916). He was instructor of music at the College of the Pacific from 1916 to 1919 and its dean from 1919 to 1921, when he was awarded a *Prix de Rome*. When he returned to the United States in 1924, George Eastman appointed him director of the Eastman School of Music. Hanson has miraculously combined four careers in his lifetime: music educator, composer, conductor, and crusader for American music. He has served as president of the National Association of Schools of Music, the Music Teacher's National Association, and the National Music Council. In 1935 he was elected to the National Institute of Arts and Letters, and in 1938 a fellow to the Royal Academy of Music in Sweden. Other honors include the D.Mus. from Syracuse University, the University of Nebraska, and Northwestern University; a Pulitzer Prize in 1944 for his *Symphony No. 4 (The Requiem);* the Ditson Award in 1945; and the George Peabody Award in 1946.

THE first performance of *The Lament for Beowulf* took place on May 21, 1926, at the thirty-third annual May Festival in Ann Arbor, Michigan. The performers were the University of Michigan Chorus and the Chicago Symphony Orchestra, with the composer conducting.[1] For this *première* the distinguished Dean of the University's School of Music, Earl V. Moore, wrote the following program notes:

[1] There is one matter which might be intriguing. On the first page of the vocal score there is a dedication to the Leeds Festival in Leeds, England. The reason for this is that the famous British conductor, Albert Coates, asked me to write this work for the Leeds Festival and to reserve the first performance. Unfortunately, it was not possible to get the work ready in time for the Festival and, for this reason, Albert Coates programmed in its place my *Lux Aeterna* for orchestra with viola obbligato. So far as I know, the work has never been performed by the Leeds Festival Society!—H.H.

Significant treatment of the mixed chorus as a medium of artistic expression is seldom achieved by composers in their early years of writing. The orchestra with its variegated shades of tone color and great range in pitch and dynamics is much more alluring. American composers have produced many compositions of medium length for chorus and orchestra, but for the most part imitation of existing models is characteristic of them rather than originality. It is possible that the choice of texts has materially influenced the resulting music, in which case the composer of *The Lament for Beowulf* gives evidence of the value of a liberal education as a background for a composer. For in this composition Mr. Hanson has created a work of commanding importance in the field of choral literature. He displays restraint as well as power of expression, a knowledge of choral and orchestral technic and capacities employed in the most telling and economical manner for the musical depiction of the scenes and incidents that are contained in the text of this Anglo-Saxon epic. The relationship of music and poem is so direct and intimate that the archaic character of each seems mutually interactive, that the mood of the text is "mistily" and "gravely" reflected in the unusual harmonic texture of the vocal and instrumental polyphony.

My own comments embodied in the program notes for this first performance reveal some of the personal details involved in the writing of this work:

It is quite understandable that the sagas of the northland should have been of great interest to me. They are the epics of my forebears. For years I read carefully a mass of this material. Then while on a visit to England I found a translation of the Beowulf epic by William Morris and A. J. Wyatt. It attracted me immensely and from this I chose one episode which is the text for my composition.

Carrying my prize with me I went to Scotland for a short stay and there, in an environment rugged, swept with mist, and wholly appropriate to the scene of my story, I began my sketches of the music. These I took with me to Rome and later brought to this country where the work was completed.

My intention has been to realize in the music the austerity and stoicism and the heroic atmosphere of the poem. This is true Anglo-Saxon poetry and may well serve as a base for music composed by an American. The music follows closely the text and the text presents with Nordic epic vigor and terse eloquence the scene of Beowulf's burial.

15

There is a brief picture of the great burial mound by the sea on which the funeral pyre of the hero is built. A great beacon mound is constructed and on it are placed the trophies of the hero, mementos of his famous battle and victories. The women lament as the mound is built by the warriors. Then follows an episode in which the wife of the hero with her handmaidens voice their grief.

The young warriors in a group surround the bier of their dead king and tell of his prowess. The work ends with an eulogy of the great hero:

Mildest of all men
Unto men kindest
To his folk the most gentlest
Most yearning of fame.

There is a brief orchestral introduction in which the mood is forecast, but *The Lament for Beowulf* is distinctly a choral work.

Some additional detail might be added. At the time of conceiving the work I was deeply involved in the type of soul-searching which a composer must do in—as Jean Sibelius has described it—"finding his own way"; in answering the questions, "Who am I; What am I; What do I want to do?"

I had in a previous summer traveled to Sweden, the land of my mother and father. I had roamed the plains of the south, the coast of the west, and the lakes of the north.

I had already written a number of youthful works for orchestra, and had just completed in Rome a tone poem which I had labeled, autobiographically, *North and West,* and my first symphony, to which I had given the subtitle *Nordic*. This introspection was, undoubtedly, youthful, romantic, and perhaps a bit conceited, and yet it is what every young composer must do if he is to "find his own way."

When, therefore, I came across Morris' and Wyatt's translation of the Anglo-Saxon epic, *Beowulf,* this seemed to me to be the one text that I must set to music. It typified to me the gray, mysterious colors of the north. It contained both its passion and its nostalgia. It was big, heroic, and yet tender.

If the story of the death and burial of the warrior king of the Vikings moved me deeply, so did this particular translation with its reliance upon words of Anglo-Saxon derivation. No Gallicisms here, no capitulation to Rome or Athens!

From the beginning, "For him then they geared, the folk of the Geats, A pile on the earth all unweak-like that was," to the tender line, "The mildest of all men, unto men kindest," the words seemed to carry their own music.

And here may I interpolate a conviction which has remained with me during the composition of many choral works and a full-length opera: a composer should not try to set to music poetry which does not "sing back" to him. I have admired many poems which I hoped to set to music but which I have never attempted because they would not "sing back" to me.

Here, then, I had found for me, the ideal text, a text which seemed to want to sing itself. I had also something very precious: a place in which to write.

I have already acknowledged my indebtedness to the inspiration of both Sweden and Scotland, but not yet to the eternal city of Rome. Here perhaps I may be permitted a brief autobiography. I was born in the small town of Wahoo, Nebraska, a community peopled primarily by Swedish Lutherans and Bohemian Catholics. I had been educated at the small Luther Junior College in Wahoo, made a brief visit to the University of Nebraska's School of Music in Lincoln, graduated from the Institute of Musical Art in New York under the genial direction of Frank Damrosch and Percy Goetschius, and followed by graduating from Northwestern University under the equally genial direction of Peter Christian Lutkin and Arne Oldberg.

I had been at the tender age of nineteen a "professor of theory and composition" at the College of the Pacific in California, and at twenty-one the dean of its Conservatory of Music and Art. I was in danger of becoming an aging administrator at the age of twenty-four!

And then the benevolent lightning struck. I was persuaded by some friends to enter the competition for the newly established *Prix de Rome* in composition at the American Academy in Rome. I have never been particularly impressed with competitions, and, so far as I can recall, this is the only one I ever entered. But this proved to be the right one, for in the Academy in Rome the most important thing in life was creation— the writing of music, the painting of pictures, the creation of sculpture. Here was also *time,* time for thought, time for introspection, time for creation. There was in addition the inspiration of the ageless city of Rome, with its glorious past, the timelessness of its present, and the infinity of its future.

It was to this city and to this Academy that I brought my poem, and it was here that I was given the opportunity of working for almost three years. Would that every young composer could have the same privilege! Would that there were hundreds of American academies for the creative arts!

I had the words, the time, and the place. Now for the music!

It is a curious experience to look back, critically, at a work written almost forty years ago. It is possible to be quite objective, for time brings many changes, changes in point of view, in philosophy, in technique, and yet there are some early works which the older composer looks back upon with nostalgic approval, sometimes even with a tinge of envy! In my own experience *The Lament for Beowulf* is such a work.

I have already spoken of the setting of words, of my conviction that the composer should not attempt to set words which do not "sing back" to him. For me the poems of Walt Whitman, the words of the Bible, *The Lament for Beowulf,* the libretto of Richard Stokes for the opera *Merry Mount* have all had this power of singing back.

In setting words to music I am reminded of a conversation with Carl Sandburg, in which he spoke of the necessity of the creator's being "immersed" in his project. Certainly in the writing of a choral work this immersion in the spirit and meaning of the words is all-important. The composer, to be successful, must come to believe subconsciously that *he* has written the words himself—that they are as much a part of him as the music which accompanies them.

The composer in this medium has another advantage: not only does the poem give him inspiration, it also furnishes him with an integrated and orderly form. In *Beowulf* the form divides itself into an orchestral introduction followed by three choral sections. These, in turn, may be subdivided, the introduction in two parts, the first choral section into five parts, the second choral section into three parts, and the third section into one part and the concluding epilogue.

There is a certain interrelationship among the three choral sections, the first part of each section having a certain similarity in melodic, harmonic, and rhythmic construction. The orchestral introduction also forecasts material which appears later in the choral sections.

A diagram might look something like this:

	Choral	Choral	Choral
Orchestral Introduction	Section I	Section II	Section III
Part 1, Part 2	Parts 1, 2, 3, 4, 5	Parts 1₁, 6, 7	Part 1₂—Epilogue

The opening of the Introduction is built harmonically of superimposed perfect fifths, the opening chord C–G–D–A setting the "color" of the entire work in a persistent, undulating rhythm, punctuated with calls in the brass (see Example I, 1, at the back of this volume).

The second half of the Introduction, built on the scale D–F–F-sharp–A–C and expanded later to include all the tones of the chromatic scale, develops increasing rhythmic and dynamic intensity.

The first choral section, to the words

> For him then they geared
> The folk of the Geats
> A pile on the earth
> All unweaklike that was

uses the harmonic and rhythmic material of Part 1 of the Introduction (see Example I, 2). It is followed by a second part built on the melodic and rhythmic material of Part 2 of the Introduction:

> Laid down then amidmost their
> King mighty famous

This leads quickly to Part 3, a pounding 5/8 meter in the orchestra against which the chorus sings:

> The wood reek went up
> Swart over the smoky glow

Part 4 is based on purely diatonic material—no sharps or flats for five pages—in a rhythmic harmonic *ostinato* over which the voices weave contrapuntal strands of tone like the wreaths of smoke from the funeral pyre:

> Sound of the flame bewound
> with the weeping

The fifth and last part of Section I begins with the "sad lay" of the wife and the mourning of her handmaidens:

> *Likewise a sad lay*
> *The wife of aforetime*

This passage employs a melodic-harmonic device which I find that I have used—quite unconsciously—for many years: an eight-tone scale using both the perfect fourth and the augmented fourth—in this case both the E-flat and E-natural in the key of B-flat, the falling Lydian fourth heightening the emotional expression of the contrapuntal lines (see Example I, 3).

Section II, Part 1, returns to the material of Section I, Part 1, but a perfect fifth higher with the words:

> *Wrought there and fashioned*
> *The folk of the Weders*
> *A howe on the lithe,*
> *That high was and broad.*

The second part of Section II describes the building of the funeral mound (see Example I, 4). Here the meter is irregular, changing from six to five to seven beats in the measure and rising to a climax with the poignant—yet philosophical—line:

> *As useless to men as e'er it erst was.*

The final part of Section II begins with a rough rhythmic motive, again in irregular meter, using a primitive four-tone "scale"—F-sharp–D-sharp–G-sharp–A-sharp—later expanded to a six-tone scale:

> *Then round the hewe rode*
> *the deer of the battle*

and rising to the highest climax of the work (see Example I, 5):

> *Whenas forth shall he*
> *Away from the body*
> *Be fleeting at last.*

The final section is a very brief recapitulation of the opening choral section:

In such wise they grieved

and ends with the epilogue (see Example I, 6):

> *Quoth they that he was*
> *A world King forsooth,*
> *The mildest of all men*
> *Unto men kindest.*

I should explain that such a technical analysis of material is easier *after* the act of composition. For a composer uses combinations of tone much as a writer uses combinations of letters. The writer does not, I am sure, think consciously in the moment of creation, "This is a noun; this is a verb" although, subconsciously, he is aware of the form and construction of his writing. Similarly, the composer has his own vocabulary, his own nouns, adjectives, verbs, adverbs, prepositions, and conjunctions, which form a part of his tonal vocabulary and which he uses—or should use—with complete freedom.

I have not spoken of the problem of orchestration, the "orchestration" of vocal lines as well as of the instrumental accompaniment. It seems to me that the voice should be used as a *voice* and not as an instrument. The voice has no valves, no keys, which when pressed down will automatically, in the hands of a competent player, give certain pitches.

Finally, as an epilogue may I say that it has been a pleasure to write these lines, to have had the opportunity of looking back analytically and yet nostalgically upon a youthful work, written almost four decades ago, but a work for which I still have great respect; to have relived once again the old days in Rome; and to have paid homage once more to that old Norse hero, Beowulf,

> *The mildest of all men*
> *Unto men kindest.*

3. *Lamentatio Jeremiae Prophetae*

ERNST KRENEK

ERNST KRENEK (born on August 23, 1900) studied in his native city of Vienna and also with Franz Schreker in Berlin. Between 1925 and 1927 he was an opera coach under Paul Bekker in Kassel. The phenomenal success of his opera *Jonny spielt auf,* often described as a jazz opera, brought Krenek international fame at twenty-six, and was translated into eighteen languages and performed all over the world. In 1928, Krenek returned to Vienna and accepted a position as correspondent for the *Frankfurter Zeitung.* He also traveled extensively throughout Europe lecturing and accompanying recitals of his songs. By 1933 he had adopted the twelve-tone method of composition—a natural evolution in view of his inquiries and interest in tonal areas beyond the late Romantic spirit of his early works. Like many intellectuals during the 1930's, Krenek found the European political climate intolerable and migrated to the United States in 1937. In 1945 he became a citizen. From 1939 to 1942 he was professor of music at Vassar College; he resigned to become dean of the School of Fine Arts at Hamline University in St. Paul (1942–47). Since 1947, Krenek has resided in California, devoting himself to composition during the winter months, and traveling to Europe, lecturing, and conducting his own works during the summers.

THE *Lamentatio Jeremiae Prophetae* was composed during the winter of 1941 to 1942, when I was professor of music at Vassar College in Poughkeepsie, New York. While I do not now remember in detail the circumstances attending my decision to set to music this particular text, I feel that the generally sinister mood of the first years of World War II undoubtedly enhanced my interest in the powerful expression of grief and anguish as laid down in the Book of the Prophet. A selection from the voluminous text had to be made. When I decided to compose the sequence of excerpts used by the Roman Catholic church in the Tenebrae services of Holy Week, I did so because this selection was sanctified by the authority of the institution that made it, an institution into which I was born and to which I had developed more intense allegiance ever since Nazi-dominated Germany had begun to threaten with extinction my native country, Austria. In this point my selection from the Lamentations differs from that chosen by Igor Stravinsky for his *Threni*. As may be seen in the subtitles given to several sections of his work, Stravinsky's choice was made in order to bring out a certain sequence of ideas and moods that he saw represented in the Scripture. I simply followed the sacred text, hallowed by the church that had prepared it in this way for reasons best known to herself and not to be scrutinized by me. The full title of my work, then, reads: *Lamentatio Jeremiae Prophetae secundum breviarium Sacrasanctae Ecclesiae Romanae.*

While using the ecclesiastical text, I did not plan to write a liturgical composition for practical use in the services mentioned, as I was well aware of the peculiar position of music in the life of the church. Although the popes, when addressing themselves to the subject, have declared that, at least as a matter of principle, they were not opposed to new tendencies in the art of music, they have surrounded such statements with so many cautious reservations that anybody not benevolently inclined toward new music may base his rejection of progressive ecclesiastical music on high authority. Curiously enough, the Catholic church (like most other religious bodies) seems to be exceptionally tolerant in accepting even very daring architectural ventures, while being rather timid and reluctant in relation to unconventional musical contributions. In passing, we may advance two reasons for this discrepancy: the impact of music on a captive audience such as a congregation attending a religious service is much stronger than that of a visual element, which one does not have to look at constantly and to which one may get used by seeing it from time to time; furthermore, music needs interpreters such as architecture does not, and one of the inherent properties of new music is that its performance seems to become increasingly more difficult for those steeped in the average specimens of the traditional type. It goes without saying that nearly all church choirs and, above all, their leaders belong to this category of performing artists.

When I decided on the style and character of my work, I went much further than just giving up the idea of making it fit for liturgical use.

I had in mind to write a work that would express as purely as possible certain ideas and ideals of composition that I had developed in those years, and to do so without compromise and concessions to so-called practical demands. This attitude was a result partly of my becoming increasingly involved in the formidable constructional possibilities of the twelve-tone technique, partly again of the despondent mood of a period that seemed to make the future of cultural activities such as performances of new music look rather hopeless.

In my opinion my *Sixth String Quartet* (1936) and my *Twelve Variations* for piano (1937) mark the high points of my preoccupation with the problems of the twelve-tone technique. The *Lamentatio*, taken up after the circumstances attending my emigration from Europe had, for a while, diverted me from the main line of my creative efforts, stands at a crossroads, as it were, in that in its intransigency it continues and perhaps exceeds the uncompromising attitude of the earlier works mentioned above, while in its compositional method it somewhat relaxes the constructional strictures of those works. It appears interesting to me that the device that produced this relaxation turned out to be the most important component of the apparatus that I developed fourteen years later when I embarked on the new "radical" and uncompromising phase of my present serial composition.

The text then offered by the Breviarium consists of three sections, each assigned to the services of one of three consecutive days of Holy Week: 1) "In Coena Domini" (Maundy Thursday), 2) "In Parasceve" (Good Friday), and 3) "In Sabbato Sancto" (Easter Saturday). While these Tenebrae (darkness) services originally were held during the nights preceding the days mentioned, they were omitted when, in November, 1955, the Catholic church altered and shortened its Holy Week ritual. The lengthy service consisted of many readings from the Psalms, alternating with prayers and excerpts from the Passion stories of the New Testament. At certain places were inserted the three "lessons" *(lectiones)* into which each of the larger sections of the Lamentation was divided. The most impressive feature of the service was that from a triangular rack holding thirteen candles at certain intervals one candle after another was removed and taken back of the altar. When the last candle was gone and the church plunged into complete darkness, a rattling noise, symbolizing the earthquake that occurred at the Savior's death, was made behind the altar, and after a short prayer the congregation left in silence.

Each of the nine "lessons" of the *Lamentatio* consists of several verses of the Prophet's text. Ever since the church's selection of verses was set to music in the Gregorian Chant (as may be seen in the *Liber Usualis*), the Hebrew letters introducing each verse were treated as integral parts of the text and sung like the other words. The letters obviously serve as a numbering of the verses. In the first lesson were used the letters "Aleph," "Beth," "Ghimel," "Daleth," and "He," which clearly correspond to the Greek "Alpha," "Beta," "Gamma," "Delta," and "Epsilon." They mean nothing different from what a modern poet would have in mind by designating his lines or stanzas by a), b), c), d), and e), or "first," "second," and so on. The fact that these sober, emotionally neutral and highly formalized announcements were to be treated as material for composition alongside with the passionate and frequently violent language of the verses proper caused rapid contrasts in the expressive temperature of the music. I found this peculiarity of the text particularly intriguing.

The verses of the Prophet are couched in the exalted prose typical of the Old Testament. They are of varying length, but on the whole rather short. Since in view of the considerable extension of the text copious repetitions of words or lines did not recommend themselves, there was a certain danger that the work might fall apart in too many short spans, become too sectionalized and choppy. The more significant, it appeared that in the sixth ("In Parasceve," III.) and seventh ("In Sabbato Sancto," I) lessons the letters were repeated within the verses and interwoven with their words, as may be seen in the Gregorian version of the *Liber Usualis,* which suggested a more continuous musical treatment over a longer span. A similar more extended structure came to mind for the last lesson, which is called *oratio* (prayer) and does not contain any letters. Another feature that would obviously be of consequence in the formal conception of the whole was the fact that each lesson was concluded with the identical invocation, *"Jerusalem, Jerusalem, convertere ad Dominum Deum tuum"* ("Jerusalem, Jerusalem, return to the Lord, thy God").

The compositional setting of my *Lamentatio* reflects both sides of my musical thinking at that time. On the one hand the work is a continuation of my pursuits in the twelve-tone technique, which began about 1930; on the other hand it reveals my increasing interest in the history of music. Already in 1936,[1] I pointed out relationships between the principles of melodic design in the Gregorian Chant and the twelve-tone technique. My studies of medieval music were greatly intensified after I came to America and had access to the marvelous facilities of the music library of Vassar College.

The setup of my twelve-tone rows was suggested by the system of the Greek modal scales. I divided my tone-row in two sections of six tones each and treated each section in the same way in which the Greeks appear to have derived their various scales from one basic mode: by gradually putting the first tone of each scale at its end an octave higher and repeating the process until the first form was reached again. Thus I obtained six forms of each of my six-tone groups. These may be called "diatonic," since they consist of the same tones and differ only in regard to the position of the intervals. We understand further that the Greeks transposed their modal scales into the ambitus of one "characteristic" octave in order to make them available within the gamut of normal voices. I applied this idea to my two columns of six "diatonic" rows by transposing them to the pivotal pitches F and B, respectively. Thus I obtained two other columns of six rows each, which might be called "chromatic" because they gradually contain all twelve tones. Inversions and retrograde forms of the patterns thus established were also prepared for use in the composition (see Example II, 1, at the back of this volume).

It may be seen that both six-tone groups present a scalelike arrangement of pitches. This is partly because of the intended analogy to the Greek modes, partly because of the idea of developing the tone-row from the tetrachord F–G–A–B-flat that is the material of the Gregorian setting of the *Lamentatio*.

The successive switching of tones within the tone-row may be called "rotation." Its introduction was motivated by the desire to manipulate the material according to the principles of the twelve-tone technique without being obliged to use constantly all twelve tones. Establishment

[1] Cf. my lectures *Ueber neue Musik*, published in Vienna in 1937, 54ff.—E. K.

of the "diatonic" columns allowed limiting at times the number of pitches to six or, by adding one or two of the "chromatic" forms, to a number less than twelve, while still handling the six-tone patterns as serial units. Most of the Hebrew letters are assigned "diatonic" six-tone groups. Nearly all of them contain in some form the melisma associated with the letters in the Chant setting (see Example II, 2).

Example II, 3 (the introductory passage of the whole work) will demonstrate the practical application of the tone-rows shown above. In this section the alto quotes, after the fashion of a *cantus firmus,* the Gregorian intonation of the *"Incipit."*

Comparing the methods used here with those of the "classical" twelve-tone technique, one might say that the "rotation," which produces the diatonic groups, means an enlargement of the number of available basic patterns by systematically modifying the original set, while the procedure by which the chromatic groups are obtained means a selective reduction of available transpositions of the basic forms. The main advantage of this selection of serial patterns was seen in the possibility of setting up distinctive harmonic flavors.

In this three-part canon (see Example II, 4) the soprano has the retrograde form of J II△ 2, alternating with O IX 4 (which happens to be the transposition by a tritone of the previous pattern). The alto uses the same tone groups, reversing their alternation. The tenor has the retrograde form of J IIX 2, which again is a transposition of the same sequence of intervals, and the form O IX 4 as above. The canonic context causes two groups of tones, F, G-flat, A-flat, B-flat, and G, B, D, E, to stand out as harmonic elements governing the areas enclosed in Example II, 4, by dotted lines.

It is in this sense that the concept of rotation loosened the strictures of the twelve-tone technique. While I used this method in subsequent compositions for several years for the same purpose, it is interesting to notice that it ultimately turned out to be of paramount importance when I approached the more advanced idea of serialism, in which not only the succession of pitches but also all other aspects of the musical process were subject to serial premeditation. Discussion of this evolution would transcend the frame of the present essay.

Another aspect of the work indebted to my historical orientation is the rhythmic and metric layout. As may be seen in the above examples, the work is notated without bar-lines. My studies of medieval polyphony convinced me that any transcription into modern notation of that music would produce adequate results only if it would avoid the free, continuous flow of the melodic lines being cut up by the arbitrary system of regularly recurring bar-lines.[2]

In the *Lamentatio,* I tried to re-create with modern means the metric and rhythmic concepts of the late fifteenth century. There was no pre-established alternation of "strong" and "weak" beats. Accents, that is, dynamic stresses, were created by the melodic lines as they went along, high and long tones automatically becoming points of emphasis. Since each melodic line would develop according to its own design, the points of emphasis were distributed freely and irregularly throughout the polyphonic fabric. Hence, bar-lines, which to us habitually suggest the imminence of a strong beat, had to be omitted.

The rhythmic organization is equally free and irregular. If, on the whole, a subdivision of rhythmic units into two or three smaller time values seems to prevail, such regularity is frequently enough interrupted, and, what is more important, the irregularities may not always occur simultaneously in the several voices. The basic unit is the semibrevis (half-note). The tempo fluctuates between $\downarrow=66$ and 120 per minute, usually staying within the medium speed zone ($\downarrow=78$–108).

As for structural features, the work consists of many relatively short sections, set for two to eight voices, these latter settings usually worked out as double choruses of four voices each. As pointed out earlier, the sixth, seventh, and ninth lessons are treated as more extended forms, the last mentioned following in outline somewhat the pattern of the classical sonata form. The work contains seven canons: one of two voices, two of three, three of four (double; by augmentation and inversion; double endless by augmentation and inversion), and one crab-canon of six voices. At the end of the first lesson the invocation "Jerusalem" is set for one voice (unison), at the end of the second lesson for two voices,

[2] More complete information on my views on this and related subjects touched upon here may be found in the two volumes of *Hamline Studies in Musicology* (Hamline University, St. Paul, Minn., 1945, 1947), wherein the results of my own research as well as that of my advanced students were collected and edited by me when I was dean of the School of Fine Arts at the university.—E. K.

and so forth, until the apex of complexity is reached in the final invocation, after the *oratio,* when the "Jerusalem" is set for nine voices. Considering that a chord of nine different tones leaves only three tones of a twelve-tone row unused and that for the next nine-tone chord another form of the basic series must be found such that its first six tones will complement the leftover three, one may evaluate the problems involved in constructing this musical configuration.

It may be objected (and such objections were raised) that for a "modernist" who admittedly was bent upon finding novel ways of musical construction and expression I was too much concerned with historical precedent. The answer, of course, depends entirely on whether a listener who does not know anything about the historical background finds my work sufficiently original to hold his attention, or whether he senses a lack of vitality to be ascribed by an expert critic to the stifling influence of my historical orientation. For myself I will say that I did not look to the Greeks, to the Chant, or to the fifteenth century for justification. I think that I used the cues wafted my way through the ether of the ages independently enough. Although I concede that I perhaps do not attach any longer the same significance to historical orientation as I did twenty years ago, I feel that practitioners of modern serialism who are inclined to wave aside precedent owe a great deal to the isorhythmic concepts of the *Ars Nova,* the proportional arts of the fifteenth century, and the spatial experimentation of the Renaissance.

It is easy to see what causes performances of the *Lamentatio* to offer exceeding difficulties. The considerable length of the work—seventy-five minutes—is in itself a deterrent factor. But even the execution of excerpts is difficult, partly because the dodecaphonic idiom, based as it is on the equal temperament, raises problems of intonation perplexing singers not endowed with "absolute pitch," partly because the absence of bar-lines makes unusual demands in regard to orientation and communication between conductor and singers. Being well aware of these difficulties, I did not expect to hear soon—if at all—a performance of the work, and I put it away as the result of an effort that I had to undertake to satisfy an inner urge, regardless of its usability.

Nevertheless a very short fragment of the *Lamentatio* was performed on April 4, 1943, by the women's section of the Hamline University

Choir in St. Paul, Minnesota, under the direction of the excellent Robert Holliday, a choir director then combining high technical competence with adventurous musical taste, keen sense of discrimination, and efficient pedagogical methods. He prepared, several years later, a rendition of a somewhat longer sequence of excerpts with a group of singers selected from students and alumni of Hamline University. The recording that was made of this artistically outstanding performance was unfortunately technically not very satisfactory and is no longer available.

The story of how my pessimistic feelings about the *Lamentatio's* public fate eventually turned out to be unwarranted is not without interest. When I, in 1955, met Mr. Gerhard Schwarz, the state supervisor of (Protestant) ecclesiastical music for Nordrhein-Westfalen (a member-state of the German Federal Republic) and casually mentioned my *Lamentatio,* he nearly equally casually asked me to leave the score with him, as he might find some organization interested in presenting at least part of the work at the following year's Heinrich Schuetz Festival in Düsseldorf. Curiously enough, the organization he found was the State School for (Protestant) Church Music in Dresden, in the eastern, Russian-controlled part of Germany. Professor Martin Flaemig, the distinguished conductor of that dedicated choir, was apparently so much interested in the liturgical possibilities of my work that he decided on a rather monumental, somewhat static style, which, although being very impressive, differed from my more dramatic and flexible conception of the work. When I met Professor Flaemig two years later, he admitted that he too would have preferred my approach, but imagined that I might have wanted the other style. I then decided to supply metronome markings to the second edition of the score so that the character of the music might be deduced from the tempi indicated.

Mr. Flaemig's Düsseldorf performance of a substantial section of the *Lamentatio* put the work on the map, as the saying goes. The Bärenreiter Verlag of Kassel published a beautifully engraved score, and the Dresden rendition was recorded for Epic Records of New York, under the auspices of the Fromm Music Foundation of Chicago. But not before October 5, 1958, more than sixteen years after its completion, was the work heard for the first time in its entirety during the *Kasseler Musiktage,* as performed by the NCRV Vocal Ensemble of Hilversum (Netherlands) under the direction of Marinus Voorberg. The rendition by this group of nineteen singers was as breathtakingly faultless as the conception of the work in Mr. Voorberg's mind was alive, meaningful, precise, and dignified. The event was the more impressive as it took place in the newly rebuilt St. Martin's Church of Kassel (Germany), which had been completely destroyed in the air raids of World War II. Jeremiah's outbursts of grief and anguish over the degradation and annihilation of the Holy City took on a new and special meaning at a place that only recently had risen from the ashes to which it had been reduced by the arrogance of false prophets.

Other performances of the whole work have occurred since. Of these I have heard the rendition by the Choir of the Vienna (Austria) Broadcasting Station under the direction of Mr. Preinfalk. It was more spirited and aggressive than any other I have heard. From a technical viewpoint it might be of interest that this fine choir had no trouble with the excessive length of the piece. Since its radio transmission was planned for the three afternoons of Holy Week mentioned above, they studied the work piecemeal, starting months ahead of time, and put it on tape as they went along, one short section after another. Radio stations elsewhere have adopted the idea of broadcasting the work at the appropriate time during the Easter season. While it is still unlikely that my *Lamentatio* will soon be used in the liturgical service which ideally is its legitimate place, it is gratifying to notice that through the medium of the radio it has at least approached its place.

In America extended sections of the work had admirably vital, eloquent, accurate, and impressive renditions through the New York Schola Cantorum and its inspired leader, Hugh Ross, at Tanglewood and New York, both sponsored by the Fromm Music Foundation. In all these cases the work was sung by small organizations of less than thirty individuals selected for their special fitness for the task at hand. Clarity of texture, highly desirable in any prevailingly linear style, was the welcome result. The massive sonority produced in the rendition of a few sections of the *Lamentatio* by the large choir of the Copenhagen Radio was not altogether inappropriate, although correct intonation had to be secured by the discreet work of a few strategically posted string players.

In conversations with some of the conductors of these performances it transpired that they encountered much fewer difficulties and that the preparation took much less time than they, or I, had anticipated. It has been an experience of long standing that any music becomes easier to perform by the simple process of aging. A composition that seems to be forbiddingly difficult at the time of its writing offers much less than half as many problems when taken up ten or twenty years later, even if it has not been played in the meantime, and certainly not by the interpreters who tackle it after such a time span. One reason for this probably is that some of the technical difficulties have become standard elements of literature of the intervening period so that players occupied with contemporary music automatically become familiar with these features. Another, less tangible, but perhaps more important reason might be found in the natural mutations of the collective mind, which largely remain unconscious to those thereby affected. A younger generation is born with somewhat different, more advanced mental patterns of perception and is therefore able to absorb more quickly and translate into practical action more readily the phenomena that baffled its predecessors because these phenomena were the expression of creative minds "ahead of their time."

It seems that generally difficulties of intonation have lost much of the fearfulness they used to hold for choir singers not so long ago. Minds and ears have adjusted themselves to interval progression and sound combinations that would have caused considerable despair one or two decades ago. The metric peculiarities of the *Lamentatio* have not caused much trouble either. As far as I gathered, the conductors set up rhythmic units of two, three, or more beats according to their own perception of the overall metric picture, or they used a simple, neutral *tactus* marking the half-notes, or combinations of these methods. The absence of bar-lines apparently has not exacted too high a price to pay in effort or anguish for the paramount goal of keeping the music freely floating and flowing.

Of the many choral compositions which I have written (see the Catalogue of Composers' Works at the end of this volume) only one other *a cappella* work is conceived in the twelve-tone technique. This is a set of *Six Motets* on German texts selected from the *Meditations* and *Journals* of the great Austrian writer, Franz Kafka. This work was commissioned by RIAS ("Radio In the American Sector" of Berlin), written and produced in 1959. While the dodecaphonic procedure is rather traditional in that the basic tone-row, its usual transformations, and transpositions are employed without rotation or other more recent, "serial" methods of writing, the choral style is more progressive in splitting syllables, isolating vowels and consonants, and utilizing other devices, some of which are reminiscent of the *hoketus* technique of the *Ars Nova*.

In my *Five Prayers* for women's chorus *a cappella,* written in 1944 after five of the sacred sonnets from John Donne's *The Litanie,* I used a twelve-tone row as a *cantus firmus.* This idea was prompted by the following lines of the poet: "Heare us, for till thou heare us, Lord, we know not what to say . . . heare thyselfe, for thou in us dost pray." I felt that these lines might be interpreted as suggesting the Lord's Prayer, in which He taught us "what to say" in order to be heard by Him. Thus at the beginning of the cycle the Pater Noster is sung in Latin by the chorus in unison on the following twelve-tone series and its derivative forms (see Example II, 5). It may be seen that the distribution of whole-tone steps and skips of fourths or fifths within the four three-tone groups of the series shows a high degree of regularity. In the five songs of the cycle one section of the Pater Noster after the other is used as a *cantus firmus,* to which the other voices furnish nondodecaphonic counterpoints. The mixture of two languages reminds one of the bi- and trilingual motets of the thirteenth century.

In 1957, I was asked by the Gregorian Institute of America in Toledo, Ohio, to write a Mass in an "advanced" idiom and yet accessible to the average church choir. I tried to solve the problem discussed at the beginning of this chapter by setting up a twelve-tone row (see Example II, 6) that would contain sufficient potentialities for diatonic context of the traditional type so that the singers would not be confused by unfamiliar skips and chromatic progressions, while the accompanying organ would supply the necessary transitions between seemingly unrelated harmonic areas. It remains to be seen whether this *Missa Duodecim*

Tonorum, carefully planned as it is to meet the demands and limitations of liturgical purpose, will eventually find its place within the church, such as the totally different *Lamentatio* has found outside, or even at the fringes.

4. Symphony No. 4, "The Cycle"

PETER MENNIN

PETER MENNIN (born in Erie, Pennsylvania, on May 17, 1923) acquired formal training at the Oberlin Conservatory between 1940 and 1942. Duty in the Army Air Force during World War II interrupted his undergraduate study, but he returned after demobilization and completed his course work. Graduate studies were taken up at the Eastman School of Music, where he earned a Mus.M. in 1945 and a Ph.D. in 1947. At Eastman, Mennin's teachers in composition were Howard Hanson and Bernard Rogers; advanced instruction in conducting was under Serge Koussevitzky at the Berkshire Music Center. In 1947, Mennin was awarded a Guggenheim Fellowship. He taught at the Juilliard School of Music from 1947 to 1958, when he accepted the directorship of the Peabody Conservatory of Music in Baltimore. In January, 1963, Peter Mennin was named president of the Juilliard School of Music, succeeding William Schuman, who became head of the Lincoln Center for the Performing Arts.

THE *Symphony No. 4, "The Cycle,"* for chorus and orchestra, was begun in the summer of 1947 and completed in November, 1948. It is scored for full orchestra, including two flutes, piccolo, two oboes, two clarinets, two bassoons, three trumpets, four horns, three trombones, tuba, percussion, strings, and four-part chorus of mixed voices. The work was first performed in Carnegie Hall on March 18, 1949, by the Collegiate Chorale and members of the New York Philharmonic, under the direction of Robert Shaw, who had commissioned it.

The text was written in order to fit the specific need of composing a symphony for chorus and orchestra. The general concept and structure dictate, to a large measure, the quality of the text. From the outset, it was my feeling that a "lean" text was needed, so as to have space "in between the words," for music. Therefore, the "use" of the text should not be confused with that of the oratorio or cantata. It is meant to be considered, as nearly as possible, as an abstract work, depending wholly on the intrinsic merit of the musical ideas themselves. This is in direct contradiction to the usual poetic setting, in which the text has already been conceived by an author before the composer brings his musical talents to the work. The attempt of a marriage between poetic text and musical medium was of prime consideration from the outset. Their interdependence was essential.

This work was conceived in quite a different manner than my own *The Christmas Story*. In that particular work, I tried to capture the meaning of the biblical text and arrived at a musical setting which I believe reflects these views. The orchestral group serves the chorus and soloists as an instrument of accompaniment and support. The objective at the outset was to translate the poetic idiom into a musical-dramatic one. The text, which was already available, indicated the direction the music would take.

The *Symphony No. 4, "The Cycle,"* posed different problems. Here it was my intention to combine two equally important musical forces, emphasizing their individual characteristics and, when the musical moments required it, welding them together into a single unit. The many and varied possibilities of these two bodies of sounds were to be explored.

The text reflects an inner feeling of mine which needed further musical fulfillment in order to complete itself. All in all, one element could not, or should not, exist without the others. As was stated earlier, it was not my intention first to seek a poetic text, then proceed to lay the groundwork for a musical setting. It was necessary that it presented musical-structural possibilities as well, and had to be simple and abstract so as to undergo repetition, variation, and development. Therefore, a completely self-sufficient text would only present major obstacles to the solution of this composition. The text was never meant to be extracted from the work and evaluated separately from the music. It exists only as part of the total concept. Conception of the general content of musical ideas and poetic text had to be realized simultaneously, and "built in" from the outset, in order to have the text conditioned by the music.

The first movement, Allegro Energico, avoids small diversionary effects, and the mood that prevails is austere and intense. Its rhythmic scheme is broad-scaled, and the interplay of rhythmic groupings and meter indicates clearly that the rhythm of the whole work is determined from its smallest unit. It opens in a vigorous linear manner with an orchestral exposition that presents several of the main ideas. It then proceeds to develop them at some length before the chorus enters in unison, moving in sustained style against restless activity in the orchestra. The opening choral statement indicates the duality of materials that typifies the first movement. The tonality hovers around E, F, C, and B (see Example III, 1, at the back of this volume).

This idea is repeated, interrupted, then varied—at M, a section in which the text, "Suppliant yet . . . ," is repeated in rhythm of three bars, while the brass punctuate in irregular eighth-note patterns. In performance, it is important to begin this section at the pianissimo dynamic that is indicated so that the imperceptible crescendo, through a series of harmonic changes, becomes dramatically powerful when it arrives at the climatic point on the words "Look where the star hurls . . . ." While the following section immediately reduces the dynamics in the new treatment of the opening choral idea, the tension does not subside (see Example III, 2). Though the dynamics are marked pp, the canonic entrances in the tenor, alto, and bass parts must be distinct. Slight accentuations on each of the first three notes may be necessary to achieve this.

The orchestral section that follows is essentially of symphonic design and further exploits the musical materials. Then the choral section, "They act not from random thought . . . ," further emphasizes the element of contrast by pitting staccato male voices against smooth-flowing women's voices. Final development of the central choral idea takes place while fragments of the opening orchestral idea ornament it and emphasize its breadth. This leads directly to a more intensely developed recapitulation of the earlier orchestral section. The movement closes dramatically with the chorus, punctuated by the orchestra, declaiming on the text, "With sounds that pierce the marrow with savage hymns of exultation."

The second movement is primarily reflective and contemplative in character, and results as a kind of musical prayer. The quality that is to be achieved is a broad, cantabile, and sostenuto style. A sense of breadth and spaciousness characterizes this movement, with its unending, irregular rhythmic flow. It has two major ideas that are rather elaborately worked out, one primarily for the orchestra, the other for the chorus.

It begins in a cantabile, *ricercare*-like subject in the strings. After a certain point of linear growth is reached, the male voices superimpose a flexible *ostinato* over the string texture, on the words "Come back to the earth," while the altos separate the repetitions with "Man forgets . . . ." The strings continue their linear development alone until the sopranos enter with a statement of a new musical idea. This is developed polyphonically by the rest of the chorus, while the opening idea is further developed in the orchestra, thereby expanding both subjects simultaneously and keeping their musical identities separate (see Example III, 3).

At K, the section for chorus alone has the effect of a stretto of the broad choral idea. It is most important that the bar-lines be considered only as arbitrary divisions of meter, since the proper phrasing and rhythm are shown in the notation by dotted lines that correspond to the interplay of the rhythmic and metric patterns (see Example III, 4). The bass and tenor lines sing the choral idea fugally in rhythmic diminution, while the sopranos and altos present it in melodic inversion, in regular rhythm. An expansion of the orchestral subject leads to a full-scaled presentation of both musical ideas that culminate in a declamatory statement of the highest intensity, with the chorus singing, "come back, come back," over the insistent motif of the beginning. The movement closes as it opened, with quiet polyphony in the strings, and the men's voices reiterating, "Return to the earth."

This movement makes use of the principle of double-fugue with melodic variation. The choral and orchestral musical ideas unfold separately, then simultaneously, always emphasizing their "separateness." Retaining clarity of expression for each of the ideas in their various uses, and adjusting the balance of the performing groups to each other at various moments, is a major consideration in the proper performance of this movement. Though the texture is at times complex, it must always remain clear, since there are no "accompaniment" parts in the usual sense of the word.

Structurally, the third movement is perhaps the most elaborate. It begins in a proclamative manner and then assumes a consistent contrapuntal texture. The canvas is broad and the musical interest is dramatic. Various technical procedures are used, always with the intention of serving the larger symphonic design of the musical structure.

A forceful homophonic passage on the words "Time passing, waters flowing" opens the third movement, and recurs throughout, separating the contrapuntal sections that lie between. Two main ideas are introduced independently and developed fugally. Later they are combined to form a double fugue, which is expanded in separate blocks of orchestra and chorus. The thematic ideas are sharply contrasted: the first, "With dark and tragic destiny . . . ," being predominantly rhythmic in character, and confined within a small melodic range; the second, "Stirring fills the air," moves in a long, slow melody over a rapid staccato *ostinato* and motivic fragments in the orchestra. They are separated by an orchestral interlude of an intensely rhythmic nature. There follows another statement from the opening declamatory section, after which, subjects from both fugal sections are combined and expanded (see Example III, 5). This is followed by an elaborate development of all ideas, culminating on a dramatic orchestral climax before proceeding to the final large portion of the work. There follow melodic antiphonal statements between chorus and orchestra, after which, to the words "Still rising," is introduced a new musical idea which is later developed canonically in the chorus, while various harmonic and rhythmic motives are pitted against it (see Example III, 6). At the height of its intensity, the orchestra breaks into an expansion of the previous orchestral interlude and drives on to the final statements by the chorus and orchestra before bringing the symphony to a close.

Since most of the texture of the third movement is linear, the motivic fragments in the orchestra should be audible to the ear against the choral "sound" when they appear. They are not merely "accompaniments." Specific attention to phrasing is needed, especially when the chorus expands symphonically and demands breadth and scope in treatment. The inherent problems of balance between chorus and orchestra become of prime importance in the performance of this work. They must cooperate toward a single end in achieving a unified expression.

The medium of the chorus as a musical instrument has not changed very much in the last several hundred years. It then follows that the changes which have taken place have been purely musical. These changes influence technique and concept, and only the individuality of the composer brings new results to a medium that cannot boast of technical advances.

5. *Hymns and Responses for the Church Year*

VINCENT PERSICHETTI

VINCENT PERSICHETTI (born in Philadelphia on June 6, 1915) began piano, organ, and theory studies at an early age and showed remarkable facility in each. As a teenager, he played in dance bands and was frequently employed as organist and choirmaster in Philadelphia churches. By the time he was sixteen, he was presenting organ recitals. Full-time music study was undertaken at Combs College of Music, where he received his B.Mus. in 1936. For the next two years he studied conducting with Fritz Reiner. Two scholarships at the Philadelphia Conservatory enabled Persichetti to study piano with Mme Olga Samaroff Stokowski and composition with Paul Nordoff. The next two summers were spent at Colorado College, where he continued compositional work under Roy Harris. Persichetti received an M.A. in 1941 from the Philadelphia Conservatory and a Ph.D. in 1945 from the same institution. After 1939 he served as head of the composition department of Combs College, until he resigned in 1942 to accept a similar post at the Philadelphia Conservatory. Since 1947, Persichetti has been a member of the composition faculty at the Juilliard School. The National Academy of Arts and Letters awarded him a grant in 1948.

WITH the exception of one dismal *Magnificat*, I had written no music for the church until 1955. I had written many secular works of various kinds, and it would not have been unusual for an American composer of that time to be primarily concerned with secular music, except for the fact that I had spent eighteen years—beginning at the age of sixteen —as a church organist and choir director. To pay for my education I held jobs in various churches and so knew the services and liturgy of many. In those years I played what were probably several thousand church services and innumerable organ recitals. I knew the hymns, the anthems, the responses, and most of the music, good and bad, used in churches in this country. And I made my own contribution to this music by extensive improvisation before, during, and after the services; the singers soon learned to join in, either with descants I had hurriedly written and passed to them, or sometimes in free improvisation with me.

Many of the orchestral scores I was learning while a student of conducting with Fritz Reiner at the Curtis Institute were performed as organ preludes—excellent score-reading practice for me and a good musical indoctrination for the congregation, who enjoyed a regular musical diet ranging from Haydn to Honegger symphonies. The benevolent members of the church became so accustomed to twentieth-century music that works such as *Pacific 231*, *The Miraculous Mandarin*, *Wozzeck*, *Le Sacre du printemps*, *La Création du monde*, *Dichotomy*, and *Mathis der Maler* were no more shocking to them than works by Horatio Parker. Over the years there developed a public of several hundred souls that adjusted easily to almost any musical idiom. It was in this fertile atmosphere that much of my nonliturgical music was written, and it was not until many years later that my compositional interests were directed to religious music.

At one late after-concert party, Carleton Sprague Smith mentioned to me a proposed project to assemble an American hymnbook for publication by the University of Chicago Press. He, Albert Christ-Janer, and Charles Hughes were in charge of a plan to invite American composers to make contributions to the book. Either Mr. Smith had planted his suggestion well, or I was overripe for such work: that same night I began work on the *Hymns and Responses*—or rather, on a single hymn, for that had been the request.

Ideas mushroomed and one led to others as I found new and tempting texts. Some became responses, some amens, some hymns. The whole summer of 1955 found me obsessed day and night with music for the church. I was anxious that the use of the hymns not be limited to a single church, and found in numerous revisits to Philadelphia's many churches a variety in attitude toward music—the universal approach I wished for the hymns.

Writing the *Little Piano Book* and the *Piano Sonatinas* was good preparation for the *Hymns and Responses*. My expression had, in this earlier music, undergone a distilling process; the hymns must be music of great essence. I wanted them to be essentially singable but musically fresh, using the best texts, both old and new, that could be found, and expressing an innate religious experience. The hymns were not easy to write, for they were made of very concentrated thematic material. Some were so compelling that they stayed with me after they were completed, refusing to be dismissed, and asking further expansion and development. Parts of the *Sixth* and *Seventh Symphonies* were made of these materials, and colleagues have used them as bases for variation pieces. To some extent the *Hymns and Responses* have for me the function that traditional chorale tunes have had for other composers.

With some hesitation I wrote Christ-Janer that a Pandora's box had been opened and that my publishers had asked for the lot. The committee graciously proposed including some of the hymns in the hymnal even though they would be printed previously elsewhere.

The *Hymns and Responses* have found wider acceptance than I would have guessed; by 1960, Elkan-Vogel was preparing the fourth edition. Some of this was undoubtedly stirred by favorable press reaction, such as an article in the religion section of *Time* magazine at the time of their publication. That churches are traditionally cautious about using new music is a regrettably accepted fact, but it has been gratifying to find so many which have been anxious and able to use this music. Because they are for both choir and congregation (some are for children), the hymns have a variety of uses throughout the church year. Churches have introduced the hymns as choir anthems and, when the congregation became familiar with them, transferred them to congregational use. Other congregations have held rehearsals before the service and incorporated the hymns into the service when they were prepared. A few of the hymns have been put into new editions of church hymnals, along with the old favorites. They are used singly and have been presented complete, interspersed with prayers, as a service of music. As far as I know, the first use of a large segment of the work was in 1956, at the First Presbyterian Church in Philadelphia, Alexander McCurdy, organist. Twelve hymns and seventeen responses constituted an entire vesper service, with all of the amens divided by prayers. They are used in music classes as a basis for study of harmony, and by professional and school choruses in concert. Probably the most unusual use to which

43

they have been put was as a piano duet, played by Nat King Cole (whose father was a minister) and myself for a television program. They have been used by many churches—from Catholic to Unitarian, from Presbyterian to the Society of Friends Sunday School.

Texts for the hymns were drawn from many sources: new and old hymnals, books of poetry and plays. The authors range chronologically from those of the Bible to Peter the Venerable and John Milton, from W. H. Auden and Wallace Stevens to myself (listed on the score as Anonymous, 20th c.). The tune of each hymn is named, and its metrical construction indicated: i.e., Hymn No. 1 (Primal. 8.6.8.8.8.6.). It was difficult to find twentieth-century poetry that was constructed so that all stanzas would fit rhythmically into one musical segment or verse.

The *Hymns and Responses* may be sung *a cappella* or accompanied, in parts or in unison. No tempi are indicated, as the music admits varied approaches. More than with most music, it is necessary that the users of church music feel that it is theirs. Dynamic color will vary with different singers, and this too is desirable, so long as the word-meaning is the motivating force. The vocal writing is natural and singable and the prosody easy and well realized. Voice ranges lie well within congregational limits. When the hymns are used as anthems, they become more brilliant if transposed to a higher tonal level. Bracketed passages may be used as introductions (an extremely useful editorial aid).

Musically the *Hymns and Responses* are, in microcosm, distilled versions of my work. Each piece is a musical entity, complete but compressed. They contain no extra notes. Amens at the ends of the hymns are integral parts of the music and are not to be sung as afterthoughts; the hymn is usually incomplete harmonically until the amen has been sounded. Often, the last measure of the hymn rests on a temporary tonic that drops, by way of the amen, to its final tonal center.

Hymns

1. General Hymn—W. H. Auden (1907–   )
   Primal. 8.6.8.8.8.6. (Our father, whose creative will)
   Tonal center—C-sharp
   Characteristic harmonic progressions—minor triad (chord No. 1)
   moving by tritone relationship to a major triad (chord No. 6).

Cadential root relationship of a second (end of first line and before amen).

Color chords—freshness created by shifts of harmonic areas on "creative" and "Primal."

Sequence—("the freedom of The actually deficient on The justly") —a study in sequential alteration in which the passage is freed from the bonds of this precarious device.

Close—The C-sharp minor tonic at the end of the hymn proper is not firmly established until the amen's bass line drops below the tonic note C-sharp, giving the key center its harmonic balance.

2. General Hymn—W. Romanis (1824–99)

Traveler. 5.5.8.8.5.5. (Round me falls the night)

Origin—first musical setting by Adam Drese (1698)

Tonal center—A. The tonic chord has an added sixth and, at the beginning, appears in first inversion: C-sharp–A–E with an added F-sharp.

Characteristic harmonic progressions—Harmonic tension is created by the movement to the fresh, bass G-natural in measure 2 from the preceding G-sharps. This tonal drop savors the word "night." At the phrase return (line 3) the harmony retains the G-sharp on the word "shine," and the listener senses the approaching close.

Sequence—Each measure of the second line is written in strict rhythmic sequence, but no two measures have the same harmony—an interesting sequential study.

Close—The hymn proper ends on the supertonic (B) with an added sixth. The amen establishes the final cadence on A. This hymn demanded harmonic elaboration and a descant and became the slow movement of the *Symphony No. 6, for Band* (see Example IV, 1, at the back of this volume).

3. General Hymn—Emily Dickinson (1830–86)

Robin. Irregular. (If I can stop one heart from breaking)

Text: *Poems by Emily Dickinson* (Roberts Bros.), 18.

Tonal center—E-flat with a tendency toward C. E-flat mixolydian moving to E-flat Ionian and C Ionian is followed by a progression

through the sharp keys to G-sharp mixolydian, shifting enhar-
monically to the flats of the tonal center.

Harmonic rhythm—Irregular changes of harmony are characteristic of the quick-pulse poetry. Regular harmonic rhythm underlines the positive ends of the first two phrases and the entire last
phrase, "I shall not live in vain."

Sequence—The third-line sequential construction is freshened by
moving from a ninth on "help" to a six–three on "robin" to successive octaves in outer parts on "next again."

Close—The hymn proper ends on the supertonic (F–A–C), and the
amen ornaments a plagal descent to the tonic. This tonic has an
E-flat root, G third and C sixth, and bears only a superficial
resemblance to a C-minor six–three.

4. General Hymn—John Dryden (1631–1700)
   Foundations. L. M. (Creator Spirit by whose aid)
   Tonal center—C, with fluctuating modes
   Harmonic rhythm—regular rhythm and ornamental chorale-type
   writing suggested by such phrases as "The World's foundations."
   Harmonic materials—Seventh-chords form the characteristic tex-
   ture from which ninth-chord traces of quartal harmony evolve.
   Close—The hymn proper ends with a C-tonic with an added sixth.
   The mixolydian amen anchors the seventh texture on a solid and
   unadorned C-major triad, thus establishing musically the firmness
   projected by the Dryden words.

5. General Hymn (or Christmas)—e. e. cummings (1894–   )
   Star. Irregular (purer than purest pure)
   Text: *Poems, 1923–1954* (Harcourt, Brace & Co.), 430.
   Tonal center—G aeolian, progressing to G melodic minor
   Harmonic characteristics—close voice-spacing on words "whisper"
   and "silence," and open spacing on "innocence." Sudden shift of
   mode on words "miracle may grow."
   Form—a circular hymn form in which the harmonic momentum
   carries one verse into another without a halt. The last time around,
   the hymn rides out of the key: "begins a star." The amen, in this

case, backs up the harmony (as in traditional hymns) and attempts to establish the tentative, foreign key.

Performance—This hymn can be sung in unison with organ or piano, or the parts may be hummed under a soprano solo. It forms some of the basic material of the *Seventh Symphony (Liturgical)*.

6. General Hymn—John Quincy Adams (1767–1848)

Adam. C. M. D. (Send forth, O God, Thy light and truth)

Tonal center—G. Has the chorale-squareness of the Foundations Hymn (No. 4).

Harmonic characteristics—antiphonal writing between unison and chordal textures. At the end of each phrase there is a sudden shift in key or modal area. The hidden tritone at the cadence of the third phrase resembles the opening of the *Sixth Piano Sonata.*

Close—The tendency of the modal areas to change from dark to bright creates a cadential brightness of the hymn proper which is converted to a darker, more contemplative amen close.

7. Evening Hymn—Anonymous (20th c.)

Fortune. C. M. (Motionless share of thought at last)

Tonal center—F-sharp moving to A

Harmonic characteristics—The thematic kernel moves in strict parallel harmony. The first phrase ends with free parallel (or similar) motion on the words "prayer unfold." The word "motionless" suggests a partial freeze of parallel motion with the absence of contrary and oblique part of movement. The second appearance of "motionless" is set in a sharper texture, created by the cross relation between the soprano A-sharp and the tenor A-natural. This device increases the harmonic tension, making possible the relaxed harmony for the setting of the words "So pure the star we hold."

Close—The F-sharp hymn closes on an added sixth A tonic. The amen inverts this chord to a chordal structure that has both F-sharp and A root feeling.

8. Advent—Charles Wesley (1717–88)

Release. 8.7.8.7. (Come, Thou long expected Jesus)

47

Origin: a traditional setting of this hymn, adapting a melody by the eighteenth-century Christian Friedrich Witt. Exists in many hymnals.

Tonal center—modulatory, leading to C

Formal characteristics—strong unison writing leading to modulatory part-writing on "Born to set Thy people free." The second half of the hymn employs unison with wider melodic skips, leading to non-modulatory harmony on the words "Let us find our rest in Thee." The amen disturbs neither the key center nor the mode of the C tonic.

9. Christmas—John Milton (1608–74)

Sages. 10.11.10.10.11. (This is the month)

Tonal center—C mixolydian

Harmonic characteristics—The minor six–three triad is used as a tonic. The opening measure consists of a six–three triad on the lowered seventh scale step moving cadentially to a six–three on the tonic. The typical progression in this hymn moves from VII to I; the amen confirms this chordal movement.

Harmonic rhythm—This hymn should be conducted or felt in dotted-quarter pulses, alternating with quarter-note pulses. Measuring the hymn by jagged eight-note beats destroys the flowing movement. The word "morn" is always a pure C-major triad, falling on a strong beat, but the second insistent appearance of "For this is the month" has a quickened harmonic pulse and additional harmonic color.

10. Christmas—Anonymous (20th c.)

Laurel. 6.7.7.7. (Joy will come at Christmas)

Tonal center—G mixolydian

Harmonic characteristics—simple G-major music with two harmonic "side-slips," the parallel harmony in measure 2 and in measure 6. The major-seventh chord on the lowered leading tone at measure 7 pulls the major mode down into the mixolydian area, confirmed by the amen.

Performance—often used by children's choirs in unison or in two parts.

11. Lent—John Marckant (16th c.)
    Contrition. C. N. (O Lord, turn not Thy Face from them)
    Origin: Original musical setting can be found in *Este's Psalter* (1592).
    Tonal center—D Aeolian
    General characteristics—a quiet Lenten hymn moving in solemn
    quarter-notes. It is strictly diatonic until a chromatically altered
    chord is generated by the word "sinful." The amen is built upon
    the first three chords of the hymn.
    Performance—often sung in unison by junior choirs, and used as
    a *cantus firmus* for organ improvisation. The hymn has been in-
    corporated into church hymnals.

12. Passiontide—Padraic Colum (1881–   )
    Lament. 6.6.6.6. (Now in the tomb is laid)
    Text: Devin-Adair Co.
    Tonal center—A
    General characteristics—An inverted F major seventh chord, in-
    troduced on the word "tomb" and used at the end of the hymn
    proper, is not an F chord but an A minor seventh with an added
    minor sixth. Several root interpretations of this chordal structure
    are possible. This is the same chord that is used as a key chord in
    the prism song, "Theory" from *Harmonium*, the song cycle for
    soprano and piano. Much of the "Gethsemane" music of the
    Seventh Symphony stems from this chord. In any transposed
    form, the meaning changes radically, and in the *Symphony* the
    formal course makes a sharp turn when the hymn is introduced
    in a new key.
    Close—The amen converts this A–F–C–E chord into an A major
    tonic triad, giving the Passiontide hymn a hopeful ray.

13. Passiontide—Phineas Fletcher (1584–1660)
    Prince. 10.10. (Drop, drop slow tears)
    Origin: first musical setting by Orlando Gibbons in 1623.
    Tonal center—modulatory to C-sharp
    Harmonic characteristics—chromatically descending bass line that
    rises on "beauteous feet." A sudden harmonic shift from chromatic
    to diatonic is motivated by "Prince of Peace" in the plagal cadence.

49

The chromatic harmony in this hymn is created by the tendency of each voice to move melodically to a fresh note.

14. Easter—Peter the Venerable (1092–1156)
Venerable. C. M. (The gates of death are broken through)
Tonal center—G. The final tonic is a ninth chord, G–B–D–F-sharp–A. The hymn opens with the ninth and seventh of the G chord, and even though the root G is not present, it is felt as the tonal center.
Harmonic characteristics—Unison and two-part coupled writing are the prevailing textures. "The gates of death" is set in diatonic unison; "broken through" is in two parts; "hell is tamed" is in sudden chromatic harmony; "holy cross" is in four parts; and "king is shamed" culminates on a major ninth. The *Seventh Symphony* culminates on material from this hymn.
Performance—This Easter hymn is effective when sung in unison with a rich organ background or when sung in parts, *a cappella* (transposed up a major second).

15. Ascension—Thomas Kelly (1769–1855)
Diadem. C. M. (The head that once was crowned with thorns)
Tonal center—D mixolydian
Harmonic characteristics—The opening unison writing is shifted to four-part writing by the unexpected cross-relation on the words "was crowned." The remainder of the phrase moves to three fresh tonal areas. The second phrase grows progressively more diatonic until the final mixolydian V–I cadence on "victor's brow." The amen recalls the root movement of a second at "is crowned" and "adorns."

16. Communion—Anonymous
Sacrament. C. M. (O God unseen yet ever near)
Origin: The original musical setting can be found in *John Day's Psalter* (1562).
Tonal center—G
Harmonic characteristics—Both phrases begin with an indefinite key and modulate to the G tonic. The first phrase ends with a VII–I cadence and the second with the stronger V–I. The cadence on F

formed by the amen serves as a plagal contrast. The word "reveal" promotes a cross-relation in which all voices skip upward to a crystalline minor triad.

17. Children's Hymn—Sarah Betts Rhodes (1830–90)
Careth. 5.6.6.6. (God who made the earth)
Tonal center—D. (The final B minor triad in first inversion is used as a D tonic.)
General characteristics—"Careth" is a simple unison hymn that is frequently sung by children's choirs. Successive perfect fifths of the first phrase are answered by the successive sevenths at the end of the second phrase. The lowered leading tone in the harmony of the first half and the raised leading tone of the second half do not disturb the simple melodic line, in which no leading tone exists. The syllabic distortion of the word "careth" (the longer and higher note on "eth") was suggested by the unique manner in which children sing. (Actually, they shorten "careth" very often to two quarter notes, followed by a quarter-rest.)

18. Children's Hymn—Isaac Watts (1674–1748)
Berceuse. 8.7.8.7. (Hush! my dear, lie still and slumber)
Tonal center—D minor
Harmonic characteristics—Successive perfect fifths are used throughout the hymn and move in a motion contrary to the upper voices. The harmonic effect is one of three-part harmony with a voice coupled in fifths. The picardy third amen balances the major triadic sound which occasionally arises from the minor texture.
Performance—The hymn is sung by two-part Junior choirs. Low instruments may play the fifths below the melody.

Responses

19. Opening Response—Edna St. Vincent Millay (1892–1950)
Text: Millay, *Collected Lyrics* (Harper & Brothers), 13.
General characteristics—The tonality is E-flat Lydian progressing to F Aeolian and F Lydian, progressing to G mixolydian (via A mixolydian). In this response there is quiet two-part writing in a crescendo to six-part chords. This textural design occurs twice.

The second time it extends to reach the culminating, high sounds on "God shine through." The subito pianissimo amen has antiphonal effectiveness.

20. Opening Response—Conrad Aiken (1889–   )
    Text: Aiken, *Brownstone Eclogues* (Duell, Sloan & Pearce), 59.
    General characteristics—This response may serve as a quiet opening of a service of worship. Although the tonal center is definitely D, the response progresses by triads in free root relationships. They form a chromatic texture of independent voices that is relieved by the magical parallel harmony on the word "miracle."

21. Introit—Psalm 95:6
    General characteristics—In the traditional musical setting of these opening words, there is a tacked-on amen that can be sung or omitted. This indefinite cue to the minister often causes confusion. In this new musical setting, the amen must be used to complete the harmonic phrase, and there is no uncertainty about whether or not the choir will sing an amen. The obvious melodic descent on the words "bow down" is counteracted by the melodic ascent on "Let us kneel."

22. Scripture Response—Psalm 119:18
    General characteristics—This response may follow any reading of the Scriptures. The key shift at "wondrous thing" and the inverted E-minor final chord help allow the momentum of the service to continue.

23. Prayer Response—William Shakespeare (1564–1616)
    Harmonic characteristics—The music of this response is completely wedded to the poetry. "My ending is despair" drops harmonically into a foreign tonal zone. "Unless I be relieved by prayer" moves to a hushed polychord. "Which pierces so that it assaults" moves, by way of two-part coupled writing, to a bold E minor triad. "Mercy itself and frees all faults—Amen" gradually decreases the harmonic tension, clearing on an open and clear E minor triad (see Example IV, 2).

24. Prayer Response—Psalm 19:14

Harmonic characteristics—These traditional prayer-response words are set in a major-minor context of fused compound harmony. The dissonant harmonic progression is effective when sustained by the organ playing under the unison choir.

25. Communion Response—Louis Untermeyer (1885–   )

Text: Untermeyer, *The Singing World* (Harcourt, Brace & Co.), 67.

General characteristics—A useful Communion response that can be used effectively as a harmonic pattern for quiet organ improvisations during the Communion service. The double arriving points, "blooms" and "shrine," are both suspended from a soprano E. "Blooms" is closely spaced and "shrine" is open and relaxed. The amen is created by a dropping harmonic sequence of "shrine."

26. Evening Response—Wallace Stevens (1879–1955)

Text: Stevens, *The Collected Poems* ("The Rock") (Alfred A. Knopf, Inc.).

General characteristics—This response begins with a forceful unison that branches into two-part coupled harmony before the full chords of "lights the dark." The amen is subito pianissimo that, as an echo, completes the response.

27. Closing Response—P. B. Shelley (1792–1833)

Harmonic characteristics—An A-minor response that begins with imitative writing. The words "Life, like a dome of many coloured glass" introduce four-part harmonic writing which crescendos to a ninth chord on "Stains." A diminuendo to the high soprano G on "radiance" is continued to the ethereal amen close.

28. General Response—Anonymous (20th c.)

Text: Originally based upon a text by T. S. Eliot, whose permission for reprinting could not be secured. The present text was written by the composer.

Harmonic characteristics—E center is the underlying tonality of this longer response. The first part, "O Light Invisible, we praise Thee," moves toward the sharp keys. The second part, "The Holy

Light our hearts touch," is slower, quieter, and progresses to the flat keys. The last phrase counterbalances the first two modulatory parts by remaining firmly in the E area.

The Kyrie, Sanctus, and Agnus Dei (Nos. 29–31) are concise settings of the traditional words; the Gloria Tibi and Amens (Nos. 32–39) are simple four-part statements. The Sevenfold Amen (No. 40) is a response which progresses from diatonic to chromatic harmonic textures, while moving from a Neapolitan G-flat area to a tonic F area. The *Seventh Symphony* closes with this material.

Autogenesis is always a strong factor in my music. Many of the hymns and responses are related to each other in a way that is somewhat mystical; and the *Hymns and Responses* are, in turn, related to music which followed them. It is curious that most, if not all, of the hymns and responses were built on or generated by a response which was never finished and is not, therefore, included in the volume.

Much of the *Seventh Symphony* is a direct outgrowth of the lost response, which begins with the words "Who art One God, One Lord; not One only Person but Three Persons in One Substance" (see Example IV, 3).

The *Seventh Symphony* opens with a prayer in low strings suggesting the profile of the response which serves as a *cantus firmus*. It presents a minor-major third indecisiveness that functions as a harmonic irritant throughout the work. All five sections of the *Symphony* are motivated by the *cantus firmus* response, and as it passes through many transformations, hymns and responses emerge as outgrowths of the *cantus*. Most prominent in the *Symphony* are the e. e. cummings, Padraic Colum, and Peter the Venerable hymns, and the Edna St. Vincent Millay, William Shakespeare, and Wallace Stevens responses.

Although several instrumental works which followed the *Hymns and Responses* were built upon material of the collection, my other sacred choral music seems to have escaped their potent musical influence. *Seek the Highest,* for SAB chorus, and *Song of Peace,* for male chorus, are simple and independent statements of faith. The *Mass* for mixed chorus, *a cappella,* has a Gregorian motivic kernel, and bears no apparent resemblance to the *Hymns and Responses for the Church Year.*

I think that I am able now to escape the *Hymns and Responses;* they have been expanded and transformed to my momentary satisfaction. It has occurred to me, however, that I might let Hymn No. 7, "Motionless share of thought," become a Chorale Prelude for Band, so perhaps I am not yet free of them.

6. *The Passion*

BERNARD ROGERS

BERNARD ROGERS (born in New York City on February 4, 1893) studied architecture before beginning his career in music. Arthur Farwell was his first teacher of composition; later he studied under Ernest Bloch in Cleveland. Rogers' symphonic work *To the Fallen,* first performed by the New York Philharmonic Orchestra in November, 1919, earned him a Pulitzer Traveling Scholarship which he used for study in Europe. From 1927 to 1929 he held a Guggenheim Fellowship, and consequently continued compositional instruction with Nadia Boulanger in Paris and Frank Bridge in London. Returning to the United States in 1929, Rogers accepted an appointment as instructor of composition and orchestration at the Eastman School of Music. Since that time, he has remained at Eastman teaching and composing.

THE thought of composing music for the Passion story came to me quite by chance, arising casually during a conversation with a visiting composer (Mark Wessell). "Someone," he remarked, "should set anew the tragic narrative of Jesus, drawing upon the full palette of contemporary sounds." Although we spoke nearly thirty years ago, I recall the moment clearly, and the suggestion lodged and remained with me.

I had been a pupil of Ernest Bloch for three years. His intense vision, nourished and charged by the Old Testament, had set some mark on me. He had touched me, as every great teacher must, with something of himself: his enthusiasm, boldness, ardor, and courage. Four years earlier, in 1927, I had composed a biblical cantata based on the resurrection of Lazarus from the New Testament. At that time I was in France on a Guggenheim Fellowship; again I was fortunate in my teacher, the many-gifted Nadia Boulanger. How strong and lasting is the gift of a great teacher, liberating the younger mind as it works!

My own predilection has always been for the pictorial and dramatic;

my youngest ambition was to become a painter. (My book, published by Appleton-Century-Crofts in 1951, was titled "The Orchestral Painter," altered by the publishers to *The Art of Orchestration*.) That attraction, while it exchanged materials, has remained, emerging mainly in music of narrative character. For such natures the appeal and challenge of words, the fragile fabric of poetry (so close in its laws and values to music) proves irresistible. The long dream of a union of the arts, practiced beguilingly by such masters as Berlioz and Wagner, is still real to some temperaments. Nevertheless, music has its own reasons, and reasoning, and I had been well taught that form (the ultimate mystery) is the sovereign element, regardless of the artist's medium. The problem of the dramatic composer is that of all composers: to draw a plan which satisfies and strengthens the purpose of his work.

Here I should like to contemplate briefly another art, one which I believe is profoundly related to that of music. Architecture, which has been called the "mother-art," entered into my earliest activities, not by choice but by coercion. The fine arts (so-called) are suspect to the average American family; architecture, a "solid" art of enterprise, was more palatable in my home environment. Thus I was apprenticed to a firm of prominent New York architects and for a few years glimpsed the then fashionable *beaux-arts* point of view. I have long since come to realize that here chance had served me well; that architecture and music obey, in their own dimensions, common laws and needs. The ordering of masses, the mastery of balance and proportion, the flowering of detail and its control, above all, the splendor of simplicity—these lie deep in both media. (Pater spoke well when he described architecture as "frozen music.") I was reminded again of this attraction in reading the thoughts of America's greatest architecture, Frank Lloyd Wright. His early and enduring admiration was of Beethoven, the structural genius of tone. And Wright, whose culture was informed by all the arts, quotes again and again the penetrating thought of Victor Hugo: "Art can be no re-statement"—Hugo, whose rich-grained language and luxuriant forms deserve the term "symphonic."

When I came to study music, the ideal of form was held before me by my teachers: Percy Goetschius with his reverence for the Baroque and Classical; Bloch and Boulanger through their enthusiasm for the early schools of great religious music and the brilliant models, Beethoven and Wagner, and for that of our century. In short, my environment and experience led me to cherish the need and beauty of design.

I chose as the theme of my first choral essay the miracle of Lazarus, from the Gospel of St. John. The subject, so profoundly interpreted in paint and copper etching by Rembrandt, was singularly fitted to a broad, indeed inevitable, musical plan. Life emerging from death; the enkindling power of belief, will; the conquering power of a supreme Personality: these were the skein and solution. The darkness of the tomb, replaced through command by the light of day, is no more and no less than an ancient symbol. I used here the simple device of musical transformation, which reappeared fifteen years later in *The Passion*. The early material, set in brooding shades, returns at the end in jubilant colors.

A few years later, in 1931, I turned to the Old Testament for the libretto of a cantata, *The Exodus*. The problem and moral were not unrelated to the Lazarus legend. The turmoil and struggle were resolved in the Red Sea crossing: the denouement followed by rejoicing.

Another biblical work (1936) was set for orchestra alone. *The Supper at Emmaus* recounts the return of Jesus after his death and his encounter with the pilgrims. Again the vision of Rembrandt led me to an Expressionist setting of the mystical event.

Four years later I began the setting of *The Passion*. (Since then I have composed, for chorus, soloists, and orchestra, the cantata based on Whitman's poem of the Civil War, *Come up from the Fields, Father,* and a religious cantata *The Prophet Isaiah,* in addition to a number of brief choral works.) I composed *The Passion* during two summers. It was performed for the first time in its entirety (a few excerpts were given at the Eastman School of Music in 1942) at the Cincinnati May Festival under the direction of Eugene Goossens. On that occasion I supplied the following program note:

> The libretto of *The Passion* was prepared for me by my friend, Charles Rodda, the Australian writer, in 1930. I hesitated for ten years before beginning the setting. Two earlier religious works for voice and orchestra (*The Raising of Lazarus* and *The Exodus*) have served as studies.
>
> In 1940, a black year for humanity, I began the composition of *The Passion*. It seemed to me appropriate to make an affirmation of hope and

belief, in those days when the ancient tragedy was being re-enacted in agonizing fashion throughout the world. *The Passion* is the symbol of a universal and eternal happening; it takes place whenever truth is struck down by power and ignorance and intolerance. It occurs, in some degree, in every age. It is a sign, which we shall not abandon: that in the end, goodness will rise again, and will bear away the victory.

Since the story is immediate and vivid, I have told it in contemporary musical terms. For a long time religious music as a whole has withdrawn itself from reality. It has taken refuge in a small, complacent sphere of polite tradition. This tradition has no true link with the great religious masters of the past—Vittoria, Orlando, Palestrina, Bach. It is no more than a tired, diluted imitation: an imitation of externals. The hand of Victorianism lies heavy upon religious music. The result, except for a few significant modern works, is hardly religion or music.

The Passion is a story of suffering for truth; of the death and life that follow. It is touched with violence, anguish, despair. ("My God, why hast thou forsaken me?") The range of feeling is profound. I have not avoided colors and accents that seem to me faithful. For myself, the influence in this work is largely that of two religious painters, Rembrandt and El Greco.

The Passion is formed of six episodes. In the first, Jesus enters Jerusalem hailed by the people. The second is set in the Temple; He expels the money-changers, and castigates the Pharisees. It closes with the lament over Jerusalem. Scene III is in Gethsemane: the Last Supper: the agony of Christ, and His taking by the soldiers. The fourth scene portrays the trial before Pilate. It is followed by the drama of Calvary, Christ's excoriation of Jerusalem, the taunting of Jesus, and His death. The last scene depicts the earthquake and the resurrection, followed by a rejoicing. Most of the text is derived from St. Matthew, a few extracts are drawn from the version of St. Luke, others from the Psalms.

Thus the work is set as a continuous dramatic narrative, told by various characters—men and women—who surround the principal Figure. Until the last scene, few of the conventional forms are used. Near the end, however, a fugue on two subjects is heard, and two tonalities (C major, D major) are strongly asserted. A large orchestra, including piano, celesta, and many percussive instruments, is employed. A few brief motives (one of them drawn from my *Raising of Lazarus*) enter into the organic fabric. The conception of a pervasive creator is represented by a motive of a superimposed 5th and 4th.

59

The work is dedicated to my daughter, Anne Thacher Rogers; my wife, Elizabeth Clark Rogers; and my librettist, Percival Charles Rodda.

Although a new interest in large-scale choral works has appeared in the years since the above lines were written, the attitude toward religious music has broadened. Yet the scores that have emerged—notably those of Stravinsky, Honegger, Walton, Bloch, Vaughan Williams, Martin, and Britten, among European composers—stand in a somewhat lonely landscape. However, it would be wrong to say that the impulse and fervor which produced, somewhat earlier, the memorable religious works of Brahms, Bruckner, Verdi, and Janacek has been spent. As for the whole body of choral music, the present book is sufficient testimony to its growing stature. Brilliant American practitioners of the medium in both religious and secular vocal music are not lacking: they include Harris, Thompson, Schuman, Hanson, Copland, and Blitzstein, among a number of familiar names.

The poetic-dramatic scheme for *The Passion* followed a simple course: a first rejoicing leading slowly to the trial and tragedy, culminating in the mystical ascent and exultation. In this conception one figure stands in eminence: around the presence of Jesus are grouped the populace, some of whom describe the events and emotions of the changing story. Here the people, the crowd, from whom emerge a few spokesmen, are ranged against—and for—the individual—victim and hero. (In principle a similar pattern is found in Mussorgsky's *Boris:* the protagonist and populace occupy opposing roles.)

In broad plan, the dramatic, and ultimate, musical scheme resembles an inverted arch. After a tumultuous beginning, set in bright colors, the line descends, follows a jagged course, gaining in thrust to the scenes of trial and execution, mounting at last to its radiant picture of rejoicing.

To erect a structure at once simple (in the largest sense) and organic, I used the familiar device of thematic transformation. For example, the choral music in Scene Two ("The Temple") reappears in the final episode ("The Triumph"); the setting of the words "Mourn, Weep, Jerusalem" returns against the text "He is risen." Another instance of this technique is the use of the vigorous march music which opens the work for the closing mood of celebration. The cyclic principle is practiced freely through the entire work; indeed it seems to me impractical to build an extended, complex structure without resorting to this lucid device. In the nature of a mural, breadth is everything; detail arising treelike from a few powerful root forms. In this belief I employed a few simple motives, in the Wagnerian sense of association, recall, and portraiture. These are terse and invariably tonal, as brief in some instances as three tones. The governing key of the whole is D major; in a sense this proves the "popular" tonality, associated at vivid moments with the crowd. The character of Jesus is sometimes given color; more strikingly He is heard against the sounds of B-flat which play, ray-like, about Him. (The frequent association of this key with the character of Christ occurred without premeditation. Its presence was pointed out to me by Robert Shaw.) One interval, the ascending minor third, pervades the music as a whole; this tiny inflection, bearing a host of modal seeds, appears in a multitude of guises, varied and conditioned by its harmonic and instrumental appendages. The motive expressive of the gentle and candid nature of Christ was drawn from the first three bars of *The Raising of Lazarus* (composed fourteen years before *The Passion*); here, from the oboe, the minor third is twice heard (see Example V, 1, at the back of this volume).

For the beginning of *The Passion* the librettist suggested the mood and scene as follows: "In the introductory march there should be a militant note of revolt to suggest the rebellion against Roman rule. The Jews are hailing their King." After a mysterious pulsation of rhythms in the percussions, the opening march motive, based on D tonic, has a kinship with Glinka, who bequeathed it to Rimsky-Korsakoff (see Example V, 2).

The motive undergoes a series of vertical and modulating shifts, approaching nearer, reaching a powerful statement in the mode of E-flat (mixolydian), and reverting swiftly to the tonic of D; on a sudden pianissimo a solo tenor announces the first words: "Behold, thy King cometh unto thee," followed by a spirited choral "Hosanna to the Son of David" (distant triad of F-sharp major). A baritone voice asks, "Who is this?" The massed chorus rejoins, "He is Jesus, the Prophet of Nazareth. Hosanna to the Son of David." The hosannas continue, reaching a vivid culmination in the key of B-flat (again the tonality that will mark the figure of Jesus). Angry questionings by the Pharisees are answered by choral groups, leading to a resonant close in the gleaming key of D major, suggested ambiguously (lacking the third) in the opening measures of the scene.

Early in the second scene the voice of Jesus is first heard—He castigates the Pharisees: "O, Jerusalem, thou that killest the prophets." His lament over the city is followed by a poignant chorus, "Weep, Jerusalem, Weep! Desolate your house." Here the seminal interval of a rising minor third governs the thought (see Example V, 3).

It will be seen that the same interval appears in the shifts of the voices: third and fifth measures. The imitation of the soprano motive by the alto voices produces an expressive change of color. Another coloristic, but more dramatic effect is produced by the occasional retention of a high soprano voice after the mass chorus has cut off.

Part three describes the Last Supper. For a single time a tenor takes the words of Jesus (a baritone), beginning "Take, eat: this is my body, which is given for you," concluding "This is my blood of the new testament, which is shed for many." The disembodied timbre of the tenor voice placed on low D lends a desolate shade to the final sentence.

A hymn for men's voices drawn from the Psalms follows; it is doubled faintly by four solo cellos. The scene at the Mount of Olives is formed as a brief *passacaglia* mounting to a vehement climax colored by powerful rhythms of high trombones. Judas "cometh with a great multitude . . ." and kisses Jesus. The soldiers seize Jesus.

Part four brings the trial: the interplay among Jesus, Pilate, and the multitude. Yielding to the piercing shouts of "Crucify," Pilate takes water and washes his hands; the tonal background is strange (see Example V, 4).

Next a clamorous scene of exultation opens with a *whispered* episode of strange nature, erupting into full song; it ends the first half in a tumult of sound. The harmony is violent (see Example V, 5).

After a brief pause the tragedy of Calvary unfolds. The soldiers place on Jesus a scarlet robe and on his head a crown of thorns. This is given to a soprano alone, her phrases echoed by a solo clarinet. The taunting of Jesus with mock hosannas is given in bitter sounds from the chorus. A lamentation set for a woman's voice is based (orchestrally) on the ascending minor third (see Example V, 6).

The lament is taken over by sopranos and altos *a cappella,* singing on the syllable "Ai."

The voice of Christ is heard in an arioso. His compassion changes to a vehement prophecy of the tragic days to come.

At Calvary, He is crucified. The crowd, mocking again, bids Christ to save Himself, even as he built the temple. Priests, scribes, and elders join in the angry tumult. Jesus asks His father to forgive them. He cries out in despair (see Example V, 7). (Here, at the sign ⟍⟍ the notes are to be sung slightly flat.)

After a brief pause a strange chord, colorless and barren, is heard. Strings, muted and playing *senza vibrato,* sound the twelve tones of the chromatic series, arranged in perfect fifths. Used thus, the twelve tones sound filtered, utterly consonant. The effect is like a sigh, distant and disembodied.

The music of the Passing is played by a flute.

The earth trembles; the graves open. The populace, "fearing greatly," sing, "Truly he was the Son of God." A music of lamentation, given only to massed cellos, ends the scene.

Part six begins with the famous words "I will lift up mine eyes unto the hills," sung by a soprano. She is answered by full chorus. An alto, solo, is heard through the choral fabric: "He that keepeth thee will not slumber."

Joseph places the body of Jesus in "his own new tomb"; the two Marys come to see the sepulcher. Follows the earthquake, the descent of the angel, the rolling back of the stone. This scene, expressionistic and ashen in color, mounts to a searing peak, culminating in a motive suggestive of a pervasive Being.

A solo baritone tells the people, "He is not here, for He is risen." The full chorus echoes the last words in a jubilant cry in D (this time with major third). A fugal episode begins the final section (see Example V, 8).

After a second subject of homophonic character rising to a massed chorus of praise, the voice of Christ is heard from afar, *quasi parlando,* promising "I am with you always, even unto the end of the world." The serene chant, "He is risen," is built upon the "Weep" motive described earlier which appears in Scene Two. It reaches a majestic height upon chords suggesting the two tonalities E-flat and F-sharp. A final *presto gioioso* is based entirely on the D major triad and the rhythmic motive heard in the first bars of the scene, now much accelerated in tempo.

Following the Cincinnati *première*, *The Passion* has been performed twice, in New York, by Robert Shaw—at the Juilliard School of Music and at Carnegie Hall. At each of the three performances there seemed to be immediate communication with the audiences, despite the dissonant musical language and unsparing realism of many of the episodes. The break with traditional formulas caused no visible (or audible) discomfort; a personal approach couched in a strange syntax was readily accepted. Indeed, anxiety and doubt were far more apparent among the performers, particularly the chorus. Among the latter there were coolness and confusion until they were joined by the orchestra. From that point their hesitations (and hostilities) changed to a growing sense of conviction. That altered attitude prevailed at each performance.

The technical and psychological problems offered by this work are indeed severe. But not insuperable. Mainly the difficulties are metrical (frequent alterations of time signature), rhythmic, and modulatory. But the strange harmonic language and curious cadential evasions need only the supporting and comforting orchestra to achieve security. And like much contemporary music, *The Passion* proves, after acquaintance, much less difficult than it appears in score. Like all new music, it asks for good will, courage—and belief.

7. *The Throne of God*

LEO SOWERBY

LEO SOWERBY (born in Grand Rapids, Michigan, on May 1, 1895) obtained his early musical instruction in Chicago under Arthur Olaf Andersen (theory) and Calvin Lampert (piano). During World War I, Sowerby served in the army. He was awarded the first *Prix de Rome* for musical composition (1921–24). In 1925, after returning to the United States, he was appointed to the faculty of the American Conservatory as instructor of composition. Two years later he accepted the post as organist and choirmaster of St. James Cathedral in Chicago. Sowerby retained both positions until his retirement in 1962. His choral work *The Canticle of the Sun* after St. Francis won a Pulitzer Prize in 1945. At the present time, Sowerby is director of the new College of Church Musicians in Washington, D.C.

In the early spring of 1956, I received a letter from the Very Reverend Francis B. Sayre, Jr., dean of the National Cathedral in Washington, asking me to accept a commission to compose a work for mixed chorus and orchestra, to mark the fiftieth anniversary of the founding of the Cathedral. The anniversary was to be celebrated in November, 1957; since the Dean had thoughtfully allowed more than eighteen months for the preparation of the work, I accepted the commission. The question of a text was, of course, of paramount importance. The Dean had asked that the words "Alleluia, for the Lord God omnipotent reigneth" should be employed as either the climax or the conclusion of the piece, so it seemed logical that the entire text should be chosen from the Book of Revelation.

The reason for this request, or shall I say condition, of the Dean was that this very text is inscribed in stone on the outside of the apse of the Cathedral, the first part of the superstructure to have been built. The words inevitably brought to mind Handel's immortal music in *The*

Messiah, which would, quite naturally, give any composer an inferiority complex, so at the outset I resolved that my treatment of the text must be totally different from that of the magnificent "Hallelujah Chorus."

I proceeded to get down my paternal grandmother's copy of the Bible, given her in the year 1849 as a reward for excellence in her work in and attendance at a small church school in the north of England, and made a careful study of the entire Apocalypse. In addition to that, I asked Canon Wedel of the Cathedral in Washington to make suggestions for a text. We had considerable correspondence in regard to this; as a musician, I felt that the selections to be chosen should allow plenty of latitude for contrasting musical treatment; as a theologian, Canon Wedel was completely consistent in his choice of passages that should tie in with each other. The final result was therefore a compromise, and though I insisted on bringing in material which Canon Wedel had not at first included, I could not have arrived at the text which was actually used without his very valuable assistance.

The choosing of a text, therefore, took considerable time, and the choice of a title, which was up to me, took even longer. I finally settled upon *The Throne of God* after discussion with several clergy friends, in particular with Bishop Chilton Powell of Oklahoma. I commenced work on the music long before this, however, actually sometime early in May, 1956, writing the choral parts and a sketch for the orchestral part. Various engagements and duties made it necessary to suspend work after the first sixteen pages had been done. I was able to continue, however, later in June, and on July 10 the first draft was completed. The work was done principally in Chicago, although a section of the middle part of it was written at my summer cabin at Palisades Park, Michigan.

After such a sketch has been completed, I like to forget about it for a few weeks and then come back to it with the idea of making corrections and necessary alterations. Therefore, after having a holiday in late July, I commenced preparing a vocal score, with a reduction of what was to be the orchestral part, for the publisher. It was most important to have the printed copies of the vocal score ready for study by the chorus in Washington so that immediately after Easter Day in 1957 rehearsals of the work could get under way. Naturally, the score should have been made first, and the reduction afterward, but there was not time for this. Late in September, back in Chicago, I commenced work on the orchestral score; this was finished shortly after the New Year.

The first performance took place in the Cathedral in Washington on the evening of November 18, 1957, under the direction of Paul Callaway, organist and choirmaster of the Cathedral. Paul and I have been good friends for more than twenty-five years, and I have always had the greatest admiration for his excellent and careful musicianship and for his brilliant work as a director. I should also say that he is one of the finest organists in America. The choral group was the Cathedral Choral Society of Washington, augmented by the men of the choir of the Cathedral itself. The orchestra was the National Symphony Orchestra of Washington.

The orchestra with the choir behind it sat in the nave, just in front of the chancel steps. I recall that I was the guest of the Dean, Dr. Sayre, and that immediately in front of us sat the Bishop of Washington, Dr. Dun, with his guest, Mr. Neil McElroy, who was then the new secretary of defense. The Dean gave a gracious talk just before the performance of the new work began, saying that, although it was poor form to applaud in a church, considering the occasion of the anniversary, he not only believed applause would be in order, but he would gladly permit it. Therefore, at the conclusion of the thirty-six-minute performance the Cathedral rang with the unaccustomed sound of hand-clapping, and Mr. Callaway and I repeatedly acknowledged the plaudits of a very large and enthusiastic congregation. Many people came from New York for the performance, and some from as far away as Boston. The only other work on the program was Beethoven's *Mount of Olives,* which preceded the new work.

There are no passages for solo voices in *The Throne of God,* but the part of the Evangelist is written for a special group of men, singing sometimes in unison, and sometimes in two, three, or four parts. At least the group should be large enough so that the four parts can be made effective. Generally speaking, in works designed for performance in the church, I have not favored the use of solo voices. My feeling was, therefore, that the words of the Evangelist would have greater force and a more universal potency if they were divorced from the personality of a solo singer, and given to a group. I might add, as a practical suggestion, that the men of the regular chorus could also sing the Evangelist's sections, though it is unquestionably more desirable to have a special group, if male singers are plentiful.

The work is scored for the following orchestra: two flutes, piccolo, two oboes, English horn, two clarinets, bass clarinet, two bassoons, four horns, three trumpets, three trombones, tuba, kettledrums, triangle, bells, cymbals, snare drum, bass drum, and the usual strings.

I called the work "a poem for voices and orchestra" for the reason that the structure of the composition is similar to that of a symphonic poem. In other words, the music is not divided into separate sections, and in performance the music carries on without pauses or breaks. This, I feel, helps to maintain a feeling of unity throughout the work. This is assisted by the frequent reappearances of certain sections or themes or motives. In attempting to give an analysis of the structure of the work, I shall refer to the page numbers and rehearsal letters as found in the printed version of the vocal score, published by the H. W. Gray Company, New York City. The vocal score has a reduction of course, of the orchestral score which is more or less playable on the piano. The idea was to get into it the gist of the music itself, but not to attempt to make it pianistic. It was most certainly not designed to be played upon the organ. However, I heard of a recent performance of the work given at the Union Theological Seminary in New York under Mr. Callaway's direction, in which Searle Wright, organist of St. Paul's Chapel at Columbia University, played the orchestral part on the organ—so brilliantly that it excited the admiration of all the astonished auditors. Even though I am sure that Mr. Wright worked very hard over it, this sort of feat can only be brought off by those who have the very special gift—which Wright has in abundance—of making a really organistic accompaniment out of something written with only the possibilities as well as the limitations of the piano in mind. And if one asks why I did not make the reduction for organ, I can only say that I did not really think that it could be done satisfactorily; besides that, I did not relish the thought of the ordinary bumbling organist trying to plow his way through the piece, the whole conception of which is completely unorganistic. However, it is quite possible that in the near future an edition with a real organ accompaniment may be prepared and published, for purely practical reasons.

68

Before actually beginning to write any of the music, I prepared a number of pages of sketches of thematic material to be employed in the course of the work. This was done, naturally, after a thoughtful and minute study of the text upon which I finally decided.

The Throne of God opens quietly, even ethereally, in the higher register of the violins with a theme which will be heard again as the work progresses. Under this is a counter-theme in the oboe. The time is 4/2 and the key is C major, which seems to be the focal tonal point of the piece (see Example VI, 1, at the back of this volume).

(I find that I react better to music in long values than to music in short values, which is the reason for my preferring 4/2 to 4/4 time. I suppose this is due to my long association with the church and with its traditional music. Perhaps it is just that I find *black* music [like that of Max Reger, for instance] more difficult to see and to read. There may be something psychological about this—a greater feeling of dignity, or serenity, as the case may be, when the unit is the half-note or minim rather than the quarter-note or crotchet, which is so very common, especially in secular music.)

The theme quoted continues on its way, other parts and instruments are added gradually, the brass finally enters, and a climax is attained in the fourth score on page 2. There is a quick subsiding and a short pause at the top of page 3, after which the original motive is heard, now in lower registers, in brief canonic entries, coming to rest on the empty fifth C–G. The introduction is now completed, and the stage is set for the entry of the Evangelist, "And I heard the voice of many angels." This grows quickly in intensity to the words "and thousands of thousands," where occurs the direction "faster" (letter D, page 4), and where a nervous rhythmic motive makes its appearance and leads to a sudden brilliant flash in the orchestra (top of page 5). The continuation of this leads to the first choral section, which is in E major and is fugal in character. At letter E, page 5, the sopranos, to the text "Worthy is the Lamb that was slain," lead off (see Example VI, 2).

This entire section gives a feeling of breadth and spaciousness, which is reflected in the orchestra as it moves on its contrapuntal lines in a deliberate manner, mainly in the strings. The altos and then the basses and tenors present in turn answer, subject, answer. Later there is a retard and an interruption (letter G, page 8), and a return is made to the music which was set to the Evangelist's first announcement on page 3.

The key is one half tone higher than before; the Evangelist sings, "And every creature . . . heard I, saying" (top of page 9). The nervous rhythmic motive again makes its appearance and leads directly to a resumption of the fugal section, now in G major (letter I, page 10), the subject being sung by altos and basses in octaves, and the answer four bars later by the sopranos and tenors in octaves. The scoring is now somewhat heavier than before, with the addition of wood winds to the strings. Much of this section employs similar two-part writing for the chorus. I have always found this to be a singularly effective way of treating the vocal sound when clarity is desired, and, of course, when there is an accompaniment, particularly an orchestral one.

On page 15, as it is obvious that a climax is in the offing, the orchestra sings the fugal theme in canon while the chorus, now in octaves and unisons, has a new counterpoint to the text "and unto the Lamb for ever and ever." The brass instruments enter; the chorus rises higher and higher in sequences with the text "for ever and ever"; there is a gradual broadening over a pedal point on the tonic G; and the approach to a final cadence seems imminent when there is a sudden interruption (first bar, page 15) with two sharp, almost blinding chords (with two piccolos at the top), followed by a rushing passage in G minor leading to the highest D. The time has now changed to 4/4 and the direction "with animation" indicates the quicker-moving and more agitated character of this new section. The Evangelist, the part now divided into four, sings, "And I looked, and lo, a Lamb stood on the mount Sion." (This may be the place to point out that having a group of men for the part of the Evangelist minimized the problem of the orchestration, since there is now no absolute necessity for light scoring simply to provide an accompaniment over which a solo singer can be heard.)

A new theme appears in the upper instruments of the orchestra, and there is a greater surge generally, with the horns playing important inner parts. This commences at the bottom of page 17.

The Evangelist sings, "And I heard a voice from heaven," the orchestra plays the same music, now in A minor, and there is much brass and percussion to complement the text, "as the voice of a great thunder."

Now the Evangelist continues (letter P, page 20), "And I saw another angel fly in the midst of heaven," while the orchestra does its best to depict in sound the flying of the angel. Momentarily a calmer mood prevails as the Evangelist sings, "having the everlasting gospel to preach unto them that dwell on the earth" (page 21), but there is still a surging melodic passage growing out of the theme last quoted, with horns ever more important in the middle register, as a gradual accelerando is called for and the orchestra rushes in a torrent of sound to the key of D major (letter Q, page 21). The chorus enters: "Fear God, and give glory unto him; for the hour of his judgment is come," over a fanfare in three trumpets with long sustained chords in the rest of the orchestra. This climax is not long maintained and soon the orchestra is quieted, and the Evangelist, now again in unison, sings, "And I heard another angel out of the altar say" (top of page 25). The altos in the chorus (see Example VI, 3) continue immediately with "Even so, Lord God Almighty" (letter R, page 25).

This theme too is the subject of a short *fugato*. The direction is "quietly," and the key is B major. A more sober mood is in order here as this entire section is to lead eventually to the text "Write, Blessed are the dead which die in the Lord" (page 30). The *fugato* just mentioned dies away and the orchestra plays a rather somber passage (letter S, top of page 28), which eventually works into a crescendo leading in bare octaves to a high A-sharp, fortissimo. Then the trombones play a rough motive which mirrors the one just heard, and the Evangelist intones, "And I heard a voice from heaven saying unto me" (letter T, page 29). The chorus now brings in the text "Write" (note again the double octaves in the voices), and time slows down considerably, and "Blessed are the dead" appears (see Example VI, 4).

This is accompanied by pale wood winds on the perfect fifths with a pedal point on A-sharp in the lower strings; the music moves toward C-sharp major with a prominent clarinet solo over "that they may rest from their labors," based on the same motive the chorus has just sung. Then in unison and octaves the chorus whispers, "And their works do follow them," ending in a hushed pianissimo, over which the violins rise to the astral regions in a long octave passage (top of page 31, bar 3).

At this point a return is made to the music which began the work,

71

but there are two differences. The pitch is now a minor third higher, and the time is now 6/4 instead of 4/2 (page 31, letter V). The reason for this was that I felt this change would create a sense of more fluid motion than did the original version (see Example VI, 5). A climax is attained, as at the beginning, but this time there is no build-down, and the orchestra plunges ahead into an exultant theme (letter X, page 33). This serves as the basis for the Evangelist's entry, "And they sing the song of the Lamb, saying," and the chorus, "Great and marvellous are thy works" (letter Y, page 34). In contradistinction to some other parts of this work, this section is quite definitely diatonic. In fact, there is a strong hint of the Lydian mode. The color of the music soon darkens, however, and a move is made through E minor to the remote tonality of C-sharp minor (page 37), where there is a long vocalize in seven-part writing on the word "Name," pianissimo. This section ends with a subdued "For only thou art holy." There is a *fermata* on the C-sharp minor chord with an unresolved F-sharp (end of the first score, page 38).

Following the *fermata* and the resolution into the open fifth a new section, marked "Fast," is inaugurated by a trombone with a chromatic motive which is immediately imitated in diminution by the other brass (see Example VI, 6). A related rhythmic motive is introduced in the lower strings and bassoons (page 39, second score), developing into a rhythmic ostinato to accompany a bold progression in octaves in the horns. At letter BB, on page 40, the Evangelist announces "And after these things," which leads to four excited alleluias sung by the chorus, as a prelude to a fugue, beginning at letter CC, page 41, on the text "Salvation, and glory, and honor, and power unto the Lord our God," announced by the chorus basses (see Example VI, 7). Unlike the other fugal passages in this work, this one moves quickly, and the accompaniment is rather lightly scored with sparse chords. A short stretto is eventually formed on the word "Alleluia" (bottom of page 46), after which the chorus sings at a constantly accelerated pace an almost frenzied series of alleluias. Note might be taken of the fact that this fugue makes a return to the central key of C major, so that the alleluias just mentioned occur over a subdominant pedal point, leading to a subdominant eleventh chord, under which the kettledrum unexpectedly introduces a roll on a totally unrelated B-flat, which serves abruptly to change the tonal center.

Immediately the trombones intone a menacing motive fortissimo; this introduces perhaps the most exciting section of the work, all having to do with the fall of Babylon (page 48, bar 6). Rhythmic motives introduced on page 39 are still prominent, and the chromatic cast of the music observed on page 38 is still to the fore. The chorus declaims several times, "Babylon the great is fallen." The tonality becames more and more vague at the text "And is become the habitation of devils" (page 50, second score). In a slightly slower passage the chorus, again in the two-by-two pattern, with imitative entries, sings "For her sins have reached unto heaven" (letter GG, page 51). The principal melodic idea, however, is at the top of the orchestral texture; this is continued to page 54, where the chorus pauses while the orchestra rushes to a powerful and exciting climax. Here the Evangelist sings, "And again they said" (page 55), the chorus following immediately with the alleluias of page 41 now a semitone higher. The tonality is once again definite, and it is D-flat. The effect of the final of the four alleluias is strident, with the orchestral instruments all in high register and brilliant timbre.

The orchestra continues in the same vein until at letter II (top of page 57), over a pedal E-flat, a rustling figure commences in the strings, ascending higher and higher until a tremolo passage in the highest register of the violins leads to an inverted pedal on the upper E-flat. During this passage the Evangelist has been singing, "And her smoke rose up for ever and ever." The musical effect may be similar to the impression of smoke ascending and floating away into the air.

At letter JJ the time changes back to 4/2 and the concluding portion of the work sets in. Under the high tremolo in the strings the brass instruments intone solemnly a chorale-like passage leading to the text "And I saw a new heaven and a new earth," presented under a quietly moving duet between strings and horns, all over a low B-flat (bottom of page 58).

Note the motive in the horns in the sixth bar of this section (see Example VI, 8). After a hushed repetition of "And there was no more sea," there is a gradual increase in the orchestra in both speed and dynamics, in which this motive plays a prominent part.

The focal point of this is reached at the beginning of page 61 with a motive hurled out by the trumpets (see Example VI, 9). In connection with this the Evangelist sings, "And I heard a great voice out of heaven, saying," which announces (at letter MM) the text "Behold, the tabernacle of God is with men, and he will dwell with them," set to the identical music of the fugal section on page 5 (letter E), now transposed to the key of E-flat. The music eventually proceeds differently, and at letter OO (page 65) there is a short continuation similar to the one at the top of page 15. At the end of page 65 another accelerando commences in the orchestra, and the trumpet figure (first announced on page 61) is again heard. Another climactic point is attained, and 4/4 time is again introduced (letter QQ, page 66) by a fast-moving chordal passage of tempestuous character in the brass, with a kettledrum roll on G as an underpinning. This leads to the Evangelist (in four parts, as on page 17), singing, "And I heard the voice of a great multitude." There follows the theme in the higher instruments which appeared at the bottom of page 17, now in C minor. It is combined with the brass as the Evangelist sings of "mighty thunderings," after which there is a further hurrying and increase to a great fortissimo.

At letter SS this climax is interrupted by the sopranos and altos singing a subdued alleluia, answered in a different tonality by the tenors and basses. The sopranos and altos are accompanied by two flutes while the male singers are supported by two clarinets (see Example VI, 10). This was simply a device to ensure that the voices would not stray from the proper pitch. The alleluias mount in intensity, and the final one (following letter TT, page 70) is an amplification of the alleluia on page 56, although the key of C is by now definitely re-established; the orchestra continues with an equally intense, and completely diatonic, passage leading down into the lower middle register of the violins.

At this point the theme which opened the work is heard once more, though now "very broadly" and two octaves lower than at the beginning. For the last time 4/2 meter is reintroduced, and there is a rhythmic accompaniment in broad triplets (page 71). A rush of clashing chords ensues (page 72), the chorus again commences soft alleluias, and there is a mighty crescendo to the jubilant chordal alleluia at letter WW, marked "joyously." Here again we hear the fanfare of brass used at the bottom of page 22, but now the music is solidly orientated in the key of C. The text "For the Lord God omnipotent reigneth" is declaimed by the sopranos and tenors, then by the altos and basses, and finally by all together, interspersed with numerous alleluias and fanfares.

At letter ZZ (page 78) the orchestra plays a broad fragment of melody heard nowhere else in the work; this is actually the first motive I jotted down when I commenced planning the thematic content of the piece (see Example VI, 11). Following this there is another rush of alleluias and fanfares, and the work is brought to a conclusion with all possible sonority on a final prolonged alleluia. (Note that the first sopranos are directed to hold their high G on the syllable "ah," which is much easier and more effective than having the actual words screeched out at so high a pitch.)

Such a résumé of the work as I have just given can, of course, mean little unless the reader has a copy of the vocal score in front of him. Even then, a bare recital of what takes place cannot bring the music to life, unless one can hear music mentally, and even relatively few musicians can do this with any degree of accuracy. One might ask a composer why he did this or that, and in many cases he could only answer that he had been impelled to do such and such, or that once the music got started it led itself on, as it were, to the various keys and themes and in the various speeds. But the composer must, in his flights of imagination, use his craft to hold himself in check, and his technical equipment to preserve an order in what might otherwise be chaos. I feel that this is particularly true when one is setting words to music, or I should better say, making music to fit the words. The words must definitely dictate the music and even how the music is put together. In this work of mine there have been no repetitions of musical sections unless the text concerned itself with the same or closely related ideas. The same is true of key. One does not wander willy-nilly about the tonal spectrum; where modulations are unclear or vague, the text should provide the reason for this kind of treatment; I believe this to be the case particularly on pages 52 and 53 of *The Throne of God*. It may be noticed that I do not make use of key signatures. I long ago dispensed with this practice, since with the frequent modulations encountered in much contemporary music, the continual canceling of sharps or flats in a signature is a great nuisance. In any case, did not I state that the central key of the piece is C major?

It has been suggested that the composer could give instructions to the performers in regard to interpretation. I can say little in this regard beyond the fact that if the performers, and, of course, particularly the conductor, will place a certain amount of faith and trust in the composer's indications, of whatever sort, and then follow them implicitly, the "correct" performance will undoubtedly emerge, provided the singers and instrumentalists are capable musicians. I have indicated metronome marks throughout the score, but these need never be followed slavishly, as they are, after all, relative. Many years ago I learned that for a time I used a metronome which was inaccurate, and discovered that for a while I had been indicating speeds which were too quick. I disposed at once of the offender, and bought two electric metronomes which seem to me to be far more satisfactory than the old wooden ones. However, I feel that a real musician does not need a metronome, at least for this purpose; he should be able to sense the correct speed after careful study of a piece of music. Wasn't it Widor who became enraged at a prospective student for playing an organ work of his at the speed he (Widor) indicated?

Mr. Callaway told me recently that the only entry problem he had in directing *The Throne of God* was the first one for the sopranos at letter E (page 5); they could not seem to find F-sharp. It seems to me that if they had mentally sung the preceding line of the Evangelist as though it were their own, and had simply thought the perfect fifth from B to their own F-sharp there would have been no trouble. Granted that F-sharp is an appoggiatura (I once had a student who called it an "arpogitory"), the progression is nevertheless a simple one (see Example VI, 12).

Generally speaking, I felt that I had taken good care that in the case of all entries the singers were prepared by what had gone on before to sing their first note without difficulty. The entry for altos and basses at letter I (page 10) is, I believe, a more difficult one, but here, if singers think of the melody in Example VI, 13, they should have little trouble. In the last two bars on page 29, I anticipated some hesitation in the successive entries by having instruments come in on the note of each vocal part one beat earlier than the singers themselves.

It seems not inappropriate to conclude this essay with a review of the first performance of *The Throne of God* by Mr. Paul Hume, music critic of the *Washington Post and Times-Herald*. (Mr. Hume is certainly well known to the general public as the recipient of a famous letter from President Truman, who was one who had no hesitation in doing what many have longed to do—bawl out the critic in well-chosen colorful language. Mr. Hume finally sold the letter to a collector for $6,500.) The review follows:

Applause, contrary to all tradition, shattered the sacred precincts of Washington Cathedral last night to honor a great living composer.

The unrestrained enthusiasm was in tribute to Leo Sowerby, whose *The Throne of God* had just been given its world premiere by the choral societies of the Cathedral. The work was commissioned by the Cathedral to celebrate its 50th anniversary year, now drawing to a close. In asking Sowerby for a score, the Cathedral gave proper recognition to the man who is surely the outstanding composer of music for the Anglican church in this country, if not indeed the finest of all church musicians of any denomination.

Placing the emphasis on the proper musical resources, Sowerby scored his vast panorama of sound for large mixed chorus augmenting it with a group of men's voices used as choral narrator. These he undergirded with an orchestra of the largest proportions to create a big machine in the grand manner.

All of this becomes entirely appropriate when the magnificence of the selected text is studied. That text is taken from the Apocalypse of St. John the Apostle also known as The Revelation of St. John the Divine. Here in language of unparalleled splendor is a revelation of things that were, and are, and will be, language filled with symbols of infinite color and power, mixed with words that create images that frighten and reassure.

For such language Sowerby has drawn on the resplendent sound of the full orchestra, placing above them his tremendous authority in choral writing. Voices move in long lines, or rise to shout "Alleluia," filling the air with sounds of everlasting praise. The atmosphere of the book is conveyed with striking grandeur, though the means are often conservative in foundation. Perhaps the nearest score, in texture and effect is Walton's *Belshazzar's Feast,* though the parallel is by no means precise.

Paul Callaway, employing his full chorus plus the men of his regular choir, and the glee club of St. Albans School, also had the National Symphony Orchestra to voice Sowerby's sacred festival piece with power and beauty. The men's numerous entries in unison, as narrators, might have been more imposing: otherwise it was a masterful affair. Sowerby, a Pulitzer Prize winner in music for an earlier work of similar proportions, has given Washington Cathedral a worthy memento of its anniversary.

PART TWO

English Composers

8. *The Vision of Judgement*

PETER RACINE FRICKER

PETER RACINE FRICKER (born in London on September 5, 1920) began advanced musical training at the Royal College of Music. World War II interrupted his studies, but after demobilization he continued composition instruction privately under the Hungarian composer Mátyás Seiber. Fricker's *String Quartet* in one movement, first performed at the Brussels Festival of the International Society for Contemporary Music in 1950, was the initial work to bring him to the attention of the music world. The *First Symphony*, which won the Koussevitzky award in 1949 and was first performed the following year at the Cheltenham Festival by the Hallé Orchestra under Sir John Barbirolli, firmly established Fricker as one of the most important English composers in the second half of the twentieth century. Following these successes, Fricker composed a steady stream of compositions in all media, which confirmed previous critical acclaim. In 1952 he was appointed musical director of Morley College, succeeding Michael Tippett.

THE English choral tradition is a strong one. Even at times in our history when our musical reputation was low, choral singing and particularly the organizing of large-scale choral festivals flourished. There are fewer of these than there once were, but the survivors—the annual Three Choirs Festival, for example, or the Leeds Triennial Festival—show the same pattern: a week of concerts, with the accent on full-scale works for large chorus and orchestra. As the singers are usually the best from all the local choral societies, the standard of singing is high. The music ranges from the great classics to recent or specially written works.

English composers have taken advantage of these conditions to produce some of their most elaborate works. Very often these have been written comparatively early in their careers, and so have helped both to establish their reputations and to give them the chance to work at large-scale musical forms. There have of course been many minor works and failures, but the contributions in this century from, for instance, Elgar, Vaughan Williams, Walton, and Tippett show that this choral tradition can still stimulate the composer's imagination.

It is possible to argue that the day for the large-scale oratorio or cantata is past. Certainly the tendency now is all in the other direction—composers tend to be more interested in the single note, in delicate patterns of sound for a few performers, than in the broad strokes and massive effects needed for music in the grand style of the late nineteenth century. This is often a pity; there is room for, and indeed need for many approaches to the art of music, and the composer who is most happy when "thinking big" is handicapping himself unnecessarily when he tries to thwart his natural instinct and become a miniaturist.

The fact must be faced that some types of compositional techniques today are not really suited to the limitations of the average human voice. Choral music is in a way set apart from the normal course of music-making for a composer. The contemporary composer is to a very large extent preoccupied with techniques often serial in one form or another, but in any case usually chromatic; the rhythm is likely to be subtle and varied, and the texture anything from very sparse to very dense. When we get to the stage where even a trio needs a conductor (and this I have seen myself at a European festival), it is not surprising that the performer sometimes feels that the composer is asking too much of him.

This is not quite a new situation in music; we can remember that Beethoven and even Schubert were considered difficult by their contemporaries. Nevertheless, it is new that a great deal of music being written today demands a top-class professional to perform it. In the field of instrumental music the challenge can be met, though any composer will be able to tell of performances of his work which were badly under-rehearsed. There are, too, solo singers who can cope with the most awkward problems; it is when we come to the field of choral singing that we find the biggest difficulty. There are a few professional or semiprofessional choruses which can be expected to sing the most testing music, but in general choral singers are amateurs, and sing for pleasure. In this country (England), at least, they come along to the weekly rehearsal to "have a good sing," and are exasperated or bored when they have to spend a long time working at problems of intonation and rhythm. A work which is difficult, but which holds out promise of ultimate reward, can be dealt with, but too often contemporary music for chorus is awkward, frustrating, and unsatisfactory in performance.

There is, of course, no doubt that many problems tend to disappear in the course of time—that today's passages of great difficulty become tomorrow's commonplaces, but that is not always of much help to the harassed chorus trainer. It is certainly a great advantage to a composer to have had the chance to work with a chorus; even more than is the case with instrumental music, choral music needs long and intimate experience before it can be tackled with success.

My own choral works are four in number: two unaccompanied, one with small orchestra, and an oratorio. The two unaccompanied ones are *Three Fragments from the Song of Roland,* set to medieval French words, and *Two Carols* on fourteenth-century texts, a setting of macaronic English and Latin words. In these I have tried to avoid using a musical language which would be incongruous with the direct simplicity of the words. There are few passages of polyphony; the texture is for the most part homophonic, with triadic harmony and a non-chromatic melodic line. Especially in the *Roland* settings there is a tendency toward doubled two-part writing (octaves between soprano and tenor, and between alto and bass), with a preponderance of bare fourths and fifths.

The work with small orchestra is another matter. The text is Andrew Marvell's *Musick's Empire,* a poem of some elaboration and artificiality. The work is not a long one, but I felt myself free to use such devices as fugue and canon, and even double fugue. Moreover the poem is so shaped as to allow a recapitulation of the opening soprano theme, so that there can be an attempt at formal unity not always possible in word setting. In short, the work has perhaps something in common with the *Odes* of Purcell; not of course in musical language, but in the use of set formal devices, and even to an adaptation of the typical Purcellian cadence, with its simulatneous tonic and leading note.

In 1958 the Leeds Triennial Festival was in its hundredth year, and the organizers asked me if I would write a full-scale oratorio for the

83

occasion. In spite of some initial doubts about whether the "traditional" English oratorio would fit into the mid-twentieth century, I accepted with eagerness; I had long had in my mind the possibility of setting part of the remarkable poem *Christ,* by Cynewulf. Practically nothing is known of this eighth- or ninth-century English poet, and probably only a few of the poems attributed to him are actually his. Nevertheless, those that are certainly by him show a quite astonishing dramatic and imaginative power, and it was particularly those passages in his poem dealing with the Day of Judgement that made a deep impression on me when I first read them.

In preparing the text of *The Vision of Judgement,* a good deal of cutting and rearranging was necessary; the original is long and somewhat repetitive, and I was conscious of the need for a satisfactory overall musical form as well as a logical poetic one. The final shape is of two main movements (or acts, if the work is considered dramatically), divided by an interlude, an unaccompanied chorus. The first of these movements falls into five sections:

I (Introduction)—A choral recitative, depicting the terror of the people of earth at the approach of the great day of the Lord Omnipotent. This is a homophonic setting with sharp contrasts in dynamics. The main orchestral motif, a succession of superimposed fifths, is used frequently in the first part of the work (see Example VII, 1, at the back of this volume).

Interlude—Dona Nobis Pacem—Sancta Maria, Ora Pro Nobis. This is for the two soloists, soprano and tenor, and semichorus, accompanied by organ. (The Latin words, here and later, are not in Cynewulf's poem; I added them to express the prayer and anguish of the people of earth, and to act as dividing points between the main sections of the work.)

II—A "symphonic allegro" in two sections, describing the sounding of the trumpets by resplendent angels. The second section, the longer and more important of the two formally since it is used again later, is preceded by the first entry of the additional brass groups, stationed on either side of the orchestra. The climax is the sequence of piled-up fifths of the opening, leading into:

Interlude—Miserere Nobis (chorus)—Ave Maria (unaccompanied tenor).

III—A short choral introduction, "Then shall be heard a people sorrowing," in the form of a slow march, leads to a soprano aria telling of the coming of Christ, stern to the sinful, and blessing those he loves. This, like the later tenor aria, is self-contained, and thematically quite independent from the rest of the work. At the end, an *ostinato* flute solo accompanies the women's voices singing, "Well shall it be for those souls who in that stern time shall please God" (see Example VII, 2).

A short linking passage for the orchestra on a theme prominent in the second part (see Example VII, 3) leads to:

IV—Another and longer "symphonic allegro." This is also in two parts; the first depicts the destruction of sun, moon, and stars. The orchestra and chorus are reinforced by the additional brass at another reference to the trumpets sounding, and there is a recapitulation of the second part of Section II. The climax, "Of all great sounds this shall be the greatest, bringing fear to men," is followed by the final appearance in its full form of the passage in fifths of the opening.

A solo trombone echoes the Ave Maria sung earlier by the tenor, and this acts as introduction to:

V—A tenor solo, telling of the destruction of earth. It ends in mourning, with a different version of the coda to the soprano solo (Section III), "Well shall it be for those souls . . . ."

This completes the first part, or "act." The emphasis has been on destruction, and on the fear and agony of sinners. The second part considers the joys of the blessed, but before this there is a long unaccompanied setting for tenor, semichorus, and full chorus of the "Libera Me." This is in a way the core of the work; the Latin of the *Requiem Mass* takes us from *"morte aeterna"* to *"lux perpetua."*

The second "movement" is shorter and more compact than the first. It opens with an allegro chorus, starting quietly and building up gradually, describing the host of the blessed ascending the hill of Heaven. It is cast in the form of a quick march, and may be thought of as a parallel to the slow march of the sorrowing which preceded the soprano solo earlier. Its theme is derived from the orchestral link in the first part, between Sections III and IV. A scherzando version of this theme leads, via a sequence of ascending triads, from the trombones (a sequence of which considerable use is made from here on) to a quiet alleluia for eight-part chorus.

85

The second section of the finale is a duet for the two soloists, the picture of the joys of "the home that never shall know end." These words suggest the use of the most elaborate orchestral textures of the work, with perpetual canons for divided violins and for the voices, and quiet *ostinatos* for percussion and harps. It ends with a decorated version for the soloists of the earlier choral alleluia.

The final tripartite chorus begins softly with an echo of the opening of the duet. The central section is a *passacaglia*, "There is angels' song"; the theme, a succession of dropping and rising fifths, is derived from the piled-up fifths which were prominent in the first movement (see Example VII, 4). The final section is a prolonged and joyous alleluia.

I have gone into the form of this oratorio in some detail because for me the construction is an extremely important part of the business of composition. *The Vision of Judgement* is planned to fall into two parts, the first dealing with terror and destruction, the second with joy and praise. The only direct quotation of a theme is in the opening section of the second part, which is, as I have said, foreshadowed in an orchestral link in the first part. The motive of piled-up fifths in the first part becomes that of successive fifths in the *passacaglia* of the second part, a case of transformation which is probably not at all obvious to the listener, but which is necessary to me as a composer.

There is, too, a harmonic link between the two halves of the work. The opening shows a tendency toward D major, with a prominent A-flat as a kind of dominant. This A-flat–D major relationship is repeated in the final bars—again this is not likely to be noticed by the listener in a work lasting nearly an hour, but it satisfies my sense of shapeliness. Incidentally, I realized after the performance that A-flat used as a dominant of D is the basic harmonic factor of my *Second Symphony,* written nine years before—a coincidence of which I was entirely unaware when I was working on *The Vision of Judgement.*

It will be seen that I have tried to give the work an overall unity by dividing it into scenes and set-pieces in somewhat the same way that Berg did in *Wozzeck.* These scenes are separated from each other either by the piled-up-fifths motive of the beginning, expressive of despair and anguish, or by the Latin interpolations. In only one case are two scenes run together; these are the second and third of the second part, the duet and the final chorus. In addition to sharing thematic material, they also share a common tempo. The quaver (eighth-note) remains at a constant speed, so that 3/8 (allegro), 3/4 (moderato), and 3/2 (*maestoso*) are, so to speak, geared together. Most of the 3/4 sections feature a saraband-like rhythm which is intentionally used as a unifying factor, and can be seen in Example VII, 4.

The chorus needed is a large one—nearly 350 at the first performance. Both double four-part and single eight-part choruses are called for— which I admit raises problems in arranging the seating. A five-part semichorus is also needed. The most elaborate textures are to be found in the unaccompanied "Libera Me," in which the semichorus and full chorus occasionally provide thirteen separate strands. The writing usually avoids the use of such a strict device as fugue, which would be out of place in a generally dramatic work. However the "Libera Me" is treated more formally, as a point of repose between the two "acts," and here a good deal of use is made of imitative counterpoint (see Example VII, 5).

My description of the work has not dealt with the musical language used. This is deliberate; to use words to interpret music is usually very misleading. As far as idiom is concerned, I tried to strike a balance, to create a work which would take its place in a somewhat conventional field—the traditional English oratorio—without sacrificing my own natural style.

I should like to be able to give an opinion about the future of choral music, but I do not think that this is possible as things are at present. There should not really be much limit to what a chorus can undertake, and the sound of massed human voices should stimulate the composer to his greatest heights of inspiration. But we are all bound by convention —the caution of chorus trainers and managements, the timidity of singers, and the weight of public and critical opinion all combine to prevent us from seeing just what could be achieved. I find it difficult to believe that extreme serial techniques will produce choral music of stature, however interesting the results may be in other fields. Perhaps the massed effects of some of the works of Carl Orff are a pointer to a new style in large-scale choral music. Perhaps, too, we might think out again the very structure of the chorus—in view of the drastic and almost universal shortage of good chorus tenors, composers might experiment with a three-line rather than a four-line texture. I know of many re-hearsals where a work for sopranos, altos, and baritones would have been welcomed. This might also relieve us of some of the muddily thick writing which has produced so many dull and unattractive works, works which, however interesting on paper, prove to be disappointing in performance.

In my experience in writing choral works, and especially with *The Vision of Judgement,* I have come to realize that choral music is not only very much alive, but is a most necessary and rewarding field for a composer. For one thing, it is a real chance for the composer to work with amateurs, and to get to know their needs, their likes and dislikes. It is all too easy to get into the habit of writing for a small group of highly skilled and experienced professionals, forgetting that the amateur has just as great a part to play in the development of our art. If there is a gap today between the composer and his public, as is sometimes alleged, this kind of thinking has helped to create it.

Secondly, choral music is a largely unexplored field today because many composers are so conventional in their approach to it. There are a great many I can think of who in their orchestral music show origi-nality and invention, but who, when they write for choirs, seem to be unable to forget the counterpoint exercises of their youth. It is rare now-adays to find a work that shows an awareness of choral color (the equiva-lent of orchestration) that we can find in Monteverdi or Gabrielli. I know of nothing to compare with the forty-part motet *Spem in Alium,* of Tallis, with the almost stereophonic effect of blocks of sound shifting from one side of the auditorium to the other. We are, as composers, often too cautious and unimaginative, and too suspicious of the amateur's skill.

Thirdly, music for the human voice is the very foundation on which our musical heritage is built. It is often a temptation for a composer to immerse himself in a private and even overrefined world of his own. It is difficult to retain this attitude when considering the writing for choirs; here we must remember that warmth and humanity must always be a part of the art of music.

9. *The Water and the Fire*

ANTHONY MILNER

ANTHONY MILNER (born in London on May 13, 1925) was educated at Douai School, Woolhampton, Berkshire, between 1939 and 1943. As a scholar at the Royal College of Music (1945–47), he studied composition with R. O. Morris and piano with Herbert Fryer. Between 1944 and 1947, Milner worked privately on composition with Mátyás Seiber. Morley College (London) appointed Milner tutor in theory and music history in September, 1947. Since 1954 he has been an extension lecturer for the University of London. The Royal College of Music placed him on its staff in 1962. Since 1952, Milner has been director and harpsichordist of the London Cantata Ensemble, a group specializing in the performance of Baroque literature. The presentation of his choral work *Salutatio Angelica* at the International Society of Contemporary Music festival in Oslo in 1953 brought him international recognition. In addition to composing and performing, Milner is a frequent contributor to periodicals and books on music. His most recent book is *Music in Performance: An Anthology of Descriptions from Centuries Past, with Comments* (London, 1963).

A dramatic oratorio, *The Water and the Fire* has four scenes and calls for a large choir (divided into two choirs in Scene 4); a boys' choir (singing mainly in unison); and soloists—soprano, tenor, and baritone. The necessary instruments are two flutes (doubling piccolo), two oboes, two clarinets, two bassoons, four horns, three trumpets, three trombones, bass tuba, timpani, percussion (two players), two harps, organ, and strings. Its duration is roughly fifty minutes.

This work was written for the 1960 Three Choirs Festival at Worcester but, since an illness prevented me from finishing the fourth scene in time to allow sufficient choral rehearsal, the performance had to be canceled. Its structure and textures were planned to take account of the considerable resonance and echoes of a large medieval cathedral, the generally straightforward choral writing being designed to suit the necessarily limited rehearsal schedule of this festival.

The libretto (consisting of Biblical extracts, a quotation from St. Augustine's *Confessions,* poems by St. John of the Cross and St. Teresa of Avila, and portions of the Easter Vigil liturgy[1]) narrates symbolically and allegorically the plight of man estranged from God and his subsequent repentance and reconciliation, viewed in the context of Christ's Passion and Ressurection. Two quotations prefacing the score—*"O vere beata nox"* and a phrase of Jacques Maritain, *"toute l'immense nuit du corps animé"*—point to the background of the drama: night seen first as the darkness of sin and separation, later as the "dark night of the soul" and the prelude to resurrection. The other two main symbols, the water and fire of the title, also have manifold significations: water symbolizes the storm of divine anger (Scene 1), the "waters of death" (Scene 2), yet also the presence of God (Scene 3) and the waters of baptism (Scene 4). The separation of the male and female soloists in Scenes 1 and 3 represents the disunity of fallen man; their duet in Scene 4, the renewal of human harmony of the Redemption. There is no need for symbolic commentary in program notes; symbols lose their force and savor when expounded. Since most of those employed are well known in their Biblical context, the primary meaning of the drama is easily understood. In Scene 1 the solo tenor represents mankind while the chorus is confined to narration and comment, but in Scene 2 the chorus gradually stands forth as humanity en masse with the tenor as spokesman. By Scene 4 the chorus is completely involved in the action: the mere spectators of the opening bars have now entered into the heart of the drama as the redeemed children of God; drama is assumed into liturgy and representation transformed into ritual participation. The

---

[1] Extracts from Isaiah, Chapters XLI, LII, and LIII, are taken from Ronald Knox's translation of the Bible by permission of His Eminence the Cardinal Archbishop of Westminster. Extracts from the Revised Standard Version of the Bible are reprinted by permission of Thomas Nelson and Sons, Limited, and the National Council of the Churches of Christ in the United States. *Song of the Soul That is Glad to Know God by Faith* (Stanzas 1–2, 4–7, 10–12), translated by Roy Campbell, is published by the Harvill Press, Limited, and reprinted by permission of Hughes, Massie and Co., Limited—A. M.

duration of this final scene equals the sum of the preceding three, thus ensuring a balance between light and darkness, sorrow and joy.

The swift progress of the drama is largely due to the absence of verbal repetition. Sectional forms—ternary, rondo, *ostinato,* episodic—provide the large-scale musical organization; unity is obtained by pervading motifs. While the contrast of "diatonic" and "chromatic" elements is fundamental to the conception of the work, tonality of some sort (in the sense that a note or chord acts as a center) is never entirely absent even in the sections almost completely devoid of key-structure. The main tonality is C, in which the work begins and ends. Passages where choral intonation is likely to be uncertain are either doubled entirely in the orchestra or supported by stressing their main notes in the accompaniment. Rehearsal can be simplified by making the singers memorize the chief motives before embarking on the study of extended sections.

Scene 1, "Descent to the Pit," begins with a recitative for the solo soprano, whose first (unaccompanied) phrase presents the important "motivic" intervals (marked *) that dominate the entire movement (see Example VIII, 1, at the back of this volume):

> *By night upon my bed I sought him whom my soul loveth.*
> *I sought him, but I found him not;*
> *I called him, but he gave no answer.*
> *I said: "I will arise now and go about the city,*
> *in the streets and in the squares*
> *I will seek him whom my soul loveth."*
> *I sought him but I found him not.*

The rhythmic pattern (Figure a, 𝄾♪|♫) that follows "he gave no answer" builds up under the voice to an orchestral fortissimo, at which the chorus enters over an *ostinato* of four notes with the first important theme (see Figure b in Example VIII, 2).

> *Mourns the world and withers;*
> *men have transgressed the laws,*
> *broken the everlasting covenant.*
> *Therefore a curse devours the earth*
> *and men suffer for their guilt.*

The soprano joins the lament; the falling semitone stressed by the choir at "for their guilt" (see example VIII, 3A) becomes an accompaniment figure (see Example VIII, 3B).

> *The wine sours, the vine languishes,*
> *all the merry-hearted sigh.*
> *Desire fails; and love is troubled and made cold.*
> *All joy has reached its eventide.*

The choral texture underlines the ternary form: beginning with octaves and unison the first section moves toward two-part harmony. Four-part harmony opens the middle section, which gradually returns to two-part; the last section employs octaves and unison. Another important figure appears with the final sentence (see Example VIII, 4).

A tenor aria in two sections follows, the first, allegro agitato, introduced by solo bassoon and basses (whose figures provide accompaniment material) later joined by a solo trumpet and the main orchestral body.

> *I look for peace, but no good comes;*
> *for a time of healing, but behold, terror!*
> *For I hear the sound of the trumpet, the alarm of war.*
> *Disaster follows hard on disaster. The whole land is laid waste.*
> *Suddenly, my tents are destroyed, my curtains in a moment.*

The aria's second section, adagio molto, is built on a scale motif (see Example VIII, 5) which later descends to the bass, leading to an orchestral restatement of the music of the first chorus.

> *I looked on the earth, and lo, it was waste and void,*
> *and to the heavens, and they had no light.*
> *I looked on the mountains, and they were quaking,*
> *and all the hills moved to and fro.*
> *I looked, and there was no man; all the birds of the air had fled;*
> *the fruitful land was a desert; all its cities laid in ruins.*

The orchestra hammers at the figure earlier used for the words "therefore a curse devours the earth" and then subsides to an uneasy muttering in the bass. A recitative:

> *The windows of heaven open*
> *The earth's foundations tremble.*

ushers in the approaching storm; the chorus describes its onslaught, punctuated by fragments of Example VIII, 2, in the orchestra.

> The floods lift up,
>   the floods lift up their voice,
>   the floods lift up their roaring.
> The clouds pour out water,
>   the skies thunder.

This is the commencement of a gradual rise to a choral and orchestral climax which is the central point of the scene. The storm breaks: the chorus sings either in octaves or in two parts doubled in octaves against the hissing of the rain and the surge of the sea. This is the only difficult choral entry in the work: the clue to its successful negotiation lies in the brass line of the preceding orchestral bar.

> The Lord makes lightnings for the rain,
>   bringing the wind from his storehouse.
> Deep calls to deep at the noise of His cataracts.
> The crash of His thunder is in the whirlwind:
> His lightnings lighten up the world.

The orchestra carries the storm to its height, affording the choir a breathing space before the manifestation of the Divine Majesty in large sweeping diatonic lines, rising to a thundered mixture of two major triads (E and B-flat) supported by the organ. One of the main problems of rehearsal is to keep the maximum amount of choral tone for this culminating outburst:

> Mightier than the thunders of many waters,
>   mightier than the waves of the sea,
>   mightier than the storms and the tempests,
>   the Lord on high is mighty.

The ensuing section for tenor has three parts; an arioso accompanied by demisemiquaver (thirty-second note) runs and swirls over a simple harmonic foundation:

> He has cast me into the heart of the deep,
>   and the flood is round about me.
> All His waves and billows pass over me,

93

The torrents of perdition assail me,
  the cords of death encompass me.
Save me, O God, for the waters are come in even to my soul.

a recitative employing Figure b and Example VIII, 4:

Have mercy on me, for I know my transgressions,
  and my sins are ever before me.
Against Thee have I sinned,
  and done that which is evil in Thy sight,
  so that Thou art justified in Thy sentence,
  and righteous in Thy judgment.

and a song of two strophes (see Example VIII, 6):

Out of the deep I cry to Thee: Lord, hear my voice.
If Thou, O Lord, wilt mark iniquities,
  Lord, who shall abide it?

Here the tonality of C, hitherto only suggested or adumbrated, emerges clearly. The chorus offers words of comfort, referring again to Figure b and ending with a descending scale pattern that is heard later in Scene 4.

If you set your heart aright, you will stretch out your hand
  toward Him,
If iniquity is in your hand, put it far away.
Surely then you will forget your misery;
  you will remember it as waters that have passed away.

The tenor now recapitulates the material of the first portion of the soprano's opening recitative, closing with Figure b and Example VIII, 4, blended into a single phrase.

Behold, I go forward, but He is not there,
  and backward, but I cannot perceive Him.
He passes me by, and I see Him not.
Darkness hems me in; thick darkness covers my face.

An orchestral interlude presents a melody stressing the chief motivic intervals of the scene. Its tonality seems to hover between E and E-flat minor (see Example VIII, 7), and this ambiguity persists in the middle section, where the melody is inverted and the repeat of the first section a semitone lower.

Scene 2, "Encounter" contrasts strongly with the preceding: its drama is presented more directly (it could be staged), while the Knox translation of Isaiah provides new prose rhythms to lessen the impact of the Hebraic *parallelismus membrorum*. Its tonality (centered on B-flat) is more obvious than that of the "Descent," the harmonies being fuller and the proportion of diatonic writing greater; its form, rondo, much simpler. The halting rhythms of its main theme (see Example VIII, 8), derived from the accompaniment to the soprano recitative of the opening scene, are heard throughout in various guises.

After its first statement, the choir basses ask:

Who is this in the shadows, coming in crimsoned garments?

The theme is repeated, but is interrupted by the chorus:

The world stands gazing in horror;
was ever a human form so mishandled,
human beauty so defaced?

The extended choral passage that follows employs figures from Example VIII, 8, in combination with Figure b:

There is no stateliness, no majesty here to catch our eyes,
no beauty to win our hearts,
Nay, here is one despised, left out of all human reckoning;
bowed with misery, and no stranger to our weakness;
how should we recognize that face?
How should we take any account of him, a man so despised?

The tenor (Figure b), combined with Example VIII, 3B in the orchestra, accosts this unknown outcast:

What mean you by this sacrifice?

The solo baritone answers (Example VIII, 3B, expanding in the orchestra):

For my people's guilt I am smitten: for their sins I am wounded.

The chorus comment in music related to their previous extended passage, with Example VIII, 3B, which is developed by the oboe into an extended melodic line:

> *Our weakness, and he carries the weight of it;*
> *our miseries, and he bears them;*
> *an outcast, a man God has smitten and brought low.*

The musical material described above is combined with new motives in the ensuing dialogue, leading to an aria for the tenor:

TENOR: *Where then is my hope? Will it go down to hell?*
           Shall we descend together into the dust?
BARITONE: *It is I, the Lord thy God, that hold thee by the hand*
(CHRIST)   *and whisper to thee: Do not be afraid.*
           For if I be lifted up, I will draw all things to Myself.

The rhythm of Example VIII, 8, becomes insistent, emphasizing heavy dissonances in preparation for the solo tenor's cry of recognition.

> *Late, late have I loved Thee, O Beauty so ancient and so new!*
> *late have I come to love Thee!*
> *For Thou wert within me, and I outside;*
> *Thou wert with me, yet I was not with Thee.*
> *Thou didst call and cry to me and break through my deafness;*
> *Thou didst shine forth and my darkness was scattered;*
> *Thou didst touch me, and I burned for Thy peace.*

Example VIII, 8, appears in B-flat major, the first clear statement of a major triad in the work. After a hush the dialogue continues:

TENOR: *Now is all my hope only in Thy great mercy.*
CHRIST: *I tread the way of death. I go before Thee.*
         As thou passest through the waters I will be with thee.
         Take up thy cross and follow me.

The music of the tenor's aria in Scene 1 (Example VIII, 6) is repeated:

TENOR: *Whither Thou goest I shall go,*
         and where Thou dwellest I too shall abide.
         For by Thy grief my fall is stayed
         and by Thy bitter agony I am healed.

Over repetitions of Example VIII, 8, in A-flat, the chorus closes the scene:

> *And there is darkness over all the earth,*
> *darkness so thick that it may be felt.*

Scene 3, "The Waters by Night," a soprano aria with a choral refrain, represents a pause in the drama, a period of waiting expressing hope and trust, symbolizing the interval between Christ's death and resurrection. (Compare Romans 6:3–4: "All of us who have been baptized into Christ were baptized into His death. We were buried therefore with Him by baptism into death, so that as Christ was raised from the dead by the glory of the Father we too might walk in newness of life.") The opening bars of the orchestra and the soprano's first stanza (see Example VIII, 9) contain the basic material of the movement, which is varied and developed in subsequent stanzas, the choral refrain either repeating or inverting the four-note motive first heard in Figure d (in Example VIII, 9).

SOPRANO: *How well I know that fountain's rushing flow*
Although by night
Its deathless spring is hidden. Even so
Full well I guess from whence its sources flow
     though it be night.
Full well I know its depths no man can sound
     and that no ford to cross it can be found

CHOIR: *Though it be night.*

SOPRANO: *Its clarity unclouded still shall be:*
Out of it comes the light by which we see

CHOIR: *Though it be night.*

SOPRANO: *Flush with its banks the stream so proudly swells;*
I know it waters nations, heavens, and hells

CHOIR: *Though it be night.*

SOPRANO: *The eternal source hides in the Living Bread*
That we with life eternal may be fed.
Here to all creatures it is crying, hark!
That they should drink their fill though in the dark,

CHOIR: *For it is night.*

SOPRANO: *This living fount which is to me so dear*
Within the bread of life I see it clear
Though it be night.

The final scene, "The Easter Fire," owes much to the shape of the Easter Vigil liturgy, the ritual element being emphasized by musical repetitions, antiphonal singing, and three quotations from the liturgical chant. It commences with an orchestral processional (lento) in three sections, whose function in the general structure corresponds to that of the interlude ending Scene 1. The melody of the first section (in F-sharp) is played by low brass over thirty-two-foot organ pedal notes. After a moment's silence a solo boy treble "from a great distance" sings "Lumen Christi" (see Example VIII, 10, taken from the procession that follows the Blessing of the New Fire in the Vigil rite), answered by the rest of the trebles, "Deo gratias."

I had intended that in the cathedral performance the boys should come from the back of the church down the nave. If possible this should be adhered to for performances in a cathedral or a very large church; in a concert hall the boys should be placed high up in the choir seats, preferably where they cannot be seen by the audience. The second section, *pochissimo piu mosso,* is again followed by "Lumen Christi," this time a minor third higher and "a little nearer." In the third section the melody of the first returns augmented over an *ostinato* bass derived from Figure c (in Example VIII, 9), combined with the melody of the opening chorus (Example VIII, 2), moving to a massive climax. All the trebles intone "Lumen Christi" (one tone higher than the preceding entry) and are answered by the full choir "Deo gratias," with a chord of C major supported by organ and full orchestra while the trebles ring hand-bells (an imitation of the procedure followed at the solemn intoning of the Gloria in the Vigil Mass).[2] The demisemiquaver (thirty-second note) runs in the orchestra and the gradual mixing of G major harmonies with the C major triad recalls the music for "the Lord on high is mighty" in Scene 1. An invocation for the solo tenor follows:

> Rejoice, O choirs of angels in the heavens:
>   rejoice, ye mysteries around the throne of God.
> Let the triumph of salvation sound the triumph of our mighty King!
> Rejoice, O earth, in the radiance of this great splendour:
>   know that from all Thy globe the darkness has been scattered.
> O dear brethren, who are here with me
>   at this wondrous lighting of the holy flame,
>   join me and proclaim the mercy of our God.

2 Special bells are not required: the "dinner-bell" type will suit very well.—A. M.

Throughout the scene the main tonality is that of a "free" C major: the music frequently departs from it episodically but returns at strongly emphasized cadence points forming the terminations of sections. Over shifting six-note chords (see Example VIII, 11) the chorus sings a four-phrase tune, allegro moderato alla danza, beginning with octave doubling and closing in four-part harmony.

> *This the night wherein Thy chosen people passed out of the*
> *house of bondage.*
> *This the night when Israel walked dryshod through the sea.*
> *This the night which purges away the blackness of sin*
> *by the light of Thy pillar of fire.*
> *This the night when Christ burst the bonds of death*
> *and rose victorious from the grave*

An antiphonal section for choir and soloists follows (see Example VIII, 12), the soloists at first interjecting comments but later combining with the choral invocations; the last of these ends in a fortissimo B major chord.

CHOIR: *O holy night,*
SOPRANO: *the very time and hour of Christ's rising from the dead.*
CHOIR: *O truly blessed night,*
               where heaven weds earth and God restores mankind.
SOLOISTS
AND CHOIR: *O holiest night as bright as day which lights up our joy.*
CHOIR: *Lo, the old things have passed away: all is made new.*

In the new key, accompanied by roulades for the wood winds, the tenor addresses the soprano:

> *Arise, my love, my fair one, and come away.*
> *For lo, the winter is past, the rain is over and gone.*
> *The flowers appear upon the earth*
> *and the time of the singing of birds is come.*

As a refrain the choir basses sing the first statement of a threefold "Alleluia" (a chant from the Vigil Mass). The soprano joins the tenor in a duet in which ornamental melismata appear for the first time in the work:

And the voice of the turtle-dove is heard in our land.

A second statement of the "Alleluia" by the choir tenors (in E major with additional accompaniments) leads to another duet, ecstatic and passionate:

SOPRANO: *The fig tree puts forth her figs*
and the vines are in blossom.

TENOR: *Arise, my love, my fair one, and come away.*

SOPRANO: *My beloved is mine, and I am his.*

TENOR: *Arise and come away.*

BOTH: *Alleluia* (repeated several times in rapid coloruturas).

The full choir sings the third statement of the chant "Alleluia" in C major. The vernal joy of the preceding section now yields to liturgical exaltation: the tenor is no longer merely the spokesman of humanity but its priest, and thus summons the choir to join him in the Eucharistic sacrifice. Trumpet fanfares accompany the harmonized Gregorian responses.

TENOR: *Per omnia saecula saeculorum.*

CHOIR: *Amen.*

TENOR: *Dominus vobiscum.*

CHOIR: *Et cum spiritu tuo.*

TENOR: *Sursum corda.*

CHOIR: *Habemus ad Dominum.*

TENOR: *Gratias agamus Domino Deo nostro.*

CHOIR: *Dignum et justum est.*

The tenor begins the Preface of the Vigil Mass in the ritual Latin and traditional chant, the choir accompanying him with a translation of his text:

TENOR: *Vere dignum et justum est, aequum et salutare, Te quidem, Domine, omni tempore, sed in hac potissimum nocte gloriosius praedicare, cum Pascha nostrum immolatus est Christus.*

CHOIR: *Always, O Lord, is it right and good to thank Thee, most of all and loudest on this Night when Christ offers Himself a Victim for us all;*

The choir continues alone, referring to Figure a before resuming the homophonic, antiphonal setting of the text:

Who by dying overcomes our death, and by rising again restores our life, taking away the sins of the world. And therefore with Angels and Archangels, with Thrones and Dominations, with Virtues, Princedoms, and Powers, Cherubim and Seraphim, and with all the heavenly host,

leading to a condensed recapitulation of the *alla danza* section by two choirs, begun by the solo soprano and tenor with the words "On this night." While the first choir repeats "This the night," etc., each phrase being answered by a phrase of the second choir's repeat of "O holy night," etc., the soloists weave coloraturas over both to the words of the second choir. The dance quickens with a new melody shared between the soloists to the words "And therefore with angels," etc., over a variant of the *ostinato* Figure c; this is repeated with added harmonics by the two choirs, leading to a blazing tutti of full orchestra with bells and organ to the words:

We sing a hymn to Thy glory abiding unchanged for ever.

The tonality of the *ostinato* shifts under the C major of the choir; the bells recede into the distance, moving to E flat. A semichorus of boys and men begin the central prayer of praise:

Sanctus, sanctus, sanctus, Dominus Deus Sabaoth

joined by the full choir for the second phrase:

Pleni sunt coeli et terra gloria tua. Hosanna in excelsis.

An instrumental interlude presents a transfigured version of Example VIII, 7, descending (in inversion) from the heights in violins and wood winds to the lower strings and brasses. The semichorus, *con intimissimo sentimento,* continue the prayer:

Benedictus qui venit in nomine Domini

to be joined by the full choir for a (transposed) repeat of

Hosanna in excelsis.

The music for both Sanctus and Benedictus is deliberately ecclesiastical in style, to point the contrast between the previous drama and present ritual. As the final chord of "excelsis" dies away, the cellos recall Example VIII, 2, *con alcune licenza quasi un recitativo;* as it continues, the memory (as it were) of past sin and evil rises threateningly but sinks after a few bars into an agonized dissonance. Over this the tenor joins an inversion of the melodic pattern of Figure b to Figure d:

> *Lord, I am not worthy that Thou shouldst enter under my roof,*
> *but speak the word only and my soul shall be healed,*

the choir repeating "speak the word only" in a whisper. The following arioso for Christ (baritone) starts with figures that recall the opening of Example VIII, 7 (inverted), and the "motivic" intervals of Figure b, moving to quotations from the Sanctus and Benedictus sections.

> *My peace I leave you, My peace I give you,*
> *not as the world gives do I give to you.*
> *Let not your heart be troubled nor let it be afraid.*
> *For lo, I am with you all days, even to the consumation*
> *of the world.*

The final section, *calmato quasi berceuse,* a coda to the work, presents an entirely new melody in D-flat. First heard in the trebles (see Example VIII, 13) it is taken up by the choir, the violins repeating the new version of Example VIII, 7, above it, leading to a double statement of the chant "Alleluia."

The tenor and soprano soloists and choir embellish the continuation of Example VIII, 7, with coloraturas. Example VIII, 13, returns shared between the two soloists and softly accompanied by the choir. It fades into repeated statements of Figure c by the choir and of Example VIII, 10, by the trebles, over a variant of the chord patterns of Example VIII, 11, in the orchestra (Example VIII, 14), settling firmly on a chord of C. The night remains, but it is lit by the brightness of Christ.

10. *Missa in Honorem Sancti Dominici*

EDMUND RUBBRA

EDMUND RUBBRA (born in Northhampton on May 23, 1901) received his first instruction in music (piano) from his mother. At fourteen, he left school and worked for several years as a railway clerk, devoting spare hours to the study of contemporary music and composition. Cyril Scott taught him in these early years. Reading University awarded him a scholarship, which permitted compositional studies under Gustav Holst (1919). Later at the Royal College of Music, Rubbra was strongly influenced by R. O. Morris. Other teachers in composition were some of England's finest composers: John Ireland, Eugene Goossens, and Ralph Vaughan Williams. An excellent pianist, Rubbra has frequently appeared in recitals of chamber music over the years. Since 1947 he has been a lecturer in music at Oxford University.

ALTHOUGH this work was preceded two years earlier by the *Missa Cantuariensis,* the latter, in spite of its Latin title, was written to fulfill a commission from the Anglican Cathedral of Canterbury for a festival, double-choir setting of the Anglican Communion Service. This, therefore, is in English, whereas the work under discussion is in Latin.

The difference of approach in the two works is largely caused by this difference in language, for although the sense of the words remains the same, there are in the Greek and Latin words of the Mass universal overtones that undoubtedly exercise a subtle influence upon the style when they are set to music. It must be understood, of course, that I am here putting forward my own personal reasons for the differences between the *Missa Cantuariensis* and the *Missa in Honorem Sancti Dominici.* There is, for me, a great subtlety of distinction between the English "Lord, have mercy upon us" and the Greek "Kyrie eleison." The former is a localized English transliteration of the meaning of the original, whereas the original words themselves have an aura of universality by reason of an agelong accumulation of religious emotion without distinction of nationality. In setting the English version of the words of the Mass, I am, for better or worse, immediately in contact with the English Cathedral musical tradition, and, intuitively placing myself within it, the result—without, I hope, being less personal—shows where the music is rooted. The Latin words, on the other hand, release me from any allegiance to national traditions, and I approach them with, perhaps, greater awe, but certainly with less inner restrictions, emotional and musical. There is, in the *Missa Cantuariensis,* a musical reserve and objectivity that seem to stem from an inherited uncommittedness to Anglican forms, but in the *Missa in Honorem Sancti Dominici* I am inside the words, warmly and emotionally identifying myself with their universal appeal. This is the reason why I have chosen to discuss the shorter, more concentrated Latin Mass rather than the larger, more complicated Anglican setting.

The intention in writing the Latin Mass in 1948—there was no commission involved here—was to provide a contemporary work that could be used liturgically. This meant, first, that each movement had to be as concise as possible, each point being made with the utmost economy and clarity, with no word repetition beyond that permitted in the liturgy. Secondly, it meant reconciling contemporary musical language with the ideal of liturgical music stated in recent Vatican pronouncements: namely, that such music should help and not disturb the worshiper in Catholic ceremonial. Thirdly, it should aim to be simple enough for the average choir. Above all, I wished to write something that would be a *personal* expression. The reconciliation of all these ideals makes the task of writing such a work immensely difficult. What I have *not* succeeded in doing is to write a work that, at the moment, the average Catholic choir in England can effectively sing without long preparation. But, provided the spirit of the work fits the occasion, it is good for the evolution of choral singing that liturgical works should be written that demand more from the singers than the Mass settings and motets in general use.

The work under discussion is simple in diatonic substance, and there are very few acute dissonances. What personality I have been able to give to the music comes about partly through chordal relationships and the consequent fluidity given to the harmonies. It is here that the choir's ability is tested. For instance, one such passage from the Agnus Dei contains no single chord that by itself is strange to the most untutored choir: the difficulties arise in the transitions (see Example IX, 1, at the back of this volume).

The rhythms are also very free, and adjustments have to be made fairly frequently to different lengths of measure. (This, in fact, is not very different from the practice of the great polyphonic period, for as R. O. Morris has pointed out in his book *Contrapuntal Technique of the Sixteenth Century*,[1] there is rarely metrical regularity in the individual parts, or coincidence of accents when together.) Again, measures of five and seven beats are of common occurrence; the Sanctus, for instance, being in 5/2 throughout, with the exception of one measure. All these echoes of contemporary musical thought, even if the sources of them can be traced back to a much earlier period, somewhat hinder wide liturgical use of the work in England, and by far the greater number of performances have been given by professional or semiprofessional secular choirs in concert or broadcast performances. Indeed, the first performance was given on October 27, 1949, at the Royal Academy of Music, London, by the Fleet Street Choir, the personnel of which was recruited from the ranks of English journalists. It was this choir that recorded the Mass for Decca. (Another recording has been made for ARGO by the Schola Cantorum Choir of Wellington, New Zealand.) Nevertheless, some performances have been given liturgically, notably by the Westminster Cathedral Choir under George Malcolm.

In the Anglican Communion Service the Gloria is placed last, thus giving an opportunity to the composer for an impressive climax to the whole work. But the ritual of the Roman Catholic church, in putting the Gloria second, makes the solving of the overall musical form peculiarly difficult. This difficulty is not present if the work is used exclusively for liturgical purposes, for the spacing of the various numbers so cuts up the music that, if each section is formally self-contained, there is no need for a more unifying thread than is given by, say, a basic key and its related centers, or, as in Byrd's *Five-Part Mass,* a kind of leitmotiv that links the various sections together. If, however, the composer—as is

[1] Oxford University Press, 1922.

most likely—envisages concert performances in which the relatedness of the various movements adds to the overall musical effect, then special attention must be given to the formal unity of the whole. In my Latin Mass, I have treated the Kyrie, Gloria, and Credo as together constituting three related sections, linking the Sanctus, Benedictus, and Agnus Dei in like manner. In effect, there are two movements, each of three sections. Moreover, the C-sharp in the A major chord of the final "pacem" of the Agnus Dei clarifies the ambiguity of the unfilled-in fifth with which the Kyrie begins and ends, thus completing the tonal circle of the music.

In the first three sections (constituting the first "movement") the linkages are by key, rhythm, and interval. The Kyrie is in A minor, but with an inner modal content which includes B-flat and G-natural instead of the usual B-natural and G-sharp: the Gloria is in C major, with B-flat again prominent (see Example IX, 2). The rhythmic linkage between these two movements is found in the dotted rhythm of measure one of the Gloria, which is a diminished version of the rhythm of the ending of the Kyrie (♩. ♩ | ♩♩).

In the Credo, the alto voice has the same interval (fourth) and notes in measure one as in the beginning of the Gloria, and the idea is extended canonically, the slight time-lapse serving to emphasize the fourth, and to break up rhythmically what would be two not very interesting consecutive fifths.

The linking procedure is altered in the last three sections (constituting the second "movement"). Here the note A is the basic starting point—and the interval of a third is predominant in melodic movement. This is illustrated below. (The same process was more extended in the *Missa Cantuariensis,* in which all six movements start from a G that has no fixed significance in any particular scale until a certain direction has been taken.)

In writing choral music I have been in the fortunate position of not having to modify my general style, so that what I write chorally has an idiomatic affinity with everything else I write, whether a symphony or a string quartet. My basic musical thinking has always been diatonic (even if not in the strictly classical sense), and it is likely to remain so. I am in no way convinced that nothing further can be built on diatonic foundations. Diatonicism is not a static concept, and it can continually reveal fresh things by finding new and unexpected relationships. In my particular diatonic thinking, the fifth has assumed an enormous significance. Its very openness and ambiguity—although it is an ambiguity that, paradoxically, is at the same time completely clear—makes it ideal for affecting subtle shifts of tonality without leaving them unbased. Perhaps I may make this clear by quoting from the beginning of the slow movement of my *Sixth Symphony* (see Example IX, 3). Here the changes of harmony have been determined by a simple movement of fifths, and the melodic clothing of these fifths, although apparently in C minor, does not seem to take away from the basic A minor feeling.

Similar shifts are found in the Christe section of the Kyrie in the *Missa in Honorem Sancti Dominici* (see Example IX, 4).

The C-sharp of the tenor voice (and later of the alto voice) becomes temporarily, by reason of the chromatic shift of the fifth, a part of a new triad, which dissolves back again to the original chord. The difference between the effects of the two C-sharps is caused by the particular movement of the accompanying fifth, rising on the first occasion and falling on the second. This, to my mind, is entirely diatonic procedure, and the difficulties inherent in the progressions are largely solved if the accompanying fifths can be kept absolutely steady in pitch. This steadiness gives anchorage for the chromatic movement of the tenor and alto lines.

The canon at the end of the Kyrie is an example of an extension of time-honored procedures, for the octaves of the upper parts move canonically against chords and not against a single line.

An unusual feature of the Gloria is that the opening words, "Gloria in excelsis Deo," are formally set instead of being given in a plain-song version to be sung by the priest. I did this because I felt I wanted a strong choral opening (which, as I wrote earlier, would link itself rhythmically to the end of the Kyrie), should the work be given a concert performance. Liturgically, the opening three measures can be left out, the choir, after the intonation of the Gloria by the priest, entering piano at "Et in terra pax." When the music at the lento ("bonae voluntatis") settles into a clear D-flat major, there is a pronounced melodic movement between D-flat and E-flat in the soprano and an augmentation of this in the tenor. This influences the melodic lines of the polyphonic allegro that follows ("Laudamus te"). The interchanges of material among the voices is constant, creating a unity of texture even if some of the points of imitation are lost in the general *élan* of the movement. Dotted lines on Example IX, 4, show some of the relationships of the parts. It will be noted that movement in fifths is very frequent, and that the bass line, although related melodically to everything above it, has a strong movement within a fourth (D-flat to A-flat), making a link with the fourths of the opening of the movement (C–G, F–B-flat, in Example IX, 5). The next section ("Domine Deus") is a cumulative four-part canon in C-sharp (or D-flat) minor, exact imitations being between the bass and alto voices, and between the tenor and soprano voices a fifth higher. Counterpoint gives to homophony in the next section ("Domine, Fili unigenite"), but it is again dominated by the fifth, often in open form. Here occur occasional stress lines, and a word should be said about my idiomatic use of them, as they are often misunderstood in performance. The marking (—) signifies a combination of stress (very slight) and a correspondingly slight lengthening of note-value; in other words, it indicates nuance. It is impossible to indicate the exact values of these nuances, but the words and syllables themselves will often give an idea of the amount of stress and lengthening required. This homophonic section is continued, for three voices, in the setting of the "Qui tollis," the tenor having a seemingly independent and highly expressive line that punctuates the flow of chords with the words beginning "miserere nobis." In performance, it is the tenor voice that must be prominent against the quietly sustained yet shifting harmonic background of soprano, alto, and bass, *and the crescendos and diminuendos of the tenor voice must never be echoed by the accompanying voices.* The "quoniam" is very quietly harmonic before the final allegro setting of the "Amen" and "Cum Sancto Spiritu." Although all the parts here are marked forte, the "Amens" should in fact be a background to the alto line (see Example IX, 6). One difficulty of balance is nearly always experienced here, unless the basses are strong in tone down to bottom E. To counter this, the basses can be put up an octave, but that obviously alters the spaced harmonic color that I need.

The Credo, like the Te Deum, is very difficult to make into a formal unity when set to music, unless it is divided into many self-contained sections. This is not possible in a liturgical setting: I have, therefore, been content to let the general style of the work, with its many bare unisons, fourths and fifths, create its own unity of feeling. Two sections call for particular comment. First, the Crucifixus (see Example IX, 7). In the example I have quoted the music that precedes this to show how the fifth (B-flat to F) of the Crucifixus has been prepared. This held fifth, which acts as a double background pedal, and which must remain undeviating in pitch, expands and contracts by the contrary motion of the tenors and basses. *The equality of tone of these two lowest voices must remain exactly the same until the end of the section.* Experience has shown that the tenors in this contrary-motion, two-part writing tend to predominate.

The second section to which I would like to draw special attention is the setting of the "Et in Spiritum Sanctum" (see Example IX, 8). Here is seven-part medieval organum expressed in terms of consecutive spread-out triads. Again every part must be balanced so that no voice in the pianissimo texture overweights any other: nor must there be expressive crescendos and diminuendos until the marking at the top of page 17.

The Sanctus is divided into two halves, one pianissimo and one forte. The tonal effect desired in the first section is that of the reverberations of a bell after the main note has been sounded. On paper, it looks as though the overlapping A's in all four voices lead to an accumulation of tone, but that is not desirable, the individual entries merely adding a vibrational throb to the sustained note. Similarly, the notes with a stress and *tenuto* line over them should never be preceded by a crescendo. The forte second section uses the same melodic material, but a diminished fifth higher. Finally, this material is raised another tone, so that the ending is in a clear F major. This key, or rather this chord, is taken over by the Benedictus, which then proceeds to dovetail the basic melodic material of the Sanctus in such a way that five keys are stated in as many bars (see Example IX, 9). Once C-sharp minor has been established, this remains the key of the music from the "qui venit" until the end. The contrapuntal entries of the voices in the "qui venit" are characterized by the progressive enlargement of the interval with which the phrase begins:

D-sharp–E	(second),	tenor.
G-sharp–B	(third),	bass.
B–E	(fourth),	soprano.
E–B	(fifth),	alto.
A–F-sharp	(sixth),	tenor.
C-sharp–B	(seventh),	bass.
B–B	(octave),	soprano.

These enlargements must be made as clear as possible in performance.

The Agnus Dei, apart from expressive accents, is pianissimo throughout. There is very little counterpoint, and the whole effect of the piece depends on retaining clarity of pitch when moving to unrelated triads. Its slowness does, though, give time for this accuracy of pitch to be prepared.

The attitude of the performers toward this work—and indeed to my work generally—should not be one of a withdrawn austerity, just because the look of the printed page is plain and unadorned. Everything, from a hushed pianissimo to a fortissimo, was dramatically conceived, and every marked nuance should therefore be overstated rather than understated. As the exact degree of statement can never be indicated, this must of course be left to the individual intuition of the conductor. But I do want to stress that this is not austere music: it may seem emaciated in its printed appearance, but red blood runs in its veins! The textural reserve of my music comes from an inherent dislike of padding and an unmotivated busyness. Every voice in the texture—and this applies to a symphony as well as to the work under discussion—has its melodic part to play in molding the architecture of the music.

Perhaps I may mention here, in conclusion, that since writing the four-part Latin Mass, I have completed a *Missa a tre* (soprano, alto or tenor, bass). This was commissioned by the Church Music Association of England to meet a demand for a liturgical work that asked for fewer voices and that would be more accessible for general use. This work has six movements, omitting the Credo, and although simpler than the four-part *Missa in Honorem Sancti Dominici,* it still needs adjustment to a style that does not adhere to the tonic-dominant basses of classical music.

11. *A Child of Our Time*

MICHAEL TIPPETT

MICHAEL TIPPETT (born in London on January 2, 1905) began serious musical study at the age of eighteen at the Royal College of Music, where he had composition under Sir Charles Wood and R. O. Morris, and conducting under Sir Adrian Boult and Sir Malcolm Sargent. In 1940 he was appointed musical director of Morley College, London, a position he held until 1952, when he resigned to devote full time to composition. During his tenure at Morley College, Tippett exerted a strong influence on all students and professionals who were associated with him. As a result of his intense interest in music from all periods, the Morley College Concerts Society programmed an unusually fine series of concerts of old and new music. Tippett has often appeared as a lecturer on BBC radio. A collection of these radio lectures, found in his book *Moving into Aquarius* (London, 1959), attests to his searching and comprehensive inquiries into many spheres of music as an art.

I have decided to write about *A Child of Our Time* in the detailed way offered by this collection of essays because I have recently found buried in a drawer a copy of the first draft of the text in the form in which it was shown, twenty-one years ago, to T. S. Eliot. This means that not only have I the advantage of looking back now from a sufficient distance to be reasonably objective about this work, but I can also, at need, think myself back into the time when all was still in the flux of conception.

The matters that seem most generally interesting are how the traditional elements of construction fare with such a contemporary story; how the popular can be joined to the sophisticated, textually and musically; and what are the special problems, if any, that face a composer who writes and constructs his own text.

But first we need a short biographical account of how the work came to be conceived at all, and the role played in its composition by T. S. Eliot.

Large vocal and instrumental works are generally either operas or oratorios. Twice already—with *A Child of Our Time* and with the nearly completed opera *King Priam*—I have been uncertain at the very first whether the work growing in the mind was for the stage or the concert hall. *A Child of Our Time* began in fact as an opera on the Irish rebellion of Easter, 1916. I eventually discarded the material not only because it was unsatisfactory, but also, and principally as I see now, because the dramatic impulse was receding before the contemplative. This is the decisive matter. Only when I had passed that point of decision was I certain the work belonged to the concert hall. I also saw that it belonged in the tradition of the Passions, where the story, as story, is only related as the basis for contemplation. (That is, the composer never prolongs or emphasizes the necessary narrative or descriptive music beyond the essential minimum, in order that as much attention as possible can be given to the contemplative.) But having got so far, it was some time before I found the material for a contemporary Passion which suited me.

This was in the thirties, when the climate of artistic opinion was more concerned with social problems than is general now. My concern was always chiefly compassionate. At the same time I was in many ways more emotionally affected by the growing tensions in Central Europe than most of my compatriots. When these tensions finally issued in September, 1938, as the certainty of another world war, and then when in November of that year the cruelest and most deliberate of the Nazi programs was launched on the pretext of an incident in Paris, the personal amalgam of general compassion for all outcasts and particular susceptibility to the Nazi horror fused into a clear artistic image. The period of searching and conception was over.

I then went to T. S. Eliot, who at that time often guided me in my faltering steps, to ask if he would consent to write my text. This he agreed to do, provided I give him a precise scheme of musical numbers, and an exact scheme of the number and kinds of works I considered necessary for each musical section. I returned home to do just this for him, because I saw at once what he meant. In oratorio or opera the musical schemes must finally be paramount, if the work is to live. I had not read Susanne K. Langer at that time, but, taught in part by Eliot, I instinctively appreciated her dictum: "Every work [of art] has its being in only one order of art; compositions of different orders are not simply conjoined, but all except one will cease to appear as what they are." So that while drama eats up all incidental music and painted stage sets, "music," in Miss Langer's words, "ordinarily swallows words and action creating (thereby) opera, oratorio, or song."

This then was the reason Eliot demanded that I, as the musician, prepare a musical scheme, before he as a poet did anything whatsoever. Also, since he knew as well as I did that narrative recitative needs many words, while a vocal fugue may use next to none, he asked for precise directions concerning the number and kinds of words. As he expressed it: "I need my homework set for me."

What I put down on paper for Eliot is what I have recently unearthed from a drawer. It is headed "Sketch for a Modern Oratorio" (the title had not then appeared), and I shall return to the interesting differences between it and the final text to the printed music later. Suffice it to say that Eliot considered this "Sketch" for some weeks and then gave me the surprising advice to write all the words myself. He felt the "Sketch" was already a text in embryo (as, in fact, it was), and that whatever words he, Eliot, wrote would be of such greater *poetic* quality they would "stick out a mile." While true to his belief in the primacy of the *musical* imagination in opera and oratorio, he considered the more highly poetically imaginative words of a real poet to be often unnecessary.

Thus it was that I began the somewhat unusual task for a composer: to invent or find the necessary words for my own musical scheme.

Set down in such a cold manner as this, it might almost appear as though the musical scheme which the composer needs is to be sought for or conceived as absolutely independent of his dramatic or other verbal material. But the issue is only one of *primacy*. In the case of *A Child of Our Time* the inner feelings, which could only be expressed in some artistic image, were finally given objective substance in the musical scheme of an oratorio, but the dramatic and even philosophic material which the music had to swallow was entirely embedded in the gradually forming musical apprehensions from the very start. A great deal of this fusion of words and music is of necessity traditional. Or rather, there are certain constructive or functional practices which are basic and finally unchangeable. If the dramatic material requires narrative, then this part of the musical scheme will be basically different from the musical correlative to the contemplation or expression of a single situation or emotion. The one is recitative and the other aria; and if they are to play their proper functional or constructive parts in the scheme, they will be analytically, at any rate, recognizable as such.

Narrative or contemplation, recitative or aria, whether for solo voice or for a chorus, these then are the basic functions in any and every scheme of oratorio. Being quite clear on the matter, I found it easier, when I came to prepare his homework for Eliot, to sketch out an embryo text, where of course my proposed words were already at one with my musical scheme.

But from music of the past, I also knew of two local traditions of arrangement which had always fascinated me. The scheme of Handel's *The Messiah,* and the scheme of the Lutheran *Passions.* The shape of *The Messiah* is tripartite. The first part is all prophecy and preparation. The second part is epic: from the birth of Christ to the second coming, judgment, millennium, and world's end. The third part is meditative: chiefly, the words of St. Paul. Incomplete performances, which are the rule, grievously impair this wonderful shape. But I have always observed and admired it. I decided to accept this scheme for *A Child of Our Time* by keeping a first part entirely general, restricting the epic material to a second part, and using a third part for consequential comment.

The scheme of the Lutheran *Passions* is of course more unitary, based as it must be on the liturgical gospel except for Passion Sunday. Within that unitary scheme the traditional musico-verbal functions can always be distinguished: narrational recitative, descriptive chorus, contemplative aria, and finally the special Protestant constituent of the congregational hymn. I wanted to use *all* these functional practices within the tripartite shape borrowed from *The Messiah.*

The obvious difficulty lay of course over the congregational hymn. A modern oratorio based on sensibilities of emotion expressive of inner and outer events in Europe and America between the world wars, and destined for the concert hall and not the church, cannot merely use the metaphorical language of liturgical Christianity. I mean to say that

Christian hymns could not speak to agnostics or Jews; Jewish hymns could speak to the general concert-hall public even less. For to "speak" in this sense, is to do the operation which much-loved traditional hymns do to the appropriate congregation of the faithful. But in what sense at all are we in a concert hall a congregation of the faithful?

I was for long at a loss. Then one never-to-be-forgotten Sunday, I heard a colored singer on the radio sing Negro songs, including the spiritual "Steal Away." At the phrase "The trumpet sounds within-a my soul," I was blessed with an immediate intuition: that I was being moved by this phrase in some way beyond what the musical phrase in itself warranted. I realized that in England or America everyone would be moved in this way, forcing me to see that the unique verbal and musical metaphor for this particular function in this particular oratorio had been found. But it was not until after the world war, which soon supervened, that I could test in performance the fact that the Negro spiritual presented no expressional barriers anywhere in Europe. Nor maybe anywhere in the world.

Having found the unique congregational chorus which belonged so exactly to the rest of my material, I was exercised by the technical problems of presentation. But first I sent to America for a collection of spirituals, and when these came, I had an experience I imagine very similar to those of the Lutheran composers. I opened the collection and found that it contained words and tunes for every dramatic or religious situation that could be imagined. I chose therefore five spirituals, for their tunes and their words, which provided the exact "congregational" metaphor for five calculated situations in my scheme.

The next question, of presentation, meant a further purchase from America; this time of recordings of *a cappella* presentations of spirituals by the relatively conventional Hal Johnson Choir (whom I remembered from the sound track of the film *The Green Pastures*), and by the extreme "hot" group of solo singers which was called, I think, the Mitchell Christian Singers. These latter went in for cross-rhythmical counterpoint by the spoken voice, as well as a great deal of blues-provoked ambiguity of pitch. Fascinating though this disc was, I had to forego such extreme methods of presentation for the sake of the normal European concert-hall choir. And, with regard to the Hal Johnson methods, I realized that I needed to purify the harmonies and clarify the contrapuntal texture.

This brings me to the second matter of general interest in this essay: that of fitting the popular to the sophisticated. There is nothing of course specifically choral in this problem. It is also nothing new. The European experience has been more concerned with folk song and dance, while America has been more consistently concerned with jazz (using this for a moment as a blanket term). But *A Child of Our Time* presented a special problem because of its being an oratorio. I did not need to use Negro material for its flamboyance, or its nostalgia, or its crude rhythmical exhilaration (all of which elements are drawn upon in *Porgy and Bess,* for instance). I had to see how this musical vernacular could be sufficiently purified to take the charge of feelings of a rather higher order without at all losing its immediacy of appeal. This was the basic problem, and I think it can be said that it was solved.

This venture did not lie exclusively in purifying the conventional harmonies of sentimentality. It lay rather in apparently excluding all harmonies whatsoever. I accepted the underlying conventional chord of the added seventh particular to each spiritual, and often sought variety only through rhythmic counterpoint, and by playing tonal masses of choral sound off against solo-voiced leaders. The consequently harmonically static choruses at the five critical points provided a peculiar contrast to the much more harmonically ambiguous music of the other members. They became periods of rest.

Having got so far, I had also to accept that this virtue of emotional release provided by the spirituals had to be paid for by allowing the popular words and music to affect the general style, within which the sophisticated numbers of the oratorio had to be written. I will deal with the textual matters more fully later in this essay. As for the music, I used the interval of a minor third, produced so characteristically in the melodies of the spirituals when moving from the fifth of the tonic to the flat seventh, as a basic interval of the whole work—sometimes on its own, sometimes superimposed upon the open fifth below the lower note.

These intervals (minor third, fifth, and flat seventh) could lead on one side toward a kind of sliding chromatic fugue (see Example X, 1, at the back of this volume); and on the other to a Kurt Weill-like tango (see Example X, 2), or even to a dance-like accompaniment (see Example X, 3).

Nevertheless, after the first performance, because the spirituals were so well-known and immediate, even though the rest was unknown, there was a good deal of press criticism concerning the propriety of putting the popular into the sophisticated in this way. But subsequent performances have set all to rights. The spirituals are seen to be an integral and essential part of the work, and the transitions to them seem now particularly effective.

When I took the "Sketch" to Eliot, I had already decided upon the five spirituals and observed their brand of folk poetry. There were first and foremost specific references to the Bible: "Go down Moses, way down in Egyptland"; echoes of the Apocalypse: "The trumpet sounds within-a my soul"; homely phrases such as "Nobody knows the trouble I see" and "I'm goin' to lay down my heavy load"; and wonderful poetically fresh metaphors like the line from "Deep River," "I want to cross over into camp-ground," which particularly stirred me. As with the Negro melodies therefore, when I came to take stock of how I could best indicate to Eliot the kind of words I imagined suitable, I turned first to the verses of the spirituals, and noted the various metaphors I have listed above.

Or rather the taking stock was more elaborate. I tried to set in order all the considerations of musical and dramatic shape (*The Messiah* and the *Passions*) and all the considerations which I had so long pondered concerning the dramatic and philosophic material itself. Because these deliberations had been so extensive and prolonged, I think, everything was ripe for laying down a viable scheme of numbers with their lengths and kinds, and even for indicating by actual words what I meant. That is, as I have mentioned above, indication by actual words seemed the most immediate and simple. But since I was always expecting that Eliot's words would replace mine, I wrote my words on every right-hand page of the manuscript book and wrote an explanation of what I was intending on every left-hand page.

It is clear from a comparison of the first "Sketch" with the published work that I was able to set down straightaway a musical-dramatic scheme (of three parts, each containing several numbers) which remained unchanged. I prefaced each part (but especially Part 1) with a chorus which I considered functionally as a kind of "Prologue in Heaven" on the lines of Goethe's *Faust:* i.e., everything seen in the most general terms in relation to the cosmos. I then proceeded inward from that point. In the overall tripartite scheme, the same inward movement takes place from the general to the individual, from Part 1 to Part 2 (and then out again in Part 3) as happens within Part 1 itself. It is easier to see in tabular form:

I   The overall pattern.
> Part 1   The "situation" in general terms; from cosmic to human.
> Part 2   The effects of the "situation" on an individual human being.
> Part 3   Meditations on this drama; moving outward again toward the generally human.

II   The outward-inward-outward movement of the scheme of Part 1, which was to echo the same rhythm as between the three parts:
> 1   Choral overture: the "cosmological" position.
> 2   Alto solo: a generalized argument; with Alto considered as personification of the soul, whether of the world or of man.
> 3   A scene of question and answer between Chorus and Alto concerning the Argument. (This and the two numbers above made up my idea of a "Prologue in Heaven.")
> 4   Bass solo: narration of the general human situation in our time; the Bass considered (to quote the "Sketch") "as a father-God figure."
> 5   Choral fugue: for which I first wrote no words, simply writing, "Chorus of the Oppressed"; the Chorus personifying now the generally human.
> 6   Tenor solo: statement of the ordinary man within this general mass; i.e. (in terms of my theme), his cry of anguish.
> 7   Soprano solo: statement of the ordinary woman; her cry of anguish.
> 8   A spiritual: the first hint of comfort, at least in simple generalized terms.

If we look back for a moment first at the overall pattern, we can see that if each part began with a prologue-chorus, then the choruses would be in relation to each other as well as in relation to the coming part each prefaced. Using the final text, this is how they read:

Part 1   The world turns on its dark side.
        It is winter.
Part 2   A star rises in mid-winter.
        Behold the man! The scapegoat!
        The child of our time.
Part 3   The cold deepens.
        The world descends into the icy waters
        where lies the jewel of great price.

From the above finished example the problems of writing or constructing one's own text to one's own musical-dramatic scheme can be easily seen. Thus, having decided on the function of the choral overtures and having decided that musically each was "to be a short constructed chorus on a 'text' or two 'texts,' to last about a minute or more" (to quote from the instruction to Eliot for Chorus 1), the verbal problem reduced itself from the nebulous to the particular: to that of style and metaphor.

Eschewing the poetic, which seemed to be inappropriate to the theme, I wanted a style of short statements, whether of story or comment. I called this style to myself "lapidaric." Remembering the poet Wilfred Owen, killed in World War I, who had always seemed close to me in spirit, I thought of one of his prophetic poems and the lines:

War broke. And now the winter of the world
With perishing great darkness closes in.

I joined this notion of seasons in history with personal experience concerning the "dark" and the "shadow" in C. G. Jung's terminology, and then wrote for Eliot the two texts of Chorus 1 in my own oversimple words:

The world turns on its dark side.
It is winter.

On the opposite left-hand page I explained discursively for Eliot what I needed, and quoted the lines from Wilfred Owen. I did all this for every number. That is, I considered carefully the function of the proposed number, its duration, etc.; invented or borrowed words that could stand as example; and wrote an explanation. Where I could think of no example, I wrote only the explanation and left the right-hand page free.

Now, when once Eliot had persuaded me that the "Sketch" had a viable shape, in his opinion, and that I myself had already done much of the strictly verbal work, I had to get down to filling up the gaps and the words. Not being a poet but a composer, I took endless advice, whether for whole phrases or simple words. I also hunted in literature. Thus, for the short text needed for the choral fugue "Chorus of the Oppressed," I eventually twisted a sentence from Isaiah to read:

When shall the usurer's city cease?

And I was excited, I remember, when I made use of an anonymous "folk" expression in a later declamatory chorus: "Let them starve in No-Man's-Land!" "No-Man's-Land" had a fine ring about it, expressed exactly what I wanted, and joined itself admirably to the Negro metaphors, such as, "I want to cross over into camp-ground, Lord."

Much less successful, in my opinion, were the occasional indigestible psychological metaphors which produced phrases like "I am caught between my desires and their frustration as between the hammer and the anvil." But the psychological jargon gave one tremendous phrase which is the motto for the whole work: "I would know my shadow and my light, so shall I at last be whole." The seasonal metaphor gives the final words (before the last spiritual): "It is Spring."

Summing up this matter of shape and text, it seems to me that the composer works with himself as librettist in much the same way as he would work with a poet. Unless he is willing to give over the whole conception of shape to the poet, he *must* prepare the poet's homework, as I did for Eliot. This preparation is the kernel of all choral composition. Any study of viable successful choral works to previously existing poems shows that even there the composer shapes his musical pattern for his purpose, not for the purposes of the poem as poetry. This is probably less prolonged a preparation (though Beethoven considered Schiller's *Ode to Joy* for very many years), but it is no different in kind from the less usual case of a composer trying with help and advice, to construct his own text for his own music.

Although the scheme or shape of a choral work is the primary consideration in my opinion, there remains the problem of fulfilling the scheme musically. *A Child of Our Time* makes its effect in fact more by the unity and intensity of the mood than by its formal shape. A mediocre performance draws attention to many formal weaknesses. Only the singleness of emotion saves it. This means that it is no use going to such a work as *A Symphony of Psalms* for the formal satisfaction we obtain from it. The whole musical apparatus is much more naïve.

Again, it is not this naïveté as such which has taken the work so far afield, though it helps to bring the work within range of amateur choral societies. It is the directness of the statement and the compelling power of the mood. These things move the ordinary public more than they do the fashionably smaller public which follows the *avant-garde* work.

I myself could hardly remain satisfied with this musical style, which could only fit this special theme. The opera *The Midsummer Marriage*, which is my next big work for voices and orchestra, is as texturally rich as *A Child of Our Time* is simple. Only in the opera *King Priam*, which I am writing now, have I presented myself with a dramatic material which demands declamatory power and concision of text and music, but with none of the folk-elements of *A Child of Our Time*. Each work, in fact, asks for its own style.

We are in a period when the whole world is beginning to interact culturally. There are therefore innumerable local publics with every kind of aesthetic need. It is only on a somewhat primitive level that these publics are one mass public of human beings. Popular music, through the extreme simplicity of its concern with entertainment, knows already no barriers to the provenance of its musical material, taking it from any and every source. Then by disc and film and radio the whole world, so to speak, listens to the whole world. But once composers deal with aesthetic emotions above these primitive levels, then the question of their audience is also no longer so simple and so extensive.

If looked at over the whole world, the innumerable publics need (and obtain) the greatest variety of musical works. But broken down into smaller units, then it is clear that it will depend on the particular gifts and inclinations of each composer where he thinks he fits into the world pattern. He may be gifted and inclined to cultivate one specialty of style and content, or he may need to change and develop.

The one certainty is that there will be over the world no limit to the validity of different styles. Even in Europe and America at the present moment, there are chorally interested composers as diverse as Orff and Dallapiccola; or as Stravinsky of *Canticum Sacrum* and Britten of *A Spring Symphony*. All are valid.

PART THREE

Continental European Composers

12. *Der Tod zu Basel*

CONRAD BECK

(Translated by Anna K. Neufeld)

CONRAD BECK (born in Lohn, Canton Schaffhausen, Switzerland, on June 16, 1901) began engineering studies but, after a brief time, switched to music. He attended the Zurich Conservatory and was a pupil of Volkmar Andreae. From 1923 to 1932, Beck lived in Paris and was associated with the two groups of musicians surrounding Arthur Honegger and Albert Roussel. Although Beck's style of musical composition reflects influences of both composers, he did not actually study with them. In 1932, Beck took up residence in Basel, where, in 1939, he was appointed director of the music section of Radio Basel. He still retains this position. For several decades the works of Conrad Beck have enjoyed frequent performances by prominent artists in Europe and the United States. He gained recognition in the United States while in his twenties when Koussevitsky conducted his *Third Symphony*. Among the many honors Beck has received is the Elizabeth Sprague Coolidge Prize for musical composition for his *Concerto for String Quartet and Orchestra*.

Soon after the first performance of the *Oratorium nach Sprüchen des Angelus Silesius* in June, 1936, I was looking for a new subject. My thoughts turned to the Dance of Death Motive (*Totentanz-Motiv*). While recovering from a mountain accident in 1938, much time was placed at my disposal and this enabled further study of the Basler Death Dance. Then one day I received from my friend Paul Sacher, who was informed of my plans, a book which became a guide for my study. It was the jubilee edition of the Basler Historical Society of January, 1856: "Basel in the 14th-century. Historical Presentation in honor of the 5th-Centennial Celebration of the Earthquake on St. Luke's Day, 1356." In its last chapter it contained a highly interesting treatise by Wilhelm Wackernagel concerning the Dance of Death. It also contained two chapters which fascinated me particularly and which were to aim my search in a different direction. The one chapter dealt with the *"Grossen Sterbent,"* the other with the Great Earthquake of 1356, "News of the Day and Posterity" by Christian Wurstisen.

What was the special attractive force of these descriptions, these *"Nachrichten der Zeit,"* more strictly speaking, which have come down to us? In the first place, it was the unbroken lapidary power of expression of the old language and the plainness and extraordinarily imaginative structure of the text. However, the "accounts" also contained a contrast between objective and personal, even highly personal, opinions of the individual chroniclers. That which was recorded simply as "News of the Day" is in reality a rich combination of historical recordings. The first ones were written in 1357, and the later ones about two hundred years afterward. Some were written in Basel itself and others in the inner part of Switzerland, Strasbourg, and places far removed from Basel. These chroniclers were not only open-minded historians but philosophers. Some of them were distinguished writers and, above all, poets. In the richness of their speech, in the depth of their expression, and in the fertile subject they were treating, had to be found the pure, poetic elements which would fulfill the hypothesis of the theme.

Of course, the collection had been arranged from the purely historical point of view. However, it was possible to rearrange them in accordance with freely ruling artistic arguments and produce something beyond the historical, yet generally worth-while. The most essential point of contact and the decisive encouragement for such a venture was brought about by the growing conviction that, behind all these innumerable details, a coherent meaning had to manifest itself to the researcher.

I made one additional step and attempted a systematic inspection of all the chronicles within reach—above all, a precise study of the great *Wurstisen-Chronicle.* The goal to procure the necessary material for the various subjects, later to be merged into one whole, could only be reached through patient and detailed work. At first I searched for larger descriptions but later for single expressions, especially ones with strong word coinage, and arranged them according to their inner homogeny. As a result, I had a collection of notes of the following kind: earthquake, pestilence, famine, occurrences in nature, special appearances in the sky, superstition, crime, and war but also words of exhortation and pleading for divine grace. From these larger and smaller parts, I gradually collected descriptions of voluminous size. By doing so, I allowed myself complete freedom, with one exception: not to add a sentence or even a word of my own.

Naturally, there existed no danger that the writing of the history of my city (Basel) should experience any embarrassment because of personal rearrangements of episodes from its history into a literary sketching of a general character—a lifting out of concrete fact into abstract values, so to speak. Moreover, with two exceptions of absolutely untimely character, all dates of the years remain unmentioned in my composition. Really, taking everything into consideration, it is completely insignificant in what historical succession these events have taken place. On the other hand, can an event of the remote past be described with more beauty and with calmer pre-eminence than when a writer says: "In the year as man counteth from the Incarnation of our Saviour, thirteen hundred and fifty and six years, on the feast of Luke, upon the eighteenth of October, on the third day following, from Saint Gallus' day, an earthquake did shake the land, greater than was ever there before known."

My libretto was developed into a provisional form when I was compelled to interrupt it for a long time. Return to everyday life and the fact that I had to take upon myself work that was new to me directed my activities into a different path and filled my time. In addition, the brutal force of World War II pushed aside the vague conception I had of the choral work I had planned.

Not until the end of the war did I again find the necessary distance from the present time in order to bring myself to continue work on *Der Tod zu Basel*. When I began again, I cut down the gloomy descriptions considerably, dovetailed quotations from the Bible and old poems into the libretto to form the center of dramatic and textual gravity, and clarified the form by separating the text into two distinct parts.

One more problem had to be solved! The original text with the many authors' linguistic approaches made the libretto impractical. A symmetrical linguistic flow had to be preserved to balance with the music. It was a task which I felt unequipped to resolve without being unfaithful to the strict concept of this literary collection. My knowledge of folk song was very useful, but I sought professional aid from the representatives of the Basler Archive for Folklore. They offered competent scholars and, most of all, sincere interest and heart-warming co-operation. Professor Paul Geiger and Dr. Adele Stoecklin aided me in polishing uneven passages and in leveling off sharp contrasts without endangering the force and power of the original language. My comprehension and analysis of the text was so thorough that the work of the musician could take a relatively fast course.

Today when I am asked to define my position regarding my oratorio *Death over Basel* in an analytical manner and beyond, it seems I am being given the role of the chronicler. The important thing is, I believe, not to comment on the musical construction of the work (others can do this better) but to express that which was and is essential for the inner and outer process of development of this choral composition. Therefore, I place this statement in the forefront of these comments in order to bring the listener closer to the essential, fundamental concepts I carried out in the genesis of this score several years ago. In this span of time rest my experiences not only of the first performance, perhaps in itself especially exciting, but of a series of additional performances of varied character by diverse interpreters and, above all, in new languages of varied expressiveness and dynamics. This span of time also permits a position of resignation and remoteness toward my work which almost allows me to take a neutral and objective stand toward my former work.

For the time being, let us remain with the text. It must be said that the hopes I had for its poetical wealth and power have fulfilled my expectations in the most beautiful fashion. This experience has also proven to be true whenever it was a matter of translating the libretto into other languages. The labor on these translations, guided by outstanding people —specialists—proved to be a rewarding effort. It is part of the riches of the world and is primarily a component of its cultural variety that the same things beneath a different sky undergo a different linguistic presentation. It is really fascinating to observe how a word, a sentence, in itself almost entirely music, still retains the same values when translated into different sounds. I can hardly imagine a greater enjoyment of linguistic power of expression and variety than the one experienced by a transposition of one's written or combined texts which, moreover, have been set to music. Essential in this case is the realization that every new language creates specific displaced accents but that the basic relation to the musical structure remains constant. This musical form, aided by the text, eventually grows beyond and lifts it into a new strata. Or shall we express ourselves differently? The text which serves as the foundation for the musical form ascends to a new level which corresponds to the joint expression. And these new planes are congruent in relation to each other even in different languages and modes of expression.

With these remarks, I would like to close the background discussion of my oratorio's libretto and return to a discussion of the first performance several years ago. At that time, because of shyness, I was on guard against public reaction to *Death over Basel* and abstained from taking a position in regard to its musical construction. Today, however, I have been asked to do so and shall accommodate this request. In general, I would prefer not to analyze a concluded work but, instead, continue my quest from completed works toward new ones. Moreover, I am of the opinion that it would be much more important and necessarily more self-evident that one hear a performance of this oratorio rather than read a discussion of it—even though the discussion does originate in the workshop of its creator.

At this point, I should like to make an observation. Namely, it can lead to serious misunderstandings when a composer submits an analysis of his composition after the work is completed since, without question, the composition extends much farther than he could have been conscious of at the time he began the work. It would be an illusion if the impression should originate that the conscious goal predominated the momentary form-scheme which was there merely for the purpose of serving the entire form and to point the way to the single episodes on which their creative function could proceed successfully. I do not believe that this is a confession of which a composer of more mature years would have to be ashamed. Quite to the contrary! That which we know shall serve in the best way that which we do not know. It shall prepare the terrain for the flight of our fantasy and bring forth the most beautiful fruit. In view of the whole, it shall draw the borderlines without restraint at any given time.

"Fading, fruitless and of but small worth," the motto and background from which everything develops eventually, is presented simply by unison women's voices of the chorus supported by a monotonal orchestral accompaniment with the least possible harmonic tension (see Example XI, 1, at the back of this volume). (The work requires soprano and bass soloists, three speakers, mixed chorus, and orchestra.)

Into this neutral, timeless sound, there breaks a realistic description of the earthquake at Basel. It is initially described by the speaker—alone —followed by the chorus building part by part, reserved at first, but then suddenly and forcefully exclaiming: "An earthquake did shake the land, greater than was ever there before known" (page 4).

There follows a choral interlude which is soft dynamically, transparent harmonically, but more pressing rhythmically (page 7). A new, strong, and vehement choral outburst continues: "The whole earth did tremble and they were felled" (page 12). This section is partly in four parts, partly in unison, reinforced by the orchestra joining in with strong accentuations. The speaker assumes the responsibility for sketching the event, which gradually recedes into the past. He continues with an introduction to the proverb of a child: "A thorn within a ring, three iron shoes horses bring, a woodman's axe, some pitchers by: in that year Basel all did die" (page 16). The proverb recalls in a very stylistic form Basel's earthquake in ancient times. A two-part women's chorus, accompanied by some wind instruments, sings this touching little rhyme. The description of the earthquake and the earthquake itself fades into the background. It slowly removes its former presence from view of the spectator yet hovers in the memory.

The development up to now must be considered a large, connected prelude to the entire oratorio. With it, is created the atmosphere in which further happenings can develop and, to be sure, come to their fullest intensity.

With the words of the speaker, "And many demanded and disputed among themselves whence this great mischance should come" (page 17), a door, so to speak, opens into a new line and direction. It happens to be the introduction of a new musical structure—a bass solo. The soloist develops the succeeding, fantastic sequence of thoughts by answering the speaker and the remaining unanswered basic question of the overall story of *Death over Basel*. He accomplishes this by representing the opinions of others. Then he takes his stand without hesitation. The soloist expresses it with such conviction that the chorus takes possession of the theme and brings the section to a conclusion (pages 17–24).

This too is merely another episode in the drama. A new phase begins with a new vocal color—a soprano solo. For the first time, a more severe musical form begins, an *ostinato* bass, which carries the entire description of the drought and famine (see Example XI, 2). The narrator introduces this dramatic sequence over the first statement of the *ostinato* bass in the lower instruments of the orchestra. Similarly, the aria concludes with the *ostinato* melody in the percussive basses. As seen from the harmonic point of view, this exclusive part is eminently chromatic. This chromaticism corresponds to the character of the text but also arises from the fact that the aria precedes the song of the Flagellants which is constructed from old, original melodies. These pertinent songs are tonal and monodic and called for contrasting musical material before and after their introduction into the score.

Here in this section, as before, it is the speaker who introduces us to the new situation. On cue, the choir sings the old friar's-songs which pass by in grand processions, interrupted from time to time by the verbal injections of the speaker. The narrator's role is in dynamic contrast but is complimented by the opposing motives and rhythms in the orchestra. Strictly speaking, this part does not have a real conclusion. The speaker carries it into a new and, this time, a very animated choral section by describing new trials and conflicts. The choral part corresponds to the simple A–B–B–A form. The repetitions appearing at intervals undergo musical condensation. As a result, there has been created a hypothesis which follows the hushed and ardently pleading, deeply moving text of the anonymous Strasbourg poet: "Redeemer, Master holy, nobis miserere" (page 44). In thoughtful, simple harmonies and in plain unison singing, reminiscent of the opening bars, the first part of *Der Tod zu Basel* comes to a close.

Just as the descriptions of the text expand by themselves and gradually open up new domains revealing the attitude of man toward the transcendental, so the musical setting produces hitherto untouched means of expression. The forms expand and create vast connecting ties. Two women speakers, a high and a low voice, step into the picture and assume an active part in the events. The text starts with restrained descriptions of strange natural phenomena concerning superstition, crime, and war, and advances to a point of complete collapse, caused by human helplessness, to an unreserved and desperate cry for divine grace. In a like manner, the musical structure proceeds in a parallel movement applying its means of expression, externally and internally—its sole purpose being to stress the power of the word, its meaning, and to transfer this into a musical context.

The performance proceeds further and further, commencing with narration marked by growing intensification in the form of alternating women speakers who, with the first repressed and pleading cries of the alto section of the chorus, report strange signs from heaven (pages 46–51). Male voices of the choir enter, answered by female voices, speaking the narrative over a rhythmic accompaniment of percussion instruments. Renewed pleading cries issue from the soprano and alto parts, followed by the sudden entrance of the orchestra and the first female speaker. Soon after, the basses of the chorus enter "singing" and reinforced by the entire choir. All reach a climax in the passionate, intensified Gunther's war chorus (pages 56–60). This passion suddenly gives way to a soft, heartfelt plea for grace, "Mercy, Lord. God grant us His grace and His Mercy," reiterated by the soprano soloist and the women of the choir (see Example XI, 3). The melody gradually fades away (pages 60–63). More will be said about the formal design of this entire segment later.

An exhaustion of strength could take place here! However, new inspiration springs forth from the text as well as from the music when descriptions of distantly approaching pestilence are sung by the bass soloist (pages 63–64). After this free structure, there develops a new severe one, combining recitative, arioso, and speaker, and interweaving solo, choral, and spoken elements. This episode concludes with an orchestral pedal point under the words of the narrator: "Yet could none of the learned say ought of whence this Death came, but that it was the will of God" (page 74). At this point the role of the speaker breaks off, and it is the chorus that takes over the narrative function to the end of *Death over Basel*.

Thus, a place has been reached where the wish to retreat into silence could take the upper hand. Nevertheless, the folk song "The Reaper, Death" with its clear and pure melodic features is able to inspire and bring new life to the music (see Example XI, 4). From the musical and formal standpoint, this old song fulfills the need for contrast with its simple but ever newly inflected verses. In essence, the folk tune frees and calms the tension and indirectly prepares the way for new energy (pages 74–85).

Before the development of the oratorio returns to its starting point —the vanity of all things earthly—there follows an episode which returns us to reality (page 86).

The real, the only reprise which creates the whole atmosphere on which the final development can be built is the musical representation of those prophetic words found in the Second Letter of St. Peter, in which he tells man "That one day is with God as a thousand years long, a thousand years as but a day," but also that there is hope for a new heaven and earth in which justice shall reign (pages 89–96). Here the singing takes the lead, whether it be the bass soloist or the chorus (see Example XI, 5). Several grandiose intensifications lead to the portrayal of the day "wherein all the Heav'ns shall by fire be consumed, and the Elements in the flame melt away and vanish" (pages 96–98).

In a style patterned after the end of the war chorus but now more direct, the soprano soloist enters and brings the oratorio to a meditative conclusion expressing hope.

Let us now compare the two parts of *Der Tod zu Basel* according to form and content. From this comparison, we can draw some possible conclusions which can be related to the construction of the entire work. We shall begin with the elements which bring about the result:

SOPRANO SOLO—
> Part I: a large aria complete in itself.
> Part II: twice repeated, parallel statements conclude "The Reaper, Death," and end the entire movement. Basically, the soprano solo provides all the lyrical climax.

BASS SOLO—
> Part I: an expanded aria—complete in itself.

Part II: the great pestilence aria, which breaks in during the final build-up until the soprano solo takes over. The role is predominantly dramatic.

SPEAKER—

Part I: an important narrative and bridging function. Participates in the entire drama.

Part II: enters during the development and continues to the point where the war chorus enters. Its last entrance is in the pestilence aria; its function logically concludes when the chorus assumes this role and broadens its basis.

TWO FEMALE SPEAKERS—

Part I: do not appear.

Part II: carry the drama of the opening up to the place where the speaking chorus takes over and intensifies the role.

CHORUS—

Part I and Part II: main function is to join in with variations. In Part II, chorus appears at an important dramatic moment with the *a cappella* entrance of the folk song "The Reaper, Death."

ORCHESTRA—

Part I and Part II: used to an equal extent in both parts. Of course, new colors are reserved for the second part.

This schematic arrangement of the functions of the performing powers demonstrates clearly how much the entire oratorio has been constructed on inward and outward climaxes. If, in addition, one takes into consideration the combinations and the additional compilations, this assertion affirms itself considerably.

Secondly, the arrangement of harmonic texture, a unifying element of form untouched up to now, naturally enters the performance because of its relation to all the spheres of musical and dramatic expression. Whether this happens in the most tender or passionate manner, these harmonic stages are essentially the same, or at least related to one another, and span a wide curve from the first to the last measure.

However, a wider curve spans the first as well as the second part—

namely, the recapitulation of "Fading, fruitless and of small worth" between letters Ⓐ and Ⓞ.

Perhaps it would be suitable to mention here that the shaping, the evolution of the textual as well as the musical means can proceed easier where the grouping of the text and composition can be accomplished by one and the same person.

I have anticipated this essay with the expectation that the reader will place the piano reduction of the full score of *Death over Basel* by his side. In this way he will be able to read between the lines of this essay. Hence, it should be possible to obtain a clearer understanding of what I have been invited to relate—some practical knowledge and experiences gained when creating and, later, when observing performances of my oratorio.

The first performance of *Der Tod zu Basel* took place on May 22, 1954, in the great music auditorium at Basel under the direction of my friend Paul Sacher. We were privileged to obtain the famous soloists Elisabeth Schwartzkopf and Josef Greindl for this performance. The Basler Chamberchoir had difficulties in its approach to my work, more than usual, since Paul Sacher was not able to take over the preparations for the first performance until the last moment. I was in despair and convinced that everything would go wrong. *Der Tod zu Basel* is both textually and musically exacting and not immediately accessible. Its power of communication cannot unfold until the skill of the performance has been mastered. Beforehand, everything is obscure; not only does it not present itself halfway but not at all. Therefore, I had to go through this crisis and mental agony yieldingly. Suddenly, however, everything perceivable assumed form and the performance came up to my expectations. Happily, my hope that my oratorio would radiate and carry some kind of message to my fellow man, a message that had profoundly pre-occupied me, was fulfilled.

The performances that followed did not all stand under the same lucky star. In Frankfurt the new radio hall did not have the necessary acoustical equilibrium, and this proved to be a great hindrance, particularly when the chorus spoke at the beginning of Part II.

A memorable experience, unique of its kind, was a performance in

Turin. During this performance, the grandeur and precision of the Italian language especially impressed me. The women speakers in the second part, because of their realistic approach to the text, could not have been surpassed. It was almost too good to be true! Unforgettable too was the performance of the part of the soprano by Magda Laszlo and the brilliancy of the orchestra. There I heard sounds I had well imagined but seldom expected to be realized to such a high degree of perfection.

A performance in the French language in Paris showed altogether different aspects. Thus I recoiled more and more from one established concept of *Death over Basel* and rejoiced when it appeared as an entirely different work. (It has also been translated into English by Norman Platt).

My comments should not indicate that these performances were less "perfect," less ideal as far as meaning is concerned. Not at all! Because they were permeated by another temperament, they showed themselves in a new light which proved favorable.

On the occasion of a performance in Vienna, it became apparent, even with the best intentions present, that miracles cannot be achieved as long as the practical suppositions for a successful performance meet obstacles too great to be overcome. Even at the last moment, musical sections which were considered to be on "safe ground" went to pieces. Through a tragic accident, the equilibrium of the rehearsals became so shaken up that a successful performance was no longer possible.

I remember two performances as especially impressive: the Basler Chamberchoir in Basel and Zurich. The event was the anniversary year of the earthquake (1956). Here was an example of how successful a performance can be because of repetition and how much such a performance grows in depth and maturity.

In Brussels a performance took place under the direction of my honored friend Franz André which delighted me because of the beauty and strength of the Flemish language. I am now looking forward to another concert featuring *Death over Basel*.

If I am to point out special difficulties which have appeared during performances of my oratorio, I should begin by turning to the orchestration. However, I feel that there are present in the score no problems which an experienced and methodical conductor will not be able to control. By all means, the soloists must be selected according to the character of their roles. Also, the choir should not be too small. It is better to organize a choir which is "too large," from which one can select a smaller chorus for special parts like "The Reaper, Death."

The first bass aria caused me a great deal of trouble. I made slow headway, and it was apparent that this was a part of the score where I was not too successful. But I promised myself better results and rewrote the aria for the revised edition now in print.

Another matter that caused anxiety is the place at letter ⓞ, starting with measure fifteen. Although the harmonic development is easy to comprehend at this spot, it sounds "false"—not just muddy, but false. Frankly, I cannot explain it but shall listen attentively at every new opportunity in order to find a clue to this phenomenon.

There are other dangers present, too. When the main speaker becomes pathetic, the result is that one does not believe him—not a single bit. A nuance in the voice is all that is needed to change this. On the other hand, it is an erroneous idea to think that my cautious use of dynamic markings is done to give the oratorio a certain degree of rigidity. Quite to the contrary, my intention is not to weigh down the interpreter with a coat of mail, an overload of expression signs.

There is another danger, which I cannot explain but which did show up during rehearsal. I refer to the interpretation of that section of the main speaker's text which describes occurrences which have taken place in Basel and its surroundings. These happenings should not be thought to be local events but occurrences of general significance affecting all men equally. The events, therefore, represent only the foundation on which the ethical and religious thoughts and conclusions are constructed— the foremost meaning of the oratorio *Death over Basel*.

In conclusion, I should like to sing the "Song of Songs." There is nothing more beautiful than the human voice, nothing more impressive than the beaming forth of the melodious sound and power of song, be it a single voice or the mellow lingering or mighty chord of a choir. Everything I have attempted to do in *Der Tod zu Basel* is based on this ideal.

13. *In the Hall of Mirrors* and *Anabase*

KARL-BIRGER BLOMDAHL

KARL-BIRGER BLOMDAHL (born in Växjö, Sweden, on October 19, 1916) started advanced music instruction in Stockholm in 1934. He studied counterpoint, orchestration, and composition with the eminent Swedish composer Hilding Rosenberg. Score-reading and conducting were with Tor Mann at the Royal High School of Music, and violin was with Per Carlsten. Two stipends from the government, one in 1941 and a second in 1946, permitted Blomdahl to travel to France, Italy, and Switzerland for further study in composition. Although his stature as a composer grew steadily, his name was brought into world prominence when the oratorio *In the Hall of Mirrors* won the International Society of Contemporary Music prize in Oslo in 1953. Two years later in Baden-Baden, his *Piano Concerto* was awarded a prize. In 1954, Blomdahl journeyed to the United States to lecture at leading universities and colleges. While in the states, he spent considerable time visiting relatives who had settled on farms in the Middle West.

To begin with, what kind of texts attract me? Naturally different kinds for different reasons and purposes, but, thinking of my oratorios and the opera *Aniara,* they apparently have one denominator in common: they all are written by contemporary poets—*In the Hall of Mirrors* by Erik Lindegren, *Anabase* by St.-John Perse (Alexis St. Léger), and *Aniara* by Harry Martinson. And this is not mere chance. I do not in any way deny that the essential problems and ideas of man are eternal, more or less the same, irrespective of the era one happens to be born in. But every epoch offers its own variations and finds its own formulations of the essential experiences, and for me, being a composer living now, it is not only natural but necessary to use texts written by poets who share my experience of life, the life of our epoch. Only then I feel that the essential requirements for a fusion of text and music are there. Personally, I would never dream of setting music to a poem by, let us say, Goethe, or a drama by Shakespeare. And if I am attracted to an old text, it has to be so old that it is deprived of every specific mark of period and milieu—that is to say, it has to be a myth.

In a way you could say that this view is very clearly reflected in the choice of *Anabase* as text for an oratorio. Far in the background you have Xenophon and the journey of the Ten Thousand, but the poem itself is a grand vision by one of the greatest poets of *our* time, created with poetic means that belong to *this* epoch, and reflected through the prism of a truly contemporary consciousness. I take for granted that you know this "series of images of migration, of conquest of vast spaces in Asiatic wastes, of destruction and foundation of cities and civilizations of any races or epochs of the ancient East," as T. S. Eliot describes the poem in his English translation of the work. And if you know it, you are also familiar with the specific poetic means Perse uses in *Anabase,* the compression of the metaphorical language through suppression of "links in the chain," of explanatory and connecting matter. In fact I hope you are, because then you will understand what I mean when I say that there is a close affinity between Lindegren's and Perse's way of using the poetic means. The logic of imagery, the combining of contrasting images, the unexpected, clash, short circuit between metaphors, and the tremendous potentiality are components that Lindegren's and Perse's poetic language have in common, with the compression carried even further in Lindegren's case. With Perse it is sentences or successions of words that are contrasted; with Lindegren, it is also individual words

In the Hall of Mirrors

When I first read Lindegren's *The Man without a Way,* forty sonnets, of which nine constitute the text of *In the Hall of Mirrors,* the book made a tremendous impression on me. But I was puzzled by the complexity of the poetic language; in other words, I felt the affective tension, but could not see the logical connection between this and the seemingly artificial, "intellectual" pattern of words. It took me quite a time to digest the sonnets and to discover the direct relations, to understand that the poetic image itself was the principal element of the poem. But then

I much more clearly felt the logic of the language, the tremendous compression and potentiality of the metaphors, and I felt that even if these poems were cut in small pieces, each little piece would still be loaded with expression. So I was convinced that the sonnets should lend themselves perfectly to setting to music, and should well stand being stretched over musical forms. And they were a challenge to me. I could not help returning to them again and again in my thoughts. The exciting experience of these poems demanded an outlet in musical form, and I wanted to try to find the unity in the manifoldness, try to build a big span without simplifying the complexity. So I chose nine of the sonnets and arranged them in a curve of expression which on a smaller scale mirrored that of the whole book.

The Man without a Way is an apocalyptic suite of images which describes a kind of descent into the kingdom of death, from whence those who miraculously return bring a new and hard-won confidence. The meaninglessness, the roadlessness, the absurdity of life is a preparation for this new freedom, a kind of purgatory before the liberation. But it is not the paradise of Beatrice and the Christian God that the man without a way now searches for but a greater independence, hard to regain: only there can he reach the happiness "that is dictated by all and nothing."

In the Hall of Mirrors takes its title from the opening line of the first sonnet. The series of sonnets gives the picture of a man studying his own face "in a hall of mirrors," where some of the mirrors are distorting and uglifying, others beautifying. The sum of the reflections gives the true picture on the man's "inner" face.

The first line, "In the hall of mirrors where not alone Narcissus enthroned on his column of despair *'sans vertige,'*" is the incitement to the musical shape of the first sonnet. It starts in the remote distance, in a glass-cold world of sound (see Example XII, 1, at the back of this volume), and only toward the end of the movement have the voices, which were in the beginning impassive, indolent, or ironical, obtained the warmth that is a condition for singing.

"Here in this silence, erasing the bound'ries between the dead who are living and the living wish of the dead ..." gives the initial atmosphere and sound of the second movement. The tempo is lento, *in modo di* slow blues, and the many rests give the character of this "Song of the Silence," which the *basso profundo* sings, now and then interrupted and supported by the chorus.

Not until the third movement does the expressive flow come to the surface, with the strings and the alto solo singing, "in the hollow mist there broke a water-lily-heaven, and the blinded trees swung their dreaming naked arms . . . (see Example XII, 2)."

The fourth movement, "but first must a hungertower of mercy tumble and distance illumine the weakness of fleeing . . . ," represents the first point of culmination, but the general character of expression is very labile, with sudden changes in mood, and the tempo still is slow.

The fifth movement is a strange interlude, a kind of scherzo, the character of which derives from lines such as "O, ache of longing, swing-time rhythm, rovin' fingers, love breast to breast and anaesthetic sigh. You rival of invalids, death-dances little cabin, with horror on down-payment and simplicity's compress . . . ." A crooner is foolishly singing in a microphone, not noticing the ghastliness of the words he is singing.

This scherzo is directly followed by an allegro *brutalmente:* "Can Death from his coatsleeve shake out what we do not know . . . ," a convulsive outburst, which almost blows up the form (see Example XII, 3).

The seventh movement is the lyrical center of the work, a soprano solo, accompanied by a solo string quartet: "Softly, softly as a spring the room fills with your dreaming . . . ." This dreamy love song acts as the strongest possible contrast to the following allegro furioso, the dramatic culmination of the whole work: "At the night-mare's end the lion leaps forth, in the instant of death exulting in his freedom . . . ."

The furioso fades away, and gives place to the concluding *tranquillo,* which brings reminiscences from earlier movements and closes the circle by returning to the initial sound and atmosphere.

As far as I myself am conscious of what I am doing, and taking into account the impossibility of describing a work of music in words—that would in fact be to re-create the work with literal poetic means—I shall try to explain my view of the form of *In the Hall of Mirrors*. The macro-form was decided by the over-all aural vision that gradually arose in me while I was studying the sonnets. This original aural vision included a closed architectonic curve of expression, where tension and relaxation, stability and lability, simplicity and complexity had their fixed positions. The traditional form that came closest to my intentions was symphonic variations, modified with regard to the vocal means—"symphonic" in the sense of development of themes, "variations" in the sense of structural homogeneity. Then I made the choice of sonnets that fitted my musical plan. The micro-form obviously had to be determined to a great extent by the words, influenced by both semantics and phonology, and above all by the indefinable poetic quality that we find between the words in poetry. But my aspiration was to try to establish close relations between micro- and macro-form through the use of melodic, harmonic, and rhythmic microstructures, germs, which in an organic way could be transformed into greater complexes. And from this aspect the twelve-tone technique seemed to suggest rich structural possibilities. So I worked along these lines, but guided by ear and intuition more than by theoretical speculation.

The nine sonnets are arranged in the following way: numbers 1, 2, and 3 are coupled to one block, then comes number 4 separately. Numbers 5 and 6 are coupled again, number 7 is separate, and numbers 8 and 9 form a closing block. Orchestration and dynamics are consciously used to help to give the macro-form clear outlines. The texture is spacious and transparent and the dynamics are kept on a low level in the first two sonnets; in the third the density and dynamics grow, but only the strings are used. In the fourth come the winds and dramatic shiftings in dynamics, but not until the sixth is the whole machinery let loose, and so on.

Talking of the melodic patterns of the work, the text comes in the foreground. I am of the "Palestrinian" schooling, meaning that I have a pronounced vocal-melodic thinking and experience, including an elementary evaluation and consideration of the intervals. And I think that as long as one uses tones with fixed pitches, systematically arranged, like the chromatic scale, one gets as a result intervals that are related to each other in a specific way, whether one likes it or not. And the discrimination and evaluation of these relations both horizontally and vertically are essential to all music that uses this scale—a perfect platitude. What I meant, when talking of Palestrina, was that one of the most essential features of the melodic writing in this piece emanates from this vocal thinking. The origin is a kind of word-melody, that comes from the melody of the spoken Swedish language. So under the melodic—and rhythmic—patterns, there lies the word-melody and -rhythm of the recited sonnets. And this word-melody I have used on different levels of expression, ranging from plain reciting to highly dramatic song. And in an elementary way you could say that this stylized word-melody in lyrical passages is kept within narrow limits, working mostly with minor and major seconds and thirds, but in dramatic passages is intensified through big leaps, thus becoming minor and major sevenths and ninths.

These elementary melodic features are basically the same for the instrumental parts, though naturally modified in accordance with the special possibilities and character of the instruments.

I have not much to say in respect to harmony. You find here a whole scale of degrees of tonality, from the clearest tonal patterns to formations that through the rapidity of changes and the complexity of chords are impossible to follow and define from the tonal point of view. But in this second case there is always a clear structural relation between melody and harmony in the same sense as in twelve-tone technique, the harmony consisting of vertical projections of melodic lines. And in order to make the vertical relations as clear as possible, I use only a restricted number of the most elementary and direct projections (avoiding, for instance, transpositions), arranged in an order of density and static tension.

Evidently the rhythm is completely determined by the text, as are also the tempi.

So far things are fairly simple and obvious, but they get very complicated as soon as one tries to explain other whys and hows. I certainly have no fixed system of relating words to music. I am guided by my ear and intuition, and many of the reasons are inaccessible to my intellect. The first "why," I should try to explain, seems to be why I kept the words, because after all—being a composer—I could just as well have tried to express my essential experience of these poems in a purely instrumental work. The answer is that the sonority of the words, the word-melody, was such that I instinctively wanted to *sing* them. In fact I could not help reading them as melodic lines, feeling a latent music in them even before I "understood" the poems, or more correctly, while I still had to rely completely on my intuitive understanding of them. But these melodic lines directly sprang from the recited words—were born, so to say, in them. Words and melodies were inseparable.

So the sound, the sonority of the words, the "phonological variable" as young composers nowadays say (after Valéry), played a great role from the beginning. Not only did it have a direct influence on the melodic structure (accents, duration, ups and downs also), but indirectly it also affected the general hold I applied on the text. In order to keep the flow and tempo of the poems, in the semantic but also in the phonological aspect, I did not want to have too many repetitions of words or syllables, which could slow down or stop the sonorous stream. For the same reason I did not want to split up the individual words into their phonological elements. So this wish also set the limits for the phonological influence on the musical structure. Naturally the semantic aspect had a decisive effect on my wish to "keep up the flow," and the result was that the poems were rendered, so to say, straightforwardly. Only in a few places in the work this general principle has been broken because of very special reasons. (For instance, in the half-spoken, half-sung fugue on "to the dead to the killed to the dead killed the murdered," which emphasizes the most dramatic culmination of the whole work. Also, on some rare occasions melismatic forms are used to increase the expression.) It is quite obvious that the sound and the sense of the words always are coupled together. In my way of experiencing poetry, the "semantic variable," the sense, in all its complexity, is the dominating factor. This gives the depth and width of the poetic experience. The sound is more on the surface, though by no means *only* on the surface. It stretches its tenacles also down in psychological layers below the surface.

In a general way I could say that the phonology of the words has had an important influence on the melodic structure and the micro-form of the work. But the semantics have determined the texture and the macro-form. And the phonological melodic aspect applied in this work not only resulted in a pronounced simplicity and directness in rendering the text, but also excluded any kind of more elaborate vocal polyphony. So the complexity and richness of the poems had to be re-created through other means; as for the vocal means, variety in all vertical relations, different levels of expression, from reciting to dramatic song, and distribution of the melodic lines among soloists and chorus was the only possibility. For the rest I had to use the instrumental palette of a big orchestra to re-create the total aural vision that I had in mind.

Now, what is the relation between the vocal and the instrumental parts? Is the orchestral score only a kind of sound-frame around the vocal? Certainly not, from my point of view. As I have said many times before, the *total* vision is the main thing for me, and the orchestra has been there from the beginning as an indispensable part of the whole. The material used is largely the same in the vocal and instrumental parts, though naturally it is treated in different ways. So the thematic homogeneity is there. And as I also hinted before, the counterpoint of this work is mostly established through the combining of different ideas in the vocal and instrumental parts, and the orchestral part is never meant to be only an accompaniment of the vocal.

But naturally we have the difficult question of what is effect and illustration, and what is music, in a more essential meaning of the word. As I see it, an "effect" in music is justified when it is "effective," that is, when it really brings about something that is conceivable to the ear and relevant in the context even if it is not the most important component. And the same goes for an illustration. If it really throws light upon some relevant fact, why not? Some critics have spoken in a negative way of the beginning of *In the Hall of Mirrors,* as being "mere effects." I strongly resent the word "mere" but am only too willing to admit that I use some "effects." The violins are playing arco and pizzicato behind the bridge, which certainly is an effect. But this way of playing brings about just the effect I wanted. It creates—together with the deep C of the double-bass—the atmosphere of space, distance, and glassy coldness that is one of the characteristics of the first sonnet. Thus it is relevant and not "mere" effect. The critics also must have missed the very essential fact that simultaneously the harp and the celesta present melodic patterns which have structural significance for the whole work. As I said, the "effect" need not be the most important component, but it should add something relevant to the general expressiveness of the music. And what is, on the whole, illustrative in music, and what is not? Isn't there a whole scale of melodic gestures, for instance, that, in an elementary sense, always had an illustrative, symbolic significance? I am thinking of such gestures as a falling, especially a chromatic falling line, that practically since Monteverdi has suggested death or sorrow or melancholy.

Anabase

It is practically impossible to describe what a poem deals with, what actually happens in it, as the function of poetry is very complicated, and a lot of things happen simultaneously on different levels. In a way the most important components of poetic expression you find between the words, and you can only experience them when actually reading or listening to the poem itself. The power and fertility of the visions in *Anabase,* their universal and timeless validity, and the refinement and stringency of the poetic language you have to experience by reading the poem. But I will try to tell you something about the framework, the background, the outer cause of events, and the actors in this epos, because that naturally had a decisive influence on my choice of musical means and forms for the oratorio. *Anabase* is the French word for the Greek *Anabasis,* which, as you certainly know, is the title of Xenophon's famous description of the retreat of the Ten Thousand after the battle of Cunaxa, in the year 401 B.C. This title alludes to one of the threads in the mighty tissue. The scene is Asia, which never is mentioned, but in all its majesty is present in every line. Summarily, I would characterize the poem as one long continuous dialogue between an Asiatic nation of nomadic horsemen and its leader. This anonymous sovereign has traits from all leaders: Alexander and Moses, Genghis Kahn and Jesus. But here he is in symbolic form an incarnation of the people, their aspirations and fate. A man of action, he is not only the ruler, warrior, and organizer but also the spokesman, chronicler, and prophet of the people. And thus this epos of the deeds of a nation of conquerors also is a poem of the essential conditions and efforts of human life, a symbol of spiritual fights, experiences, and conquests.

When it came to deciding the musical apparatus, I thought it necessary to have the whole palette of expression and sound of the orchestra at my disposal. But at the same time I had a feeling that I should work with limited and concentrated musical means in accordance with the way Perse had used the poetic ones. Consequently I wanted no big orchestra, but a rather small one. My intention was to try to re-create the visionary greatness through inner expression, not by mobilizing an enormous sound-apparatus. This point of view was also valid for the choice of vocal means. Besides, practical reasons strongly suggested a small chorus, for I knew that the choral part would be very difficult to sing, demanding a professional ensemble, and these generally are very small.

Then came the problem of how to distribute the vocal parts. Referring to the dialogue between the leader and the people which I earlier spoke of, I thought it sensible to divide the role of the leader into two. Simplifying the matter, you could say that when his realistic ego speaks, it is through a reciter, but when his idealistic ego has the word, he is too elevated to talk, so he sings, with the voice of a baritone. The people naturally are represented by the chorus, and out of this mass now and then individual voices rise. But they shall always remain anonymous, so they must come from and stay within the chorus. The whole has the shape of a continuous exchange among these different voices, and the technique used is similar to that of mosaic works. Musically the structural technique is that of serialism, which I thought very useful for my purposes. A twelve-tone row is the basis, but I have broken up this row into several smaller units, which I also can give different melodic and harmonic shape and thus use for building greater complexes, analogous with a mosaic (see Example XII, 4).

Perse's epos consists of two chansons, separated from the rest and forming a framework, and between them, ten great poems. Of these ten, I have left out three which seemed to me less apt to setting to music than the others. I briefly will try to characterize the different poems by quoting a few characteristic lines. Both text and music of the introductory and concluding chansons have very apparent connections, and they give the work its closed form. Already in the opening lines you find the exchange between soloists and chorus. "Il naissait un poulain sous les feuilles de bronze." ("Under the bronze leaves a colt was foaled. Came such an one who laid bitter bay in our hands. Stranger. Who passed. Here comes news of other provinces to my liking.—'Hail, daughter,' under the most considerable of the trees of the year.") (See example XII, 5.)

The first great poem I have conceived as an "equestrian" movement, and it is formed as a vigorous allegro. A central idea is "Et le soleil n'est point nommé, mais sa puissance est parmi nous." ("The sun is unmentioned but his power is amongst us, and the sea at morning like a presumption of the mind.")

The second poem has a ritual significance. It is a fast presto movement and ends abrupt and brutally: "Et la lessive part! comme un prêtre mis en piece . . . ." ("And the linen exposed to dry scatters! like a priest torn in pieces . . . .")

The third movement is heavy, saturated with atmosphere, but labial in expression: "Va! nous nous étonnons de toi, Soleil! Tu nous as dit de tel mensonges! . . . Fauteur de troubles, de discordes! nourri d'insultes et d'esclandres. O Frondeur! fais éclater l'amande de mon oeil!" ("Come, we are amazed at you, Sun! You have told us such lies! . . . Instigator of strife and of discord! fed on insults and slanders, O Slinger! crack the nut of my eye!") (See Example XII, 6.)

The fourth is a nocturne, subtle, transparent, and relatively quiet: "Pour mon âme mêlée aux affaires lointaines . . . ." ("For my soul engaged in far matters, in towns an hundred fires revived by the barking of dogs . . . .") (See Example XII, 7).

The fifth movement starts with mighty expanses, blinding sun, wastes: "L'Été plus vaste que l'Empire suspend aux tables de l'espace plusieurs étages de climats." ("The summer vaster than the Empire hangs over the tables of space several terraces of climate. The huge earth rolls on its surface over-flowing its pale embers under the ashes.") (See Example XII, 8.)

The sixth movement is a song of love, where four women "of different type and ardour" each in her turn sings a refrain: "Je t'annonce les temps d'une grande faveur et la félicité des feuilles dans nos songes . . . ." ("I foretell you the time of a great blessing and the felicity of leaves in our dreams.")

The seventh and last movement consists to the greater part of an enormous enumeration of things that simultaneously happen on the earth's surface. The poem starts: "Select a wide hat with the brim seduced. The eye withdraws by a century into the provinces of the soul. Through the gate of living chalk we see the things of the plain:

living things, excellent things." And then follows a fantastic enumeration: "sacrifice of colts on the tombs of children, purification of widows among the roses and consignments of green birds in the courtyards to do honour to the old men; celebrations of open air festivals for the nameday of great trees and public rites in honour of a pool; consecration of black stones perfectly round, water-dowsing in dead places, dedication of cloths held up on poles, at the gates of the passes . . . ." (See Example XII, 9.)

In this enumeration the simultaneousness is essential, and I have tried to re-create this through a big speech chorus, fugued, compact, where isolated words now and then can be discerned from the general buzzing of voices, but every word is not meant to be distinguished and understood. The fragmentary elements of speech-chorus earlier used in the work are here brought together and intensified in a big complex, and toward the end of the movement the prosaic descriptive speech-chorus is again raised into song.

Then the concluding chanson brings the work to an end, resuming the atmosphere and sound of the beginning: "I have halted my horse by the tree of the doves, I whistle a note so sweet, shall the rivers break faith with their banks?" ("Living leaves in the morning fashioned in glory . . . .")

If I should try to make some observations regarding the relations of text and music in *Anabase*, it perhaps could be fruitful to compare it with *In the Hall of Mirrors*.

Even though the affinity between Perse's and Lindegren's way of using the poetic means is apparent, as I have pointed out earlier, there are also differences, which have been of great importance for the form of the music. One could call the text of *In the Hall of Mirrors* lyrical aphorism. The poems are very short and concentrated, and precisely this quality gives the composer rather free hands in shaping the music. There is place and time for symphonic development, for working out musical ideas relatively independently, for creating closed music forms. In *Anabase*, on the other hand, you could talk of lyrical epic. In this case it means a great wealth of words, a never-ceasing stream of events which traverse each other and which demand permanent variation of interpretation and construction. The result must be a form that is broken up, "nervous," mosaic. You could in fact call the musical conception of *Anabase* a kind of freely conceived dramatic-lyrical recitative in monumental form as compared to the closed "aria-form" of *In the Hall of Mirrors*.

Another difference in the use of the means, which is a logical consequence of the different concepts of form, is that while in *In the Hall of Mirrors* reciter, soloists, chorus, and orchestra are handled in clearly separable blocks, they all in *Anabase* are closely woven together in a richly patterned web. Recalling what I said about the limited and restricted means which I wanted to use in *Anabase,* I also could say that I have used them in a way similar to that of the parts of a string quartet, where different ideas are contrasted and interwoven. The technique of development, which in *In the Hall of Mirrors* more or less exclusively was entrusted to the orchestra, has here been succeeded by a method that involves all the means in the development, vocal as well as instrumental.

As for the phonological aspect, the language—in this case, French— has, as in *In the Hall of Mirrors* did the Swedish, left its mark very clearly on the melodic and rhythmic structure of the work. Accents, duration, ups and downs, word-melody play the same role as in *In the Hall of Mirrors*. But naturally there is one great difference: French is not my mother tongue, and that inevitably in some respects has a restricting effect on the conception of the work, because I cannot feel free enough to do all the things I can with my native language. The inborn instinct for and lifelong handling of one's own language is a guarantee that makes it possible to take liberties which you cannot take with any other language. Therefore my attitude toward the language in *Anabase* is much more cautious than in *In the Hall of Mirrors:* I am keeping much closer to a normal scanning of the text.

14. My Choral Music

LUIGI DALLAPICCOLA
(Translated by Madeleine M. Smith)

LUIGI DALLAPICCOLA (born in Pisino, Istria, on February 3, 1904) was reared in a town that was part of the Austro-Hungarian Empire. As Italians and nationals of an enemy power, his family was interned at Graz during World War I. The degradation and suffering made a lasting impression on Dallapiccola and, as a result, the subject of liberty has been an important theme in many of his choral and operatic works. It was during his imprisonment at Graz that the composer began musical studies and had the opportunity to hear the standard repertoire of nineteenth-century German symphonic and operatic works. After the Armistice, Dallapiccola pursued theoretical studies in Trieste. Later, in 1921, he established residence in Florence, where he attended the Cherubini Conservatory. His piano studies, under Ernesto Consolo, were completed in 1924. Compositional studies were under Vito Frazzi. In 1934, Dallapiccola was appointed professor of piano at the Conservatory—a post he has retained ever since. Throughout his lifetime, Dallapiccola has been active in the International Society of Contempory Music and has served as Italian delegate. As pianist and accompanist, he has traveled extensively in Europe. He visited London in 1946, and during the summers of 1951 and 1952 he was instructor in composition at the Berkshire Music Center in Tanglewood. Queens College (New York) appointed him professor of composition for the 1956–57 school year, and during this American visit, Dallapiccola was active performing and condusting concerts of his works.

IF anyone were to ask me what was the division of music in which Italy had achieved its greatest advances—among all the many forward steps it has taken from the fall of Facism down to the present—I would answer: in choral singing. This is the reason: while for decades Italy has boasted a number of the best orchestras, its choruses (with the exception of the permanent group at Rome's Accademia di Santa Cecilia) dwindled in personnel or flourished ephemerally for a brief time; in the case of opera choruses, occasionally they would be excellent but still entirely unadaptable to deal either with the ancient polyphonic style or with the technique and style of choral works of our own day.

I remember how one time, during the war years, Alfredo Casella, earnestly wanting to give me the friendliest advice, expressed the opinion that as long as I continued to devote a good share of my efforts to writing for chorus, my chances were going to be slight of hearing my work performed; and, to bear out what he said, he pointed out how scant had been the success of some of the finest pages of Ildebrando Pizzetti and Gian Francesco Malipiero. I said by way of reply that choruses would also spring up in Italy once we had "flooded the market" (I used exactly this commercial expression) with a considerable quantity of choral music, some of it good. It may be that my rejoinder was that of a victim of illusion.

However, no one of my generation would have thought, in those years, of composing something *just because the right artist to interpret it was at hand*. There still dwelt in us a horror of prima donnas and "Tenors." They with their notes held on to and clung to without end, their cadenzas tacked on for bravura effect, their arbitrarily capricious and superficial musicianship, and their general tastelessness, had lorded it altogether too long already on our stages; and it was with distaste that we contemplated the possibility of the performing artist's setting himself up as collaborator and going far beyond what we might set down on paper.

I do not intend to afflict the reader with a recital of the various ill winds that blew upon my early choral works, those that never were published and that I will not now permit to be published. "Ill winds," including bad luck, encounters with disgusting impresarios trying by cheap and devious means to crash the gate of history, contacts with hysterical singers who felt themselves under mandate from God, all these have ever been the lot of any artist who hopes to keep his independence—one, that is, who rejects, on the one hand, entangling alliances with those who are powers in politics, and on the other, chances to shine in the "salons" inhabited by *grandes dames* as blessed with high social position as they are unblessed with culture of any sort. In these salons the maestro, be he painter or poet, sculptor or composer, finds himself night after night acting out the part of the Peacock in the third act of Rostand's *Chantecler;* and yet the salons seem so terribly important for those who seek publicity, an element of life which in this day and age is often overrated.

Estate (Summer) is a fragment from Alcaeus; the text was translated by Ettore Romagnoli. Written in Florence in December, 1932, it requires Tenors I and II and Basses I and II.

This was a piece written for a special occasion. The National Musicians' Union had sponsored a contest with several categories. What they requested, among other things, were pieces for unaccompanied men's chorus, "in contemporary style but easy of execution," suitable for presentation by workers' glee clubs, etc.

God only knows what they meant (or what anybody might possibly mean) by "contemporary style"; but in my opinion the National Musicians' Union, using a phrase like this, tried to appear "advanced and liberal"—and not, as they actually were, dominated by a gang of reactionaries.

I had only a few days in which to work, and in very few days, in fact, I did write this piece—to run approximately four minutes, as called for in the contest rules.

The Union's committee seemed to like it. I was notified that my piece would have a performance in April (1933) in the Hall of the Accademia di Santa Cecilia in Rome, in connection with the National Musicians' Festival. I quickly inquired how many singers I might count on, in order to have the parts copied in plenty of time, and they told me to plan for thirty-six to forty.

When I got to Rome for the final rehearsal, to my surprise I found only thirteen singers, and they had not the faintest idea what they were to sing the next day; and, as if that were not enough, they turned out to be conspicuously lacking in technical capacity both vocal and mental. On top of that, one of the singers departed hastily a few minutes after the start of the rehearsal, finding himself suddenly indisposed.

For about an hour we worked in the Accademian Hall, the chorus master, his twelve henchmen, and I. About that time there was another defection: it was mine. It seemed to me not possible that, by the following day, they could put together a performance that would be at least decent in appearance. Slamming the door, I left the hall and got quickly out of Rome.

What the "12 CHORISTERS 12" put on that following day I know not. Undoubtedly at any rate, there was one composition which the program attributed to me. (As can be seen, we have not only in ancient music the problem of attribution as a live and pertinent one.) I say "undoubtedly" because a few days later I was officially informed that the Committee from the National Musicians' Union had sent off *Estate* for publication by Zanibon in Padua.

This was, perhaps, one positive thing—and not the only one. The other is that my initial contact with the poetry of Alcaeus was not to remain an isolated experience. Ten years later I engaged in a second study of the Greek poet (this time not in Romagnoli's modest translation but in a soaring version by Salvatore Quasimodo) which proved much more fruitful.

As I write these lines, I receive notice that the "Pancratius" male chorus of Heerlen, Holland, has my old work, now almost vanished from my own memory, in its repertoire. I do not know of any Italian group, in twenty-eight years, which ever took it up.

Sei Cori di Michelangelo Buonarroti il Giovane (Six Choruses on Poems of Michelangelo Buonarroti the Younger) was written in 1933–36 in Florence and Trent. Its three series were published by Carisch in Milan.

First Series: for mixed chorus, unaccompanied.
    a. *"Il Coro delle Malmaritate"*
      ("Chorus of the Unhappily Married Women")
    b. *"Il Coro dei Malammogliati"*
      ("Chorus of the Unhappily Married Men")
Second Series: for two soprano soloists and two contralto soloists (or chamber chorus of six sopranos and six contraltos—possibly boys) and seventeen instruments.
    a. *"I balconi della rosa (Invenzione)"*
      ("Balconies of the Rose")
    b. *"Il papavero (Capriccio)"*
      ("The Poppy")

Third Series: for mixed voices with full orchestra.
    a. *"Il Coro degli Zitti (Ciaccona)"*
      ("Chorus of the Silent")
    b. *"Il Coro dei Lanzi briachi (Gagliarda)"*
      ("Chorus of the Drunken Lansquenets")

"The consequent knowledge [of the existence] of this manuscript, the general acquaintance with the works contained therein, is bound to prove a very great satisfaction to all of you and pleasing in connection with the research work of our Academy: for it bears within it an intact and valuable treasure of the purest and most exquisite specimens of our tongue. Through them our language will one day be enriched with new graces and beauties, and our *Vocabulary,* conserving it, will be in a position to receive from it an advantageous and most notable increase."

In these words Francesco del Furia expressed himself in the course of a lecture, given at a meeting on February 24, 1818, on "Some Writings of Michelangelo Buonarroti the Younger found in a Codex MS in the Marucelliana Public Library."[1] Michelangelo Buonarroti the Younger is not a difficult poet in his thought or syntax. (Really difficult ones, or rather "impervii"—I like this word of Bontempelli used to characterize their obscurity—are Jacopone da Todi, Michelangelo, and Tommaso Campanella.) His vocabulary, however, is so rich, refined, and uncommon that, when I published the score of the Third Series of *Choruses,* I believed it necessary to add a number of notes at the end of the text, to clarify the meaning of the words.

Notwithstanding the discovery of the manuscript of Michelangelo Buonarroti the Younger and the account that Francesco del Furia gave of it, the name of the nephew of the "divine Michelangelo" (as he was called by Benvenuto Cellini) still remained a name known only to a few specialists. The performances of his *Trancia* at the Teatro Romano in Fiesole, between 1930 and 1932, brought the name to broader strata of the population; and, after so many years, I still held intact a vivid impression of those performances, full of the most authentic peasant fascination, there in the spring sunlight, amid one of the loveliest set-

[1] *Proceedings of the Imperial and Royal Accademia della Crusca,* Vol. II.

tings in the world. I had been thinking for a long time of doing a choral work based on the poetry of Michelangelo the Younger, and so, when I actually got down to working on it, I had quite clearly in my mind the general outline of the composition. Despite the "official" date of starting work (1933), I recall very well how the impulse came to me in the summer of 1932 during a trip to Arco, on Lake Garda, to take the first definite steps. The work as a whole is divided into three sections. Each of these comprises two choruses strongly contrasted with each other. Ideally it should be programmed complete in a single concert (Radio Prague did it this way, late in April, 1938, when it presented the world *première* of the complete "opera" under the direction of Maestro Kabelač). Yet the three divisions do have a certain independence which makes possible separate performances of them.

There is no doubt that one may at first seem to hear in the First Series ("Chorus of the Unhappily Married Women" and "Chorus of the Unhappily Married Men") echoes of the music of the Italian Renaissance. But anyone who is willing to probe just a little below the surface will realize that the seemingly archaic echoes are in no wise borrowings (as was indeed customary in those years when everything seemed to revolve around an illusion of neoclassicism, a bubble that burst following World War II, and now, fortunately, has fallen into oblivion) but have filtered down through other more recent experiences. By this I mean that no names of Renaissance masters could be cited, but that the name of G. Francesco Malipiero, the master who taught my generation what the true spirit of Italian music was, would be in order. He taught us by word and example; suffice it to mention in this connection two of his basic dramatic works: *Le Sette Canzoni* (*The Seven Songs*) and *Il Torneo Notturno* (*The Jousting by Night*).

Inheritances from the Baroque are many, in this First Series.

I think one may truly and properly speak of ideograms in the passage *"Levarci a' mattutini"* ("To bestir ourselves at matins"), which with its swinging motion discreetly suggests that of a bell in the "Chorus of the Unhappily Married Women"; moreover, certain word-emphases designed to give potency to the significance of the word, or of one aspect of it, are of undoubted Baroque origin. As an example I can cite the verse *"Un buon uom mi disse 'Fa!'"* ("A just man said to me, 'Do!'") in the "Chorus of the Unhappily Married Husbands." The exclamation "Fa!" comes on the note of fa (F) in all the voices.[2]

After what I said about the state of choral music in Italy around 1930, no one will be surprised to read that, when I had finished the First Series of the *Michelangelo* in the late spring of 1933, I locked up the manuscript in a box. There seemed to be no use in sending a publisher a score that never would have a public hearing.

Three years later, having come off the winner, with my *Musica per tre Pianoforti (Music for Three Pianos)*, of one of the prizes in the international contest sponsored by the Geneva "Carillon," I decided to use the money to have two hundred copies of the manuscript score (of the *Michelangelo,* First Series) printed at my own expense, asking the Carisch house in Milan to put the title in its catalogue. The Carisch company was glad to accept. Not only that, but they agreed at the same time to publish the other two series without any further financial contribution from me. The Second Series by this time had already had a performance; the Third, I was just working on.

When the First Series was published I had a number of complimentary copies sent out, but without any results. However, toward the end of 1937, my old harmony teacher, Antonio Illersberg, undertook the first performance of that section in Trieste. I suppose that it was a more or less experimental tryout. In any case I am deeply grateful to him, as he was the only one to show any interest.

For fourteen years after that I do not recall having received word of any performance of that work, except perhaps one at Donaueschingen, which at the moment I am unable to verify. In 1951, however, Marcel Couraud with his Chorale presented it in Venice. I was in the United States at the time. Not until 1952, during the first concert of my career that was entirely devoted to my own music, conducting this work myself at the Instituto Nacional de Bellas Artes in Mexico City, did I hear for the first time what it sounded like in reality—nineteen years after composing it and sixteen years since its publication.

My generation was in no hurry; we had learned patience. Public performance was not considered the alpha and omega of an artist-composer's

---

[2] It is impossible to render into English the correspondence between the imperative "Fa" and the musical note Fa (F).—L. D.

life—just as we were not in the habit of depending on the sums that we received from the Authors' Society. We had before us the heroic examples of the great masters of the Viennese School, whose music was attracting notice from the ISCM plus a few particularly *avant-garde* radio stations such as the British Broadcasting Corporation or the Institut National de Radiodiffusion in Brussels. Neither did today's mass propaganda then exist, nor would we have based our conduct on meretricious admiration of commercial interests.

I have said that I had clearly enough in mind at the outset the whole architecture of the *Sei Cori*. Thus I felt that after the First Series, *a cappella,* some purely instrumental interlude would be desirable, to introduce the Second.

This part has two very short texts: two quatrains selected from the poet's many *Enigmas* (or *Riddles*), namely: "The Balconies of the Rose" and "The Poppy"—two poetic compositions which do not pretend to be anything other than beautifully chosen words and verses harmoniously aligned. As previously in choosing the texts for the First Series, at this point also I saw to it that there should be a chance for rather sharp contrast. The *Invenzione* has a contemplative, still, morning character; the *Capriccio* is high in color and aggressive.

Just as I was on the point of finishing the score, I was invited by the National Musicians' Union to participate in the festival that was to take place in the spring of 1935. In spite of the sad experience I had got into two years previously, I accepted, since the name of the conductor, Mario Rossi, was a guarantee in itself. In fact the work did receive a worthy presentation in the Hall of the Accademia di Santa Cecilia. (This was my last contact with the Musicians' Union.)

In this Second Series it seemed to me that I had taken a real step forward in my quest for myself. This is the reason why I resolved to dedicate the composition to G. Francesco Malipiero, as an expression to him of my gratitude for all that he had given me.

After the serenity of the Second Series comes with sudden contrasting grimness the "Chorus of the Silent," which opens the Third. The text is taken from the Vigil titled "The Masked Ladies," to be enacted in the last night of the Carnival—ghastly and ghostlike. No trace remains of the earthy, good-humored, jesting quality of the "Unhappily Married"; nor yet of the pure word-play and conceits of the *Enigmas*. "The Chorus of the Silent" is the finest of all the poems of Michelangelo Buonarroti the Younger, certainly one of the high points of Italian poetry. Nor can one be sure that the whole idea for the *Sei Cori* did not derive its original impulse precisely from my study of this poem.

The three stanzas, eight lines each, with a recurring refrain whose fascination cannot be conveyed in translation,

> *Noi siam, noi siam gli Zitti,*
> *Paggi, messaggi, ostaggi del Silenzio*

> (*We are, we are the Mute,*
> *Pages, message-bearers, hostages of Silence*)

gave me the idea of adopting the form of the *chaconne*, with a fugue in the middle stanza.

At the very first entrance of the chorus there are instructions on the score for the utmost clarity in diction. Just as in the two preceding series, but more so, I was concerned for comprehensibility in the words; for it seemed obvious to me that, when we face the problem of teaming music with words, text-comprehensibility is not a thing to be lightly and casually thrown away, without downgrading the poets to the point of using them simply as a "pretext," or worse, as a "blazed trail." Otherwise you will have merely syllables set to music, as has been done so often, in various periods of history—quite legitimately and with excellent results—from Adriano Banchieri to Olivier Messiaen. This latter way of doing is somewhat like the intention in the days when people wrote symphonic tone poems: it was hoped merely that a text would suggest and orient the thinking of the listeners. Though it can be taken for granted that our audiences know from memory the text of the Mass or of certain perfectly familiar prayers, it does not seem to me that the same can be assumed for poetry.

(I have felt obliged, it may seem, in all the choral writing that I have had occasion to do since then, to stick to very brief texts, just to achieve maximum comprehensibility through repetition. A single exception to this rule may perhaps be noted in Number 3 of *Requiescant*.)

I think it desirable at this point to make clear that if, in the *ritornelle* (of the "Chorus of the Silent") I made use of the spoken chorus gradually moving over into a *cantato,* I did it not for the purpose of making the words understandable but rather for reasons of timbre. This is true, and especially so, of the *parlato* marked "with absolutely no timbre" (*"assolutamente senza timbre"*) on the verse "Per chi apre bocca qua si stille assenzio" ("Here wormwood is distilled for any who opens mouth").

The "Chorus of the Drunken Lansquenets" (the original title of the poem was "Chorus of Rakish Youths Going off to War"), composed to a galliard rhythm, serves as an epilogue for the work as a whole. It is for this reason that I did not hesitate to recall here and there to the listener's memory (though only in variant form or with modifications) the chief themes that had already appeared in the preceding movements.

Thanks to the kindly interest manifested by Mario Labroca, who had been in Florence for a year, as head of the Maggio Musicale, this Third Series received its world *première* there, at the Teatro Comunale, in a concert of modern music in May, 1937, under the direction of Mario Rossi.

I think that my musical personality is portrayed rather plainly in the Third Series. At least it appeared so to me when I was invited to hear one of the final full rehearsals, when the work had progressed already very well. I was so encouraged with it that I did not renew my subscription to the *Eco della Stampa* (Review of Press Notices), which was about to run out. Because the Third Series gave me this feeling of being freed from any necessity of keeping up to date on all the cheap gossip scratched off in haste between midnight and one o'clock after single hearings, I feel kindly disposed even today (although my style may in the meantime have developed into a somewhat different thing) toward my *Sei Cori di Michelangelo Buonarroti il Giovane.*

Canti di prigionia (Songs of Captivity) was written in 1938–41 in Florence and Covigliaio, and published by Carisch in Milan. It includes:

a. *"Preghiera di Maria Stuarda"* ("Prayer of Mary Queen of Scots") for mixed chorus and instrumental ensemble.
b. *"Invocazione di Boezio"* ("Invocation of Boetius") for women's voices and instrumental ensemble.
c. *"Congedo di Girolamo Savonarola"* ("Farewell of Girolamo Savonarola") for mixed chorus and instrumental ensemble.

In writing about the Alcaic fragment of *Estate,* I mentioned a second contact I had with the Greek poet which happened ten years later.

A renewed acquaintance with a poem, or a poet, even after many years, is not unparalleled in my life as an artist. My unpublished "Rapsodia" (study for "The Death of Count Orlando"), on an episode in the *Chanson de Roland,* translated by Giovanni Pascoli, was written in 1932. Then in 1946, fourteen years later, I had occasion—almost an impromptu occasion—to take up the Roland legend again in my *Rencesvals,* for male solo voice and piano, this time to the original Old French text. My *Due Laudi di Fra Jacopone da Todi (Two Lauds by Jacopone da Todi)* dates from 1929; then one may hear the lofty poetry of the Umbrian mystic rising again in the second and fourth of the five movements of my *Concerto per la notte di Natale dell'anno 1956 (Concerto for Christmas Eve of the Year 1956).*

Just as the streams in my native region, the Carso, plunge for a time into deep abysses and after flowing a good many kilometers underground, emerge again on the surface with new names and other colors, so does the same process seem to occur in me with regard to certain poetic themes.

I had occasion to realize all this as I scanned the program of the International Music Festival in Venice in the spring of 1961. The program-annotator, in a perceptive note on the First Series of the *Michelangelo choruses,* which were being performed by the Monteverdi-Chor of Hamburg, observed that the sunny, serene, carefree tone of the *Sei Cori di Michelangelo Buonarroti il Giovane* has no echo in my later musical output. Too respectful to hold it against me, too objective to try to draw conclusions from it, the program editor confined himself to observing the fact; undoubtedly the fact is quite true.

Perhaps a consideration of the dates will offer some explanation for it. It is absolutely true that the Third Series of the *Michelangelo* was finished and dated in 1936; but it is just as true that it was already completely sketched out before I went to the Festival of the ISCM in Prague in September, 1935. Naturally I am not saying that Europe lived in peace between 1918 and 1935; but it was not until the fall of 1935 that a definite upsetting of the balance could be positively noted, and this was what, step by step, quickly but inexorably, probably set off World War II. This fatal breach of balance in Europe, together with the brutality of our campaign in Ethiopia and the disasters of the war in Spain, must be considered as acting upon my personality somewhat similarly to the bio-physiological changes that cause the normal individual to grow from adolescence to young manhood, thence to middle age, and from middle age to old age. Those of my generation who felt it morally not possible to "accept without discussion" (that was the standard phrase) whatever the dictatorship imposed found themselves confronted, from one day to the next, and with horribly scant political preparation for them, with problems and responsibilities which five years earlier they had not even imagined. Here ended for me, never to return again, the world of the colorful, the cheery, the anecdotal, the world of carefree serenity. With it, perhaps, the time of youth, and with this the first period of my creative activity. I had now to seek other wood in other forests.

A few years ago, in a quite exhaustive article, autobiographical in nature, "The Genesis of the *Canti di prigionia* and *Il Prigioniero*," written on invitation for *The Musical Quarterly* (July, 1953), I made an attempt to set forth with complete candor certain events of my life in which might be sought some of the underlying reasons for what one critic has termed my "claustrophobia." In that article I also thought it suitable to point out how, on the one hand, certain important factual circumstances of world political developments between 1938 and 1941, and on the other hand, certain stages in the composing of the *Canti di prigionia,* followed nearly parallel lines.

I may as well admit that the ivory-tower idea and myth did indeed attract me at one time. But I soon realized, going back over the past, how short-lived that illusion had been, just as it is always a short-lived illusion to presume to deny tradition. No matter how much we try to withdraw into ourselves, we are soon all too aware of the echo of the tragedies going on around us. And it is possible to deny tradition with words, dismissing it with a mere boutade; but tradition will creep back in no matter where we try to thrust it out.

> *O Domine Deus! speravi in Te.*
> *O care mi Jesu! nunc libera me.*
> *In dura catena, in misera poena, desidero Te.*

Languendo, gemendo et genu flectendo,
Adoro, imploro, ut liberes me . . . .

The idea of setting to music these five lines that Mary Queen of Scots wrote in one of the last years of her imprisonment came to me immediately after I heard on the radio the voice of Mussolini announcing, on September 1, 1938, that the moment had come for starting an anti-Semitic campaign in Italy too (this, of course, after repeated official denials!). The music for this fragment was sketched out some weeks later, in a very few days. (I recall that it was in fact for only a few days that I interrupted my orchestrating of *Volo di notte*.) I did not have any idea at that time whether the *Prayer of Mary Queen of Scots* would remain a single composition in itself or was destined to become part of a larger work. The political developments had been sudden, and sudden was the musical impulse that had forced itself upon me. I had had no time to think about the general plan; whereas, as I have said, I had so clear an outline in mind when I set about composing the *Sei Cori di Michelangelo Buonarroti il Giovane*.

No sooner had I finished the orchestration of *Volo di notte* than I picked up the hasty sketch of Mary Stuart's *Prayer,* and, working it over, gave it its definitive form, choosing a grouping of instruments (the only grouping that could achieve the sound I wished for) having no wood winds, no brasses, and no strings. This was in July, 1939.

There was a brief moment when it seemed that the *Preghiera* would have a first performance at the Venice International Festival, under the direction of Dimitri Mitropoulos. But on September 1, at five o'clock in the morning, Hitler bombed Warsaw; three hours after that, he declared war on Poland. So there was something much more important and more urgent to think about than the Venice Festival or my *première,* namely, the immediate future, and—why not?—the chances one might have of surviving.

I looked at my manuscript. Several months earlier, in the Introduction of the *Preghiera,* I had insistently brought in the ancient hymn of the Church, *Dies irae, dies illa,* while the chorus murmured *parlato "O Domine Deus!"* then vocalized, and finally, still with the *Dies irae* background, sang forth the same pleading invocation.

I continued to look at my manuscript without a trace of pride about my all too easy prediction. It was now some time since the invisible hand had written again on the wall the three words that once appeared to Belshazzar; we knew their full significance by the interpretation of the prophet Daniel. I kept contemplating the manuscript. The chorus vocalized on the word *libera,* then lingered over it—as it lingered also over the word *catena.* Finally the chorus repeated several times: *"imploro ut liberes me."*

The comprehensibility of the words, an element to which I have already said that I attributed considerable importance, seemed assured. Who has not at some time—and particularly in those war years—wondered whether he would be still alive the next day? I too asked myself that question. Thus it is understandable that I wanted to have this published at once; copying the score (only eighteen pages) onto transparent paper, a process that at that time, in Italy, was still in its infancy, I offered it to the publishing house of Carisch.

Despite the extremely unfavorable world situation, Carisch accepted it. When the score came out, late in December, I sent the first copy to Paul Collaer, to whom I had dedicated it. To him I owe the first performance, by the Institut National de Radiodiffusion of Brussels; I heard it over the radio in Florence, the evening of April 10, 1940.

Less than a month later, as a consequence of the invasion of Belgium, the Institut National de Radiodiffusion would also be culturally silent, and for five long years.

In the meantime, I had arrived at the conclusion that the *Preghiera di Maria Stuarda* would be the first part of a tryptich, whose title would be *Canti di prigionia.* It had not been very difficult to find the text for the second part: a bridge which should lead us to an affirming finale. Four short verses by Severinus Boetius gave the first impetus to my fancy for the middle piece, a scherzo, as it were. In this guise, the middle section, based on a series of five brief episodes, was to have repercussions from the standpoint of construction—in a number of works of mine that followed much later.

The search for a text for the last part was long and laborious. It had to contain an affirmation of faith. The search would have continued even longer had it not been for the fact that, on July 19, 1940, Hitler made a speech in the Reichstag announcing imminent aerial attacks on Great

Britain. It was with deep emotion that I read, shortly after that, the reply of Sir Samuel Hoare, which was confined to exhorting the nation to pray. That instant I happened to remember that something similar had been written by Girolamo Savonarola, shortly before he was to die, in his *Meditatio in Psalmum,* "In Te Domine speravi," which was left unfinished:

> *Premat mundus, insurgant hostes, nihil timeo*
> *Quoniam in Te Domine speravi,*
> *Quoniam Tu es spes mea,*
> *Quoniam Tu altissimum posuisti refugium Tuum.*

By October, 1941, the score of the *Canti di prigionia* was done.

The Teatro delle Arti had for some length of time been in existence in Rome; it gave concerts and stage performances in a small theater, and its management was in the hands of a wide-awake young Sicilian named Antonio d'Ajala. Not having in mind personally recommending the first performance of my choral piece to any "Institutions" that might be more in the public eye and might carry more influence (so sure I was of getting a negative response, which would have jolted me considerably), I gladly accepted an offer from D'Ajala to give the *Canti di prigionia* their first performance at the Teatro delle Arti.

I think that never before had a score so difficult (from the choral point of view) been given in Italy. Fernando Previtali, who was the conductor, had to argue with the skeptical, encourage the dubious, shake to life the sluggish. The performance took place on a particularly ill-omened day: December 11, 1941. The whole city of Rome was swarming with police troops and ordinary policemen, all assigned to keep order in the streets. It was the day on which Mussolini declared war on the United States.

I seem to remember that this first performance, given in Rome, was one that could be called a "terrific impression." However, men and circumstances conspired in such perfect agreement that the work was never again undertaken. Aside from the chronicles in the daily papers on the day following the *première,* to which I deliberately paid no attention, not an article appeared until the spring of 1945, when Fedele d'Amico devoted a penetrating and detailed study to the *Canti di prigionia* in the first number of the magazine *Società,* published in Florence.

Nor did I ever ask the why of this neglect. The answers I would have received would have been all too easily predictable—and, in a certain sense, convincing! They would have pointed out that under the Fascist dictatorship it would have been inopportune, to say the least, to make much of a title like *Canti di prigionia:* it would have been asking for trouble and actually dangerous, perhaps. Or they might have said that the chorus part was too difficult; furthermore that, outside of Rome, no city of Italy had both a vibraphone and a vibraphonist (who would ever have predicted that in a few years the vibraphone was to become the instrument by whose aid some would insist they could solve the most complex ethical and aesthetic problems?).

Once again I had to wait.

The *Canti di prigionia* were, practically speaking, discovered in London, in July, 1946, at the first postwar Festival of the ISCM.

Canti di liberazione (Songs of Liberation) were written in 1952–55 in Tangelwood, Vittoria Apuana, and Florence. The publisher was Edizioni Suvini Zerboni in Milan.

It appeared to me an obvious necessity that the *Canti di liberazione* (for mixed chorus and full orchestra) should be three in number, and equally necessary at least that the successive movements should be adagio, allegro, and adagio, and that the whole thing should run about half an hour in length.

Some time before I started writing the music I had chosen the texts and arranged them in order. I should say rather that the words of the first section, a passage from a letter by Sebastiano Castellio, an opponent of Calvin, had been considered by me years earlier, as a possibility for the *Canti di prigionia.* The idea of taking three verses from the Book of Exodus for my central section occurred to me after a reading of *Das Gesetz (The Law)* by Thomas Mann. (I had been greatly struck by the fact that the writer had thought of Myriam, the sister of Aaron, as "a timpani virtuoso," and that was one reason why my second movement was dedicated to Thomas Mann, on the occasion of his eightieth birthday.) The text from St. Augustine (consisting of five thoughts, each of which presents the yearning of one of the five senses for the

Deity), coming last, seemed to me most suitable to express the total liberation of the spirit.

Although it has been so affirmed, I do not consider that any obvious "topical allusions" of a political nature are to be discovered in this work.

In the fall of 1949, I felt that the moment to begin composing this work had come, but I was mistaken. Within a few months I had worked out a considerable part of the foundations; I then tore it up. Then, about the end of 1951, I really thought I had something, and in fact I did compose the series of twelve notes with which the *Canti di liberazione* opens; in this melody-definition are found all eleven intervals that are possible in our tempered system.

With a hefty sheaf of rough drafts in my luggage I set off for Tanglewood, at which conference I had been invited for the second time to direct a course. I had hardly got to the Berkshire Music Center when the management of the Pittsburgh International Festival commissioned me to write a piano work. Undecided whether to accept this or not, I finally yielded to the friendly urging of Roy Harris.

It was evident, in the sacred drama of *Job* (1950), that my style of writing had undergone some changes—even though the critics, as they reviewed its first performance at the Theatre Eliseo in Rome, did not notice it. This *première* was its only performance of the season, this through no fault of mine but of the management. I may add that the whole performance was carried through under circumstances which bordered on the grotesque.[3]

Job was the first work of mine of any considerable scope in which I had used a single twelve-tone row. The *cantus firmus* (the *Te Deum laudamus*), which I used here and there, was also arranged, with appropriate transpositions, in such a manner as to achieve the "full chromatic." I had made use of only one "transformation" of the row: namely, that which is obtained by the omission of six notes among the individual sounds—the one, that is, which adopts sounds 1, 8, 15, 22, etc. (Note that this transformation appears only in the passage "Beato l'uomo cui corregge Iddio: Non c'e morte senza peccato, né sofferenza senza colpa" ["Behold, happy is the man whom God correcteth: there is no

3 See Dallapiccola, "The Birth-Pangs of *Job*," *London Musical Events* (May, 1960), 26–27.

death without sin, nor any suffering without guilt"]—and, of course, in the other parallel passages. Now, this is the only passage that I did not draw directly from the Book of Job but rather from one of the writings of a Father of the Church.)

But now, as I worked on the *Canti di liberazione,* the changes were becoming more numerous and more serious. The metrics were more intricate: I was considering effects of "accelerando naturale," playing with just one interval and bringing in the voices one at a time, in succession and with steadily diminishing time-values (Number 1: basses, bar 5, to celeste, bar 8); I would exploit individual segments of the row, as in the passage for voices alone in the first movement, which ends on the notes of the name of Bach, B A C H (three times repeating notes 7, 8, and 9; then three times notes 1, 2, and 3 of the original form, and I transposed them in such a way as to obtain the "chromatic total" each time, seeing to it furthermore that they should be arranged according to quite definite metrical relationships).

The regular canons certainly still interested me and always will (I will confine myself to citing the *canon cancrizans* [crab canons] in the first movement, between bars 85 [sopranos and altos] and 90 [orchestra]), but the irregular ones did not leave me indifferent. For example, see No. 1, bars 26–31, and bars 36–43; also *canon cancrizans, irregularis,* between bars 129 and 135 of the first movement (here only the time-value of the dotted sixteenth is maintained constant); the *canon irregularis* of the voice-parts in the third movement, on the words "Fragrasti, et duxi spiritum . . ." (bars 91–96) and its reversal (bars 104–10) (see Example XIII, 1, at the back of this volume).

"Metrical cells" (Do-mi-nus), based on the values 3, 1, and 2, and multiples of these, were set forth simultaneously on one single note by all four voices in unison at four different speeds (beginning of the second movement) in such a way as to occupy the total time-value of eighteen half-notes (later, at bars 113–17, they are beaten out by the percussion at six different tempi) (see Example XIII, 2).

I felt obliged to eschew not only all octaves but all false octave-relations as well; I bade farewell to every purely decorative element in the instrumental part; I kept seeking to obtain a freer way of spacing out the periods than I had used in the past; I elaborated canonic developments in which two or three tempi were superimposed one on the other (Number 2; bars 39–46; and the corresponding 154–61). The strengthening of the word by a musical underlining, which earlier I had had occasion to call "our inheritance from the Baroque"—when writing on the first series of the *Michelangelo*—assumed much greater complexity (for example, in the second movement episode "Abyssi operuerunt eos: descenderunt . . ."), at a point where the word "descenderunt"—rhythmically set forth by the six voices in steadily decreasing time-values, starting with the sopranos and going all the way down to the second basses—makes a curve which, properly executed, cannot but suggest the feeling of being pulled downward to the depths.

As can be seen, various problems came up, and each required an individual solution. I would like to add at the same time that I did want to write something that should not be simply *Augenmusik* (music for the eye) and yet that I did feel an obligation to keep some coherence with my own past.

A preparatory labor was incumbent upon me in that summer of 1952 in America. It was to make a study of some of the possibilities inherent in the rows of twelve tones I had laid out late in 1951. Thus it was that I decided to work on the piano composition commissioned by the Pittsburgh Festival and on the *Canti di liberazione* at the same time.

In this way came into being the eleven short pieces for piano which I named *Quaderno Musicale di Annalibera* (*Musical Notebook of Annalibera*), based on the same row as the *Canti di liberazione*. (Annalibera is the name of my daughter, who at that time was almost eight; her name cannot but bring to mind the idea of "liberation," or freedom.)

Some elements in the *Quaderno* can be distinguished in the *Canti*. Numbers 7 and 11 are to be found intact in the latter (easily recognizable despite the choral passages that cut in); parts of Number 10 occur in some passages of the first movement and in the episode of the second that is called *"Currus Pharaonis"* ("Pharaoh's Chariots"); the "cell" (rhythmic pattern) of Number 8 provided the initial metrical impulse for the passage "Dominus quasi vir pugnator" ("The Lord is as a man of war: The Lord is his name") of the second movement; something like an echo of Number 3 can be noted at the end of the third movement; and there is perhaps a reminiscence of Number 1 around measure 50 of the second movement. It does not seem to me that any elements of Numbers 2, 4, 5, or 9 in the *Quaderno* return in the *Canti di liberazione*.[4]

The composition was two-thirds finished when I accepted Dr. Eigel Kruttge's invitation to write a choral work for Radio Cologne (I had for some time been hearing marvelous reports concerning the Cologne chorus, and indeed it lives up to its world renown). The publishing house of Suvini Zerboni at the same time asked me if it could publish the work, and I accepted, not omitting, however, to warn the publishers that there might be some sales for the score of the *Canti di liberazione* but very few performances, in view of their great difficulty. (The realities proved not so dire as my predictions.)

The first performance of the *Canti* took place over Radio Cologne on October 28, 1955, in a program of the series "Musik der Zeit," under the direction of Hermann Scherchen, who was ably assisted by Chorus Master Bernhard Zimmermann.

Requiescant was written during 1957–58 in Florence and Vittoria Apuana.

From the latter part of 1952 to the early months of 1953, while working on the *Goethe-Lieder* (seven quatrains from the *West-östlicher Divan* for women's voices and three clarinets), I thought of disposing the following instruments around a central focus (Number 4), in the following numbers and order:

I	II	III	IV	V	VI	VII
3 Cl.	*1 Cl.*	*2 Cl.*	*3 Cl.*	*2 Cl.*	*1 Cl.*	*3 Cl.*
Eb. Cl.	Eb Cl.	Eb Cl.	Eb Cl.			Eb Cl.
Bb Cl.		Bb Cl.	Bb Cl.	Bb Cl.		Bb Cl.
Bb Bass Cl.			Bb Bass Cl.	Bb Bass Cl.	Bb Bass Cl.	Bb Bass Cl.

My *Cinque Canti (Five Songs)* for baritone with instrumental ensemble (1956), a setting of some fragments of the Grecian Lyrics in Salvatore Quasimodo's translation, are centered on the third song, to words by Lycimnius:

> *Acheronte,*
> *Che tormenti reca agli uomini*
> *D'infinite fonti di lagrime e dolori ribelle.*

[4] See H. U. Engleman, "Dallapiccola's *Canti di liberazione*," *Melos* (March, 1956), 73–76.

(Acheron,
Bringer of agony to men,
Brews with ten thousand streams of tears and sorrows.)

Around this as a core—this song of daytime, of life, of suffering—I ranged two songs of morning (Numbers 1 and 2) and two songs of night (Numbers 4 and 5). This structure and its connection with the choice of poems did not escape the notice of Massimo Mila; he titled an article which was in large part devoted to the Milan performance of the *Cinque Canti* "L'uomo nella sfera" ("Man in the Center of a Sphere"). To Jacques Wildberger, I am indebted for other observations of noteworthy acuteness even as concerns the interrelationships of the texts: he notes how the first fragment speaks of the morning star, and the last, of the evening star; how the second brings in singing birds, and the fourth, of generations of sleeping birds. And I owe to Andrew Imbrie a concise classification: inanimate nature in the first and last poems; animate nature in the second and next to the last; man in the middle poem.

I confess that I had never thought of so rigid and so neat an organization, either during the process of composition or later. I acknowledge that I was pleased to know that others had seen it.

After the *Cinque Canti* came the *Concerto per la notte di Natale dell'anno 1956,* in five movements, of which three are entirely instrumental (Numbers 1, 3, and 5), whereas a soprano voice is added to the instruments in the two others.

Requiescant, for mixed chorus and orchestra (a boys' chorus is strongly to be recommended in the final movement), written between the summer of 1957 and the late fall of 1958, may make one think of the *Concerto per la notte di Natale* from the point of view of structure; but in that analogy lies precisely the element of its difference. In this one Numbers 1, 3, and 5 call for chorus and orchestra, but the two other parts are for instruments alone.

Since the *Canti di liberazione* I have not used full orchestra (the *Concerto per la notte di Natale* requires a group of seventeen soloists), nor is there a full orchestra in *Requiescant.* For one thing the predominantly "intimate" character of the work did not cry out for it; besides, it was easy for me to understand that, at this stage of my creative activity, I would have little or nothing to communicate through a second oboe or a second clarinet. This explains why the ten wood-wind instruments are all solo parts, and likewise the four brasses.

Even though I had set to music texts of Latin, Spanish, German, and Italian of several periods, and also Old French, I had never before undertaken an English text.

So now there is raised a question of a philosophical nature: is it actually the composer who undertakes a text, or the text that comes to the composer, at just a particular moment of his life, bearing within itself something mysteriously *pre-shaped,* by virtue of which the composer is tempted suddenly to recognize it almost as his own creation?[5]

In a particularly painful period of my life, which I shall not explain simply because the present essay is not an autobiography, one morning in November, 1956, a student at Queens College in Flushing, New York, where I was teaching, laid on the music rack of my piano a composition of his own for unaccompanied chorus, not yet finished, in order to receive my criticisms, suggestions, and corrections. The text was a piece written by Oscar Wilde on the death of his beloved sister, called *Requiescat,* which I had never read before.

It seemed as though, in that moment, I could "see," in a flash, a complete, total vision—even though it was not yet clearly defined. I realized that these words would be the central part of a composition, and that its length should be almost exactly equal to that of the other parts put together.

One other sad circumstance, shortly thereafter, made me think of a certain eight lines of verse, almost a childish thing, which had deeply impressed me in 1943, when I had first had occasion to read James Joyce's *Portrait of the Artist as a Young Man.* It had been with a *musical setting* in mind that I had copied it and learned it by heart:

> *Dingdong! The castle bell!*
>
> . . .
>
> *My coffin shall be black,*
> *Six angels at my back,*
>
> . . .

---

[5] May I point out that, whenever I composed operas, I always wrote the librettos myself, because of the complexity and diversity of all the elements which are involved in their realization, and because of my own difficulty in "collaborating" with someone else.—L. D.

It would be a serene ending for the work. And, for the beginning, nothing seemed more appropriate than a verse from the Gospel of St. Matthew:

> *Come unto me, all that labour and are heavy laden,*
> *and I will give you rest.* (Matt. 11:28)

I realized, however, that for some, who put faith in appearances and refuse to take the sound, basic viewpoint of things, the juxtaposition of St. Matthew, Oscar Wilde, and James Joyce would no doubt seem offensive.

In the spring of 1957, Dr. Herbert Hübner informed me that Lorin Maazel had presented the *Canti di prigionia* in Hamburg and asked me whether I was disposed to consent to write something on commission for Radio Hamburg. I was in New York at the time and did not know with certainty what I would be doing the following year. Therefore I replied with thanks and said that I could give a final answer later.

A year after that, when the middle part of my composition was all finished and several other parts of it were sketched out, I happened to be in Hamburg and gave Dr. Hübner a description of the work in its entirety. I had not yet decided on a title. After the central section came the impetuous introductory movement, and the serene closing number was not long in taking shape. Lastly I worked on the instrumental parts. On November 2, 1958, I signed and dated the score.

I believe that *Requiescant* represents another step forward in my creative production, both from the point of view of rhythmic experimentation (see how, in the two orchestral sections, the duration of the groups of two, three, four, and five eighth-notes is kept strictly even by means of the metronome) and from the standpoint of the freedom of accent which may be seen as one of the true aspirations of today's music (see for example the episode that I would like to describe as "schwebend," where the stanza "Lily-like, white as snow" begins); and also, lastly, for its treatment of the orchestra, which is reduced to the essentials. What I chiefly hope for, of course, is that the work might say something to men through its poetic content (see Example XIII, 3).

The first performance took place at Radio Hamburg, at one of the concerts in the series "Das neue Werk," in November, 1959, under the direction of Hermann Scherchen. I was then in New York, so that I could not attend the *première*. Nor when it was first given in Italy, over Radio Roma, was I more fortunate: I was in Lisbon that time. Nor, more recently, was it possible for me to hear it performed at the Institut National de Radiodiffusion in Brussels. I am hoping, just the same, not to have to wait nineteen years, as I did for the Frst Series of the *Michelangelo,* to get an idea of the sound of *Requiescant.*

And now to discuss the choruses in my writings for the stage: In *Volo di notte* (1937–39) the choral parts are not very extensive, and anyone who would undertake to count the words that are given to the chorus would be surprised to find how few there are.

At the opening of the first and the sixth (last) scenes, the chorus comes in with the vowel *a,* and the exclamation *Ah!,* respectively; and just before the end, it, with peaceful solemnity, sounds forth the name of the chief character, Rivière. The chorus, consisting of Mechanics, Directors of the Company, etc., represents—as is seen from the utterances I have just referred to—the anonymous mass of humanity affected by the events: first, by the arrival of the planes from Chile and Asunción; later, by the victory of Rivière, not even suspecting that to Rivière himself it seems a "heavy victory" (one paid for at a heavy price).

This anonymous mass has no words to sing; it participates in the events *from the outside;* it sings offstage.

Only at one point, right in the middle of Scene 6, does the chorus suddenly assume a most important function. It will now have a text and will appear on the stage.

From the airport (measure 880) comes a confused murmur. The mixed chorus, divided into two (placed at some distance from each other), begins, humming. The news that the mailplane from Patagonia, piloted by Fabien, has crashed in the sea, has come through to the mechanics, skeptical as they are about the bold ideas of Rivière, and they have decided to rebel. This time distinct and articulate words are heard: "E Fabien? Perduto" ("What about Fabien?—Lost."). The two choruses, now close together, alternate on the question and answer. Some voices make themselves heard more distinctly than the others: "Non si faranno più voli di notte! La colpa è di Rivière!" ("There are not going to be any more night flights! Rivière is to blame!"); and a little later, *molto forte, ferocemente:* "Rivière! Rivière!" The chorus bursts onto the stage. Now at last it participates from the *inside* in an event, not a visible event, but one none the less direct and plain. The chorus becomes the conscience of Rivière and in the same moment acquires a consciousness of itself.

In this subtle matter, Günther Rennert, at the Hamburg Opera, by changing one of my stage directions, made clear a conception that was surely evident enough in the music, but one which in the libretto I had not realized how I might get across.

On the contents page, listing the separate divisions of *Il Prigioniero* (1944–48), the headings *Primo Intermezzo Corale* (First Choral Intermezzo) and *Secondo Intermezzo Corale* (Second Choral Intermezzo) are not aligned with the rest. A typographical detail of this kind is not to be considered as without significance. It is intended to call the reader's attention (and, if necessary, the conductor's attention as well) to two factors in the work: the one is a structural point, to emphasize that, of the seven episodes which the opera comprises, the second and the sixth are for the chorus alone; the other, a dramatic consideration, to indicate that the chorus must be assumed to be almost cut off from the action unfolding on the stage. Its role is something altogether different.

At the end of the prologue, the Mother bursts out, in despair: "Mio figlio! Mio fi . . ." ("My son! My s . . ."). Her word remains suspended. The offstage chorus, on the same syllable, comes in with the quick attack: "Fi—at misericordia tua, Domine, super nos" (S . . . o let thy mercy be upon us, O Lord"). ((Obviously this identity of syllables is only possible in the Italian language.) At the moment of its attack, fortissimo, the chorus is reinforced by the organ; the orchestra comes in soon thereafter.

At the end of the third scene the Prisoner, now close to the escape, and consequently close to what he thinks will be freedom, breaks out in invective: "Filippo! Filippo! I giorni del tuo regno son contati!" ("Philip! Philip! The days of thy reign are numbered!"). Over the final measure I have put the direction: "in tempo; not ⌒!" So that there will be no waiting for the Second Choral Intermezzo to follow immediately, with "Domine, labia mea aperies, et os meum annuntiabit laudem tuam" ("O Lord, open thou my lips, and my mouth shall show

175

forth thy praise")—accompanied by a *Nota Bene:* "The tonal power of this Second Choral Intermezzo should be overwhelming: every member of the audience should literally feel himself astounded and submerged in the immensity of the sound. To this effect one should not hesitate to use mechanical devices if necessary (loudspeakers, etc.)."

Here the chorus, supported by the full organ and the orchestra, becomes the pounding voice of the Spanish Inquisition. Cut off from the action, as I said—invisible, yet omnipresent.

In the *N.B.* which I have just quoted, I contented myself, as can be seen, with a very summary and schematic indication of what I wanted; nor could it have been otherwise. (In the spring of 1948, when I finished the score of *Il Prigioniero,* loudspeakers were not considered the daily bread of composers.) This does not alter the fact that, despite my very approximate directions, the adjectives "astounded" and "submerged," studiously and intelligently thought through, made it possible, for example, for Hermann Scherchen and his admirable co-workers (in the concert in the München Herkules-Saal, of the series called "Musica Viva," in March, 1956) to achieve fully and unforgettably the tone and the volume I had dreamed of.

I repeatedly said how important I personally consider, at least within the limits of possibility, the comprehensibility of the text, and I deem it unnecessary to add how particularly important this seems to me in the case of the lyric drama. This is the reason why, although realizing that a translated libretto is always less satisfactory than the original, because the syllables of another language take away something from those that were set to music in the original tongue, I favor the theory of those who prefer operas rendered in the language of the people that are expected to hear them, at least until an opera gets sufficiently well known (with a few exceptions, however, such as *Pelleas et Melisande*).

When I say "comprehensibility of the words," it goes without saying that I mean the essential words. It is of course a matter of common experience that, on repeated hearings of a new opera, many words are caught which in first hearing had escaped us, because we concentrated in taking in the opera as a whole.

In composing the sacred drama *Job,* I kept in mind that, since it was on a text drawn from the Book of Job, the obligation of putting the hearer in a position to follow the dramatic line was even more incumbent on me than for the two operas I had written before. This is one reason why I had recourse to a "Coro parlato" ("Speaking Chorus") in the two dialogue-passages between God and Satan; it seemed to me fundamental that the audience be informed about the antecedents of the drama, in case it might not be familiar with them. And it also seemed important to me that the audience be helped in recalling them, in case it only knew them vaguely and confusedly.

The Speaking Chorus is divided into two sections and stationed on the stage at points distant from one another. Thus the interplay of questions and answers, passing from voice to voice, from register to register, will gain the full manifest character of a dialogue precisely because the parts are recited from sources widely separated. (The colorfulness of the orchestra will naturally accentuate with contrasting timbres the opposite natures of the two Speaking Choruses.)

The other reason is one of vocal timbre. I wanted to give one single passage to a Singing Chorus, namely, the reply given by God to the hard-pressing question that the protagonist addresses to Him, the boldest question that any man ever dared to address to the Diety. The Lord's reply must be the culminating point of the drama—that was obvious. And I determined to give this moment all the forcefulness and all the illuminating power possible (see Example XIII, 4).

Nothing, at this moment, do I think of that I can report in advance about the opera that is right now on my mind.

15. *L'Apocalypse selon Saint Jean*

JEAN FRANÇAIX

(Translated by Madeleine M. Smith)

JEAN FRANÇAIX (born in Le Mans, France, on May 23, 1912) is the son of the former director of the Conservatory of Le Mans. Early musical instruction was under the guidance of the elder Françaix until Jean departed for studies at the Paris Conservatory, where he studied composition with Nadia Boulanger and piano with Isidor Philipp. In 1930, Françaix was presented the *Premier Prix de Piano*. His earliest published works began appearing in 1932, when Françaix was only twenty; the *Concerto for Piano and Orchestra* was the first to be published. A prolific composer, Françaix has written in almost every vocal and instrumental media. His compositions have received performances with leading orchestras and concert artists in Europe, England, and the United States. Since its initial appearance in 1932, Françaix's music has been heard regularly on International Society of Contemporary Music festivals.

An imaginative oratorio in three parts for four solo voices, choirs, and two orchestras, *L'Apocalypse selon Saint Jean* requires soprano, contralto, tenor, and bass soloists, and choirs consisting, in ordinary proportions, of sopranos, altos, tenors, and basses. The First Orchestra (The Orchestra of Heaven) must include two flutes, two oboes, four horns, three trumpets, three trombones, tuba, organ, two harps, four timpani, and full string choir. The Second Orchestra (The Orchestra of Hell) should include a piccolo, two clarinets, bass clarinet, two bassoons, contra bassoon, cornet, trombone, three saxophones (alto, tenor, and baritone), mandolin, guitar, harmonium, accordion, two violins, and two bass viols. Composed in 1939, the work was published by B. Schott's Söhne, Mainz, Germany. It was first performed in 1942 by the Société des Concerts du Conservatoire under the direction of Charles Münch, at the Palais de Chaillot (Paris). Subsequent performances were in London (1949), Paris (1947 and 1951), Berlin (1955), and Palermo (1961).

Having been nurtured in the Catholic faith, and being a native of Le Mans, a town having a particularly splendid cathedral, and being intimately acquainted from earliest childhood with every stone of that building, I was impelled as by a mysterious force to the composition of this sacred work. I have never written anything else like it before or since. Everybody's awareness of World War II in the offing gave a rational premonition of new apocalyptic upheavals to come; this led me to my choice of a subject. But in 1937, when I first read seriously the Book of Revelation, I was far from suspecting that I would find in that book not only a magnificent subject, little used by earlier composers, but, more than that, an answer to nearly all the deep questions that were troubling my own mind at that very time.

So I set myself to studying the text closely, being aided first and foremost by a friend who—strange as it seems—was quite elderly and a complete unbeliever; he was a graduate of the École des Chartes (the great school for advanced studies in the use of historical documents and paleography). I also had the assistance of the monks of the famous Abbey of Solesmes, which is only a few kilometers from Le Mans. Lastly, I had the privilege of consulting with a very great specialist in Apocalyptic exegesis, Father Allo. My scrutiny in depth took me a full year before a note of my score to be was set down. It was really necessary and worth all that trouble, to play this game right, for in his Apocalypse (Revelation 22:18–19), St. John threatens with hell fire anyone who changes a single word of his message. So of course I was under strictest obligation to refrain from altering one word, to make no cuts, but yet I had to condense the vast Johannine vision, to make it into an oratorio text of normal length. I was under obligation to respect not only the spirit of the inspired work, but as far as might be, the letter as well, and to immerse myself in the thought, the culture, and the living presence of the beloved Apostle.

And on I went from revelation to clearer revelation—literally speaking! For example, there is one basic question—in reality it is the one greatest of all questions: what is a man supposed to be doing here on earth? Why this uninterrupted triumph of wickedness, cheating, flaunting opulence? The Apocalypse thus replies to human suffering: your suffering will never cease till the number of the martyr-elect be complete. St. John, from his isle of Patmos (a Roman concentration camp) gave his Revelation to the early Christians who were worried about when "Parousia" ("the Last Judgment") should come. They believed it was to occur in their generation, taking literally the saying of Christ: "Verily I say unto you, this generation shall not pass, till all these things be fulfilled" (Matthew 24:34).

Here is another question to which the Apocalypse provides an answer: the Jewish question. What will be the fate of the Jewish people at the end of time? The Apocalypse gives this reply: all the Jews shall have their eyes unsealed one day, by the very excess of the ceaseless persecutions laid upon them. Rather than bewailing these, they shall see the finger of God therein and shall be converted, thus effacing their fearful crime of having failed to recognize the Christ when they saw him and of having put him to death. From a race accursed they shall become once more the chosen people; for St. John has described for us his vision of the numberless host of the elect with the 144,000 "Children of Israel," that is to say all the Jews, at their head.

Like everyone else I used to think that The Apocalypse consisted just of a long series of more or less helter-skelter catastrophes; but gradually I came to realize that on the contrary it is a book of reasoned hope, fraught with true optimism for the righteous man. All the catastrophes foretold will come to blind, hardened sinners, but to no one else.

The Revelation-story for which it was to be my task to write a musical commentary is simply, then, the news that two universes exist, God's Cosmos and the World of Darkness. But these are two worlds very disproportionate in power. The true universe is God's. Satan's universe is but a paltry imitation of God's universe. Satan knows that he is beaten before he starts, and he blinds his followers by means of outward semblances that are altogether insubstantial and fantastic. But the righteous are not so easily trapped, for they know that, if they match their faith with their deeds, no magic illusions will have any power over them.

At this point, seeing the dualism consisting of two universes so inexorably divided, and unequal beyond all measure in their potency, I thought of using two orchestras that would be separated in the same way, the one to be called the "heavenly" and the other the "infernal," the first tonally noble and strong, the second grotesque and petty-sounding. Two conductors seemed to me likewise necessary and desirable, so that their presence would make clear to the eyes of the audience that there were distinct orchestras. At performances of my score this idea of two conductors has not always been respected. I confess that two conductors, one Callas and one Tebaldi, can be an explosive kind of chemical compound. But the Apocalypse is the Apocalypse—I can't help it; the only thing I have been able to do so far, in hopes of solving the problem, has been to take over the Orchestra of Hell myself. (Even this way I am not sure that God, on such occasions, will not be a wee bit spiteful toward the Devil.)

When I had achieved the adaptation of this principle of dualism to musical terms, I ran into another difficulty. The Satanic manner of thinking is absolutely Oriental. For example, its devious progress lends itself to threefold repetition of a single series of events (albeit with subtle but undeniable variations); again, it borrows an earlier form—for the apocalyptic vision is a "literary genre" in the Old Testament—and puts into it the great new element of Christianity.

To express the triple repetition, it seemed to me fitting to divide my work into three parts. As for the curious mingling of Old and New Testaments, I counted on the special atmosphere of music to render that, composed as it is of a purely Occidental rigorousness with a deeply Oriental sense of mysteriousness. To use an analogy, when you listen to a page of Schubert, you are at first struck by its inexpressible character, and not until later, perhaps after it is all over, by the fact that it dissolves into a perfectly logical succession of chords and resolutions. In the same way St. John's Revelation itself appears at first like a great symphony; only in delving deeper does one perceive within it the dogmas of Christianity made overwhelmingly explicit. This parallelism of music and literary values stimulated me to keep on with what I had undertaken.

I believe that I have now got the stage well enough lighted so that I may at this point go ahead with the detailed outline of the text I myself extracted—at great expenditure of effort—from St. John.

First Part

1. The Prologue—connecting with the Epilogue—affirms the everlasting majesty of God and of His Son, and also the all-powerful protec-

tion enjoyed by their faithful followers. This Prologue is as it were a gentle but irresistible call to the inmost soul (see Example XIV, 1, at the back of this volume).

2. The letter to the seven churches—all of which have, incidentally, been positively identified by exegesis in the temporal world (Ephesis, etc.)—is a "pastoral letter" emanating from Christ himself as the sight of Him was vouchsafed to St. John, reassuring the valiant despite all the tribulations that befall him. The letter is a threat to the lukewarm and the possessor of ill-gotten wealth, and a promise of Paradise to him who strives and conquers.

3. After the Son, the Father. He appears as one sitting upon a throne that is upheld by four beasts (see Example XIV, 2). Twenty-four elders arrayed in white wait upon him, offering up to him alone their worldly wealth and all their powers and virtues.

4. A scroll which he holds in his hand—the New Testament—is sealed with seven seals, so that none may unroll it. But a Lion-Lamb (Christ) succeeds in doing this. His sacrifice of blood has united all nations through His priests, and the whole world renders thanks to Him.

5. With the breaking of the first four seals, the famous Four Horsemen of the Apocalypse rise to view. The first horse is white, as is he who rides him. This rider is the Parthian, holding Rome in check, the persecutor of the Christians. He is "the beginning of the end." The second horseman and his mount are red, personifying war. The third horse and rider (black) and the fourth (pale green) personify respectively famine and pestilence, the inevitable camp-followers of war. The mission of these four horsemen, verily scourges of God, is to ravage the fourth part of the earth with the aid of the powers of silver and gold.

The breaking of the fifth seal calls forth the lamentations of the martyrs, shattered by their great tribulations. White robes, symbolic of purity, are given to these, until such time as the number of the elect be complete.

The sixth seal broken, now still more "apocalyptic" catastrophes crash upon the scene. The universe of the wicked is stunned; its people look to the dens and caverns to hide them from Him who sitteth upon the throne, but He who sitteth upon the throne destroys the universe. The solemn and slow triumphal procession of the elect, headed by the children of Israel, closes the first part, while the breaking of the seventh seal causes silence to reign for "about the space of half an hour"—this, factually interpreted, represents the bliss of eternity.

Second Part

6. Seven angels sound the trumpet round about the heavenly throne. Another angel casts fire on the earth (see Example XIV, 3). This heralds the curse upon the fallen angels and the opening of the bottomless pit (7).

8. Humanity once more suffers torments—this time at the hands of Lucifer; terrifying locusts (see Examples XIV, 4); and two hundred million horsemen—a forecast of the perpetual invasions that form such a great part of history (see Example XIV, 5.) But mankind obstinately persists in worshipping idols.

9. God sends forth his two witnesses, who are, as it were, "Missi Dominici." Lucifer overcomes them and kills them; laid out in the high street of the city, their dead bodies become an object of derision. But behold, they come to life again and ascend to heaven before the eyes of their fear-stricken enemies.

10. The Second Part ends on a hymn of thanksgiving intoned by the four and twenty elders.

Third Part

11. A woman (the Blessed Virgin) appears in heaven, writhing in pains of childbirth. Before her the dragon stands waiting for the Child to devour it. But St. Michael casts out the dragon and renders him harmless with a blow.

12. Even though he knows he is defeated before he begins, the dragon causes the beast of the earth to rise up, counterfeiting the lamb with his two horns, and the beast of the sea, marking with his sign the incorrigible. The dragon then raises up Babylon the Whore (this is again a personification of ancient Rome), indulging in all sorts of infamous conduct. She is destroyed and cast into the fire (see Example XIV, 6).

13. The devil is bound and locked in the bottomless pit for a thousand years (the millennium). The elect reign in peace.

14. Satan launches one last assault with the aid of Gog and Magog

(see Example XIV, 7), but he is vanquished once and for all and cast into the Lake of Fire for the second death—in other words, the Last Judgment.

15. St. John beholds the last vision, the heavenly Jerusalem, where there shall be no more night. It is a vision of perfect bliss (see Example XIV, 8).

16. Blessed is he, the Apostle concludes, that keepeth the spirit of the prophecy; for without are the dogs. Amen.

It is curious to note how evenly balanced these rhapsodic visions are, and how great an impression they have made on the multitudes through the ages. Who has not heard about the Four Horsemen of the Apocalypse, or of St. Michael's overthrowing the dragon, or of Gog and Magog? Yet how wild and how varied the interpretations for all these episodes that have been offered! The superficial reader can see in them nothing but lucubrations and aberrations. How many have perceived therein the simple truth, that it is a message "in code" set apart for initiates by a spiritual leader who, while a prisoner of the Romans, knows that his message will be infused throughout the clandestine congregation of the first Christians?

On the other hand, how can anyone fail to be impressed by that prophetic vision of the destruction of ancient Rome, itself a reflection of all the false ideologies which have striven to rouse the blind masses throughout the course of history, even the most recent history—even, perhaps, contemporary history?

I feel incapable, at this moment, of tracing through, step by step, the very process of creation of the music that I drew forth out of such an outpouring.

It will of course be possible to say that, as the demon, after his poor fashion, kept imitating whatever God did, I provided for a harmonium to echo the organ, for the harp to be answered by a mandolin, and the string choir by the saxophones; that I tried especially hard to make use of music's evocatory power in order to render the more plainly certain subtleties of dogma; and that, in order to show the kingdom of God in its opposition to that of Satan, I set a tonal system for the Orchestra of Heaven in opposition to an atonal system for the Orchestra of Hell. However, all these are but technical devices. For, to tell the truth, I believe in inspiration, preceded by perspiration—I believe in a kind of inspiration that is as impossible to arrange in advance, but also just as self-evident, as the truth of the things seen by St. John. This last has been, however, held subject to some question. Of course rationalists doubt the truth of the visions; but even dutiful believers (*les "bien-pensants"*), somewhat lost in St. John's world, so far removed from anything conceived of by the bourgeois, innocently wonder whether the Apostle's vision were real or hallucinatory, or perhaps invented out of whole cloth. Perplexities such as these will give musicians cause to smile, accustomed as they are to the world of the subjective. Has anyone ever doubted the reality of Beethoven's *Ninth Symphony?* Or the spiritual inspiration of Mozart? "Spiritual inspiration"—there I have let the key phrase out, the kind of direct, intuitive evidence that Lucifer, by his nature, never has been willing to accept. Let him stubbornly persist in his denial. It is therefore not that God has damned him: he has damned himself.

As I attempted to solve these various great problems, I realize that I took a risk. Truly it is a case of "to be or not to be." But Music is so masterly a magician that failure cannot be attributed to it. If, however, the work is a success, it must be explained as a miracle wrought by my patron saint.

16. *Missa Salve Regina*

JEAN LANGLAIS
(Translated by Madeleine M. Smith)

JEAN LANGLAIS (born in La Fontenelle, Ille-et-Vilaine, on February 15, 1907) has been blind since infancy. When he was ten years old he was taken to Paris to the Institute for Blind Children, where he began music studies. His teachers were Blazy (piano), Mahaut—a pupil of Franck—(harmony), and Marchal (counterpoint, organ, and composition). In 1927, Langlais entered the Paris Conservatory and was admitted to the organ class of Marcel Dupré. Subsequently, Langlais was awarded the *Premier Prix de Orgue* (1930). Four years later he returned to the Conservatory to attend the composition classes of Paul Dukas. Since 1931, Langlais has taught composition and organ at the Institute for Blind Children and has held several important appointments in Paris churches. He is presently the organist at Sainte-Clotilde, a post once occupied by another distinguished composer-organist, César Franck. In his dual role, Langlais has made frequent European and United States tours. Recently, his summers have been spent at Boys Town (Nebraska), where Langlais has participated in sacred-music workshops.

THIS work involves two choruses: first, a polyphonic choir, intended for three-part men's voices (these may be doubled by three-part women's or boys' voices); a second choir, singing in unison, is thought of as being sung by the congregation as a group, hence by men, women, and children alike. No solo voices are used.

The first chorus, although it has no appreciable difficulties of execution, has a very different character from the other. It develops in turn the different parts of the great traditional antiphon, *Salve Regina,* which forms the thematic basis for the entire work (see Example XV, 1, at the back of this volume). The bass part frequently intones the Gregorian chant attached to the anthem. The upper voices complete the harmony, which is very simply written, and is intentionally so done, in order to make the composition as easily performed as it can possibly be. Great care has been taken to see that every modulation is sufficiently prepared in the instrumental parts. Even these latter do not offer any serious difficulties. Moreover, the *tessitura* for each one of the voice parts is kept small; and thus the *Mass* can be sung with complete effectiveness by a volunteer choir.

The second chorus has only two small fragments of the above-mentioned Gregorian melody (see Example XV, 2a and b). This choice of the simple manner, deliberate as in the other case, makes it possible for any group to learn the parts it is to sing very quickly. Experience has proved that one hour of rehearsing is sufficient to prepare an ordinary congregation for participating as the second chorus in a public hearing of my composition.

No one previously seems to have written a Mass on these principles (participation by the whole congregation in a polyphonic work). It should be made clear that, as I planned it, no music-reading is required of these singers. They can easily learn their part by rote and sing it all the way through from memory. This also, it seems to me, is an idea never tried and carried out by any other composer. I must add that I tried it on the recommendation of someone else, and that the idea, therefore, is not mine.

Two organs are called for. One organ, a large one, provides richness and texture for the whole. Themes original with me, hence of course not Gregorian, are given to this instrument at frequent intervals all the way through. At the same time, a number of fragments from the *Salve Regina* plain-chant are set forth repeatedly on the large organ, sometimes being combined with the original themes. So the part for this organ has some character of freedom about it. For the most part it is written for fairly full registrations, with a variety of timbres, but it also affords opportunity for the use of solo stops, such as the cornet, which notably sounds forth in the Benedictus.

A comparatively sizable installation will best render my intentions, for an organ with only a few stops would not have the desired *panache* and would tend to kill the general effect.

The smaller organ supplies accompaniment. It serves to support both the polyphonic choir and the congregational chorus. But since this is a work of essentially solemn character, the small organ, if too subdued and too meager, cannot be expected to give all the effects that one would wish for. I should like to emphasize that neither of the organ parts offers any great technical difficulty.

In addition to these two organ parts, eight brass instruments are required. Two trumpets and two trombones are featured with the large organ; one trumpet and three tenor trombones are added to the small, or accompanying, organ. The brasses are never, or almost never, employed alone, but are always supported by the organs. What the single trumpet and the three trombones assigned to the accompaniment part do is to lead and amplify the vocal effects. Therefore the eight brass parts were written more in a vocal than in a purely instrumental style, and their concerted embellishing power is considerable. But aside from this active artistic value, the four instruments added to the small organ do make the choral execution ever so much easier by announcing in advance the vocal entrances, and then reinforcing the voices.

I wrote the *Salve Regina Mass* in 1954. It took me only thirteen days to complete it, since my formula was both clear and simple.

The composition was never planned with a particular group in mind, nor any one individual, either. My aim was to write something that could be put on as part of a regular church service, having the congregation of the faithful join in, along with a polyphonic chorus, as I have already explained. The *Salve Regina Mass* has been performed many times, in numerous countries, and by Protestants as well as Catholics. I have been immensely pleased at this, and can only feel joy and approval on learning of such occasions. In particular the United States has taken to this work, and glorious hearings of it have been given there.

At this point it will be worth-while to set down the circumstances of the writing of it. In November, 1954, Abbé Jullien, who is in charge of the televised Mass in Paris every Sunday, paid me a visit. "For the coming Midnight Mass for Christmas Eve in Notre-Dame of Paris," he said, "I would love to have a Mass in which all the people could take an active and really effective part. What is more, in order to take advantage of the great size of the magnificent structure, I wish we could have a work that would utilize both the organs of our cathedral, and a polyphonic choir, with some brass instruments. Can you write us such a Mass?"

My answer was: "Such a musical composition would not be possible without quite a few rehearsals; I don't see how you could rehearse the whole congregation, since they will be arriving only a short time before the sacred service begins."

"Your job," said Abbé Jullien, "will be to work it out in such a way that the people's part of the Mass can be properly prepared in one hour's time." Staggered by the good Father's unprecedented plan, I answered a second time: "This idea of yours seems completely impossible to me." But the priest was so persistent that, before saying "No" once and for all, I decided to take a few days to think it over.

Because our marvelous cathedral is dedicated to the Virgin Mary, I quite naturally thought of getting a theme to guide my work from the pages of the Gregorian chant which are in her honor; a theme also would be needed to give the work more unity. I ended my search with the great first-mode *Salve Regina,* an antiphon for which I have always had a special affection.

This antiphon of course is divided into a number of sections. Since I felt that I must think first of all about what the congregation was to sing, I had to find some passage that was both melodious and simple. The part "O clemens: O pia" seemed to me most suitable both to my liking and to the necessities of this undertaking.

I set to work at once. In four days the "Kyrie," which I had thought of as being the hardest part to work out because it has so few words, was all finished (see Example XV, 3a and b). Encouraged by this and in an enthusiastic mood, I carried the work ahead with so much intensity and confidence that nothing could stop me. As I have said, it was done in thirteen days in all. Father Jullien had won out over my fears, however well founded.

There remained the actual trial of it, and I still felt extremely apprehensive about that part. Again my guide proved to be wiser than I.

The part for the polyphonic choir was entrusted to the Seminary of the Holy Spirit in Chevilly-Larue. With the co-operation of such a competent director as Father Deiss, this part of my *Mass* was soon ready for performance. But the people's part, the riskiest unit in the construction, still remained.

In order to appreciate what I have to say next, the reader must realize that a great number of the Catholic population is attracted to the Midnight Mass at Notre-Dame. In order to try to get a seat at this magnificent service, the faithful think nothing of coming to the Cathedral two hours ahead of time.

It was agreed upon in advance that the rehearsal, with the full personnel of those who were to sing, would begin at exactly eleven o'clock. I was at the church by ten forty-five. Since I am the regular organist at Sainte-Clotilde Basilica, where I play the Midnight Mass every year, I did not know some of the special customs at Notre-Dame, and I was not informed about these. When I came to the Cathedral, I was stopped by a policeman and asked where I was going. "To the Midnight Mass," I replied. "But there is not a single seat left. You can't go in," he insisted. I explained what I was there for, and finally I was allowed to go through. But then I found that I still had to get past a second, and then a third, policeman, each one raising the same objections. The only way I finally gained permission to enter the hallowed and historic portals of worship was by waving my score.

At eleven o'clock Father Jullien appeared, explained to the assembled worshippers what was about to take place, and had very concise vocal scores passed out among them (the copies were especially prepared for the benefit of the congregation); and the rehearsal began.

From the very first minute I was amazed. Before midnight success was a certainty. The *Mass* began on the stroke of midnight, and I simply could not believe my ears. You can see how far we carried our audacity when I tell you that this *Mass* was broadcast and televised throughout France and nine other countries! This alone made the whole business much more frightening.

The enthusiasm and confidence of everyone concerned proved powerful aids, and (this point is without hesitation to be called miraculous) it was all carried through with a simplicity and perfection in every detail beyond all telling. I will never forget the following remark by a lady who had sung a role in *The Magic Flute* at the Paris Opéra and who was present to hear our *Mass:* "Anything I ever heard or saw at the Opéra," she said, "is *nothing* compared to what I have just now been hearing and seeing at Notre-Dame." Her judgment of course had nothing to do with Mozart, nor with the composer of the *Salve Regina Mass.*

A performance like this, improvised, one might say, at least as regards the congregation-choir, had never been tried before. Its success has remained in the memories of many as a clear demonstration that it is entirely possible to bring the assembled multitude into a modern-style composition. Out of nine thousand persons in attendance at Notre-Dame, we estimated that at least three thousand participated in the first rendition of the *Salve Regina Mass*.

I have made no changes in the work since that first hearing. From the standpoint of placing it, I have observed how greatly the sheer lusty volume of the brass instruments helps the voices in, on their entrances. I was careful to give the singers their pitch in advance of the attack, on the trumpets or on the trombones. Ordinary amateurs, thus given a feeling of safety, are not afraid to sing out. Consequently, and because of that, they can relax as they sing each his own part.

If one follows my musical directions precisely, one will have no trouble in re-creating the atmosphere of this first performance as I have described it. It must be said, however, that the locale of the *première,* namely the Cathedral of Paris, had much to do with it. Such impressive surroundings, while they do lend beauty to the work, are however not requisite for a good performance. Mr. Charles D. Walker of the Church of the Heavenly Rest, New York, had an excellent idea, which was to start his program containing a performance of my *Mass,* with a group of works of the Venetian school, written for the Basilica of St. Mark in antiphonal style, the same arrangement that I adopted myself for the composition we are discussing. I have heard a tape-recording of this concert, and I unreservedly admire it. Still, it was not the same as at Notre-Dame of Paris.

In writing for voice, or more exactly for chorus, my first concern is to avoid confusing the vocal sound with orchestral instruments. The voice, after all, is not a violin nor a cello but a direct and, most of all, a natural mode of expression. In a choral work each voice demands to be handled with particular care. Its peculiar *tessitura,* and also its own special character, call for equal respect from the composer. The soprano part does not pose the same problems as the alto part; and the same is true, of course, for the men's parts. Some devices for example, though excellent for a composer writing for orchestra and fairly simple of achievement, should be rejected, it seems to me, by one writing for chorus. Chromaticism has always appeared to me to be contrary to good vocal expression. On the other hand, breathing is of very great importance for voices, whereas in an orchestra it becomes purely an aesthetic problem. Being a physiological matter when it comes to singing, it is in that situation a thing of supreme importance.

Volubility (too many words crowded into a phrase) in solo singing hinders comprehension of the words. When it comes to (amateur) choral singing, it is beyond the range of possibility.

As concerns moving into a new phrase after a substantially long rest, (amateur) singers have to have "blazes" along the trail, an anticipation of the first note of each attack. This is another worry that the orchestra composer never has.

Many times I have heard fine renditions of the Fauré *Requiem* in churches—entirely unrehearsed performances. The preparation of the vocal attacks by the instrumentalists, and likewise the preparation of the modulations, certainly lie behind the fact that this beautiful work can be given a splendid hearing without extensive rehearsing, and even without any rehearsing at all.

My teacher, Paul Dukas, had a saying: "It takes twenty years of composing experience to write for the voice." How right he was!

I am not one of those who think that contemporary composers have exhausted all the possibilities in choral writing, but I do think that a great many things are impossible for a vocal ensemble.

Olivier Messiaen, my dear and lifelong friend, has demonstrated, in his *Cinq Rechants,* by his powerful genius, that it is entirely possible to make a choir sound as no one ever did before.

Intrinsic musical values aside, there is in a choral work one purely technical consideration. The question of tonic accents is firmly bound up with the business of vocal composing. On this point I think that many go at this question with too inflexible an attitude. The composers of Renaissance times, whose vocal works have given us marvelous models to work from, did not let themselves be bound by any one rule as regards the prosody. Reading certain Masses by Palestrina, for example, or by Vittoria or Goudimel, one may easily find prosodic liberties taken in writing for the inner voices, and sometimes even in the outer ones.

A weak syllable on a strong beat, in a decrescendo, does not appear to me to be a violation of the rules of prosody. The great Stravinsky, who has written for voices to words in a variety of languages, sometimes presents examples of prosodic treatment which are original with him and are pronounced false by some critics. I do not share their views. Yet it certainly is clear that originality in this respect does not entitle one to disregard all conventions. You have to be intelligent enough to reject some taboos and observe some others.

The musicians who wrote the magnificent melodies of our Gregorian chant put music before words. Their music still defies time.

The first "Christe" of Gregorian *Mass No. XI (Orbis factor)* gives us a curious but splendid example of prosody. The second syllable of the word *"Christe,"* a weak syllable of course, is sung on a strong beat. Furthermore, this second syllable comes on a note a fifth higher than the preceding syllable. An expression mark of "piano" over the higher note, that is on the weaker syllable of the word, achieves a very fine color effect. Without such a mark of expression unquestionably it would constitute a prosodic violation.

I could give many such examples.

In some unusual cases of this kind, not to say in some *wrong* spots, the choir director can often transform what might be considered an error into a success in the treatment of the poetry.

It has seemed natural to me to bring in these examples from Gregorian music, since, in a way, Gregorian music has been my guiding theme. Its modal color also has been one of several bases of my own work. But that would be because the great masters whose style so strongly influenced me in composing my own *Mass* are in fact the men of the school of Notre-Dame of Paris, Perotin "le Grand" most especially. However, I did not constrain myself to be influenced solely by that great master. The guidance of Guillaume Dufay and Guillaume de Machaut, for both of whom I have always had the highest admiration, has also been most valuable to me.

Naturally my aim was not to write pastiches of these old masters. I may say that my aim was exactly the reverse. With means at hand that those venerable composers of the distant past never knew, I have sought to re-create the medieval color that emanates from their works. The truth is that I think I prefer the haunting poetic genius of the men of the Middle Ages to the prodigious learning of the Renaissance composers.

Chords without thirds and the use of the doubled leading-tone were of particular usefulness to me in creating a medieval atmosphere, and this was what I sought. Examples: E–G-sharp–C-sharp; D–A–D.

I was provided (as I shall explain) with a wonderful chance to put side by side a model of medieval art and a composition of our own century, but the reader will readily understand that it was in no spirit of comparing the two. When the firm of ERATO asked me for permission to make a recording of my *Salve Regina Mass,* I inquired what other work they had in mind for the second side. Very kindly they offered to devote both sides to works of mine. But I, declining this suggestion, asked to have a Mass by Guillaume Dufay put with mine. When I heard the disc all the way through on both sides, my immediate reaction actually was that the contemporary writer was Dufay and I the ancient one!

In France this recording won, not only the *Grand Prix du Disque,* but also the Madame René Coty Prize. This was the only time that this distinction has ever been awarded. The former President of the French Republic had founded the latter prize at the time of his wife's death, in memory of her.

I have been happy to learn that the Haydn Society has put out this same record for distribution in the United States. Other foreign companies have done the same in their respective countries.

In writing this work, my first intention was to compose a Mass which, as a number of our Popes have urged, would give the Catholic faithful a chance to take part effectively in the singing of the service.

My second aim was to contribute a new piece of writing to the particular occasion of the Midnight Mass of which I have spoken.

This latter aim has now been pushed far into the background by the numerous hearings of my work which continue to be given in many countries.

America, great country that it is (I love it and I have visited every part of it extensively, playing a great many organ recitals)—America has taken considerable interest in seeing that my *Mass* is widely known.

At this point I wish to thank the musicians in America who have generously placed their fine talents at the service of my composition, namely: Charles Dodsley Walker of New York, Walter Blodgett of Cleveland, Paul St. Georges and Theodore Marier of Boston, Monsignor Schmitt of Boys Town, and Alexander Peloquin. I wish likewise to thank all those who may have conducted this work unknown to me. I want all the choir directors, Catholic and Protestant, who have taken pains energetically to bring before the public this particular sample of my writings to find herewith a heartfelt tribute of appreciation and admiration.

17. *Golgotha*

FRANK MARTIN
(Translated by Madeleine M. Smith)

FRANK MARTIN (born in Geneva, Switzerland, on September 15, 1890) received his early music instruction at the Geneva Conservatory, where he studied piano and composition with Joseph Lauber. Between 1918 and 1926, Martin worked and lived in Zurich, Paris, and Rome. In 1928 he returned to Geneva, where he taught at the Institut Jacques-Dalcroze and was instructor in chamber music at the Conservatory. Later he served as director of the Moderne de Musique (1933–39). The composer remained in Switzerland until 1950, when he moved to the Netherlands. Two years later, and for the next six years between 1952–58, Martin was professor of composition at the University of Cologne. Following this appointment, he returned to his home near Amsterdam. In 1947 the Schweizerischen Tonkünstlerverein (Swiss Composers' Society) presented Frank Martin with its coveted prize for composition. Schoeck and Honegger were the only Swiss composers previously honored with this illustrious award.

My oratorio *Golgotha* was written between 1945 and 1948. It calls for a four-part mixed chorus, with fairly frequent dividing of these parts, and five soloists: soprano, contralto, tenor, bass, and baritone (the last taking the role of Christ).

The orchestra consists of two flutes (one piccolo), two oboes (the first doubling on *oboe d'amore* and the second, on English horn), two clarinets (small clarinet in E-flat), two bassoons, four horns, two trumpets, three trombones, timpani, percussion, strings, and piano. There is also a substantial part for organ.

The work is in two parts, the first taking forty-five minutes and the second about forty minutes, each consisting of five scenes.

In the spring of 1945, when I was living in Geneva, there was an art show at the Musée des Beaux-Arts offering, for all to admire, a wonderful collection of etchings by Rembrandt. Of all the masterpieces there assembled, I was particularly struck by three separate "states," differing greatly each from the other, of one view of Calvary, commonly known as "The Three Crosses." Against a dark multitude, looking paralyzed with horror, the three crosses stand, with Jesus Christ and the two thieves; a flood of pale, white light falls from heaven upon the center cross, whereon Jesus is dying. There in such a very small compass that one catches a vision of surpassing majesty, the sight of the world of the spirit fighting against the world of earthly powers, with complete confidence that to the spirit will fall the ultimate triumph.

After seeing these etchings, I was literally haunted by the idea of expressing some picture of the sacred Passion in my own terms. But, for one thing, the very grandeur of the subject caused me to wonder whether I would be capable of this; and for another, I could not yet see what form I should give to such a subject, what musical means I should employ in order to carry out such a design. I wished very much that I could compress this whole divine drama, so fearful and so splendid, into a modest and very brief piece of music, as Rembrandt had done on his small rectangle of paper. Turning it over and over in my mind, I perceived that a musical composition has different requirements from a print, and a *brief* musical discourse on the Passion would be out of place anywhere; I could not imagine such a thing in a song recital, nor yet in a symphony concert. Consequently I had perforce to come round to conceiving of an oratorio which, by its very length and breadth, would be fitted to provide a framework and an atmosphere such as the enunciation of a subject like this would have to have. I quickly realized that if I confined myself to the words of the Gospel alone, I could hardly hope to be able to establish a sufficiently cohering musical form; I should only be wandering from one recitative to another. Therefore I should need to find texts in the nature of lyric commentary, and some moments of meditation on the several episodes of the sacred text, and on the meaning of what these reveal to us and for us. In this way I kept coming closer, as one step led to another, to the classic concept of Passion music, as it appears to us glorified in the great masterpieces of Johann Sebastian Bach. So no wonder I hesitated!

197

Still I seemingly could not dismiss the idea, and it appeared to me that our great respect for the works of the past ought not to keep us away from certain themes; it might well be that any period of history should have a right to try to give its own utterance to the great subjects on which our minds and spirits are nourished. It might be, at least for a few people, that a fresh vision of Christ's sufferings and victory over death might convey more truly the presence of this timeless theme, and give it greater actuality. I realized, at any rate, that there was not too much danger that I would fall to copying the classical Passions in servile fashion; for it is true that, whereas in the former musical settings we follow a narration of the death of Christ given to the assembled believers, who express their reaction in choruses, chorales, and arias, my plan was to make the sacred drama live again before our eyes, in the present tense, so to speak. What I especially wanted was to bring Christ to life in His divine person. I wanted to show Him first in action on earth, denouncing the scribes and the hypocritical Pharisees with just the same vigor and scorn as when He drove the money-changers out of the temple; later I would like to show Him at the Last Supper, getting His disciples prepared for His departure, then in His agony in Gethsemane; lastly, in Part II, at the trial, having overcome every kind of agony, giving His answers to Pontius Pilate and the High Priest with peaceable authority altogether Godlike. Comments of a lyrical character would in this case serve only to highlight these varied attitudes on the part of Christ, and to give support to the dramatic action by their stricter form, as the strophes of a chorus are seen to do in ancient tragedy. Two figures only—the High Priest in the Sanhedrin and Pontius Pilate in the Praetorium—rise opposite Jesus Himself.

It was not my intention to follow one of the Gospel accounts step by step in its relating of the Passion, but rather to give an over-all view of the sacred drama; and so I chose from among the four Gospels whatever seemed to me the most essential parts of it. Thus I worked out seven scenes, the first of which shows the enthusiastic welcome the populace gave to Christ on His entry into Jerusalem. The second is devoted to the castigation administered by Jesus in the Temple to the scribes and Pharisees. The third is the Last Supper, and the fourth takes us to Gethsemane. Here ends the first part. Part II opens with the trial, first before the Sanhedrin (Scene 5), and then before Pilate (Scene 6). The final scene leads to Golgotha.

I still had to consider what texts to use for the parts that would be lyrical in character. As I searched one day in the Geneva Public Library, I had the fortune to come upon a good translation of the *Meditations* of St. Augustine, a work not very widely known. From it I extracted a few passages that might be adapted to the several episodes of the Passion, just a few meditations of broad spiritual import.

With these elements in hand, I finally got started on my musical task. The first thing that came to my mind now was, like a résumé of all that Rembrandt's etching has been saying to us:

> *O death, where is thy sting?*
> *O grave, where is thy victory?*

And with this exultant shout I had the oratorio begin. After a time of thinking it over, when the phrase was already in its musical form, I decided to hold it for the ending, between the death of Christ and the choral heralding of the Resurrection (see Example XVI, 1, at the back of this volume). A part of this music I also used at the end of the opening chorus to the words: "But Christ died for us; in Christ we have life."

Now, before writing about the music of this oratorio, the musical language that I have employed in it, I should like to allow myself a few very general thoughts concerning the attitude which the contemporary composer may adopt with regard to religious music. It must be said, first of all, that there are several ways in which a composer may come to a sacred text. It may be that he is obliged to handle it, by commission or command, or by the nature of his functions in some church position. It was in this manner that composers of classical times, in most cases, were led to write music for the church, masses, cantatas, oratorios, or passions. For them there was no problem: it simply was up to them to provide such a type of piece for such and such a ceremony. They merely had to do their best, each according to his talents, his degree of genius, his spiritual power, and also with a musical technique not subject to incessant review. Even in our own time there can still be found some combinations of circumstances similar to these in every respect; I know composers who are organists or *kappellmeisters* and write cantatas all the time for their own parishes to use on religious feast days. From the spiritual point of view this is the ideal situation for a composer; it has given us many masterpieces in the past. It is best because the musician is at once and automatically in a certain mold. He has not to choose a subject from among an infinity of possibilities; he has not to ask himself any earnest and urgent questions of aesthetics; in a word, he is not tied up with public opinion, with the critics, nor with that elusive and redoubtable entity that is the world of art for the artist—a hundred-headed hydra, ready to weigh and to judge, to make or destroy reputations. All this type of composer has to do is treat a subject according to his own means and within his own faith, in all tranquillity of mind and in all humility.

But if this favorable conjunction of circumstances once was widespread, the church being then a power in the domain of art and possessing the material means to put on large and important compositions, it is not so nowadays. A composer writing for his own church most often has inadequate means of performance. He can only count on whatever poor resources he has, constantly, and must think about getting around all the technical difficulties. The material basis, which is indispensable to every art, is wanting. Art in our times has become a world apart, governing itself, a world in which artistic value alone counts; and it puts a religious work and a secular work on exactly the same footing.

Thus the composer in our time who proposes to write a religious work that will aim beyond the restricted demands of a given parish must first of all want to do it and take all the responsibility on himself; after that he must freely choose his own subject and decide for himself what musical means he will employ. He finds himself in this way in the same situation as he would be before undertaking any secular work. And yet it is not the same thing. To my mind, when dealing with a religious work of art, everything that is artificial—aesthetics itself, the artist's pleasure in manipulating voices, sounds, and forms—ought to be subordinated to the inner compulsion to express one's faith convincingly. And I doubt that there are many contemporary works which have aroused in men's spirits so much as one true religious sentiment, strengthened one faith, or led one hearer to a meditation such as can sometimes bring us to the brink of a mystic vision, if not all the way to it. Most modern works bring the composer to mind; in them we admire his latest success, possibly his new masterpiece.

But a truly religious work of art ought to make us forget its composer, and our era is as unfavorable as may be to the germination of such art. Ours is an age of individualism; each man seeks to create a language which shall be his alone. It is by this sign that he can be recognized as an artist of worth; for it is differentiation in art that we seek, the unique, the personal, much more than universal human values. Of course, all this applies only to the conscious attitudes of the listener and the critic, for a completely personal art would be of interest to none but its composer. There can be no genuine art but that which expresses essential and collective values but expresses them on the personal plane of the author. Thus, in the presence of a strong work of art, we feel it on the collective level, but our consciousness fastens on what is personal and differentiated about it. We find in it the proof of its own value, and, quite naturally, all our admiration and enthusiasm go to the artist himself. We are so accustomed to this that it seems strange to us and almost childish that in other periods, even in some of the greatest for art, men should have attached such great importance to the quality of the subject chosen and to its general import, and likewise to artistic qualities having nothing individualistic about them: mastery of craftsmanship, and sureness of touch in every detail as well as in over-all structure. In those days an artist was admired for staying so well within the norm, while the public was more or less unconsciously touched by any personal note that there might be in his art. Today the artist is admired for moving so far away from the norm, just so long as, though successfully concealing this, he is wise enough to stay within bounds.

All these considerations do not make creating an art work any easier —a work, that is, having a universal and quasi-anonymous character such as a true religious composition should be. Moreover, our society is not based on religion, as it used to be. This is not to say that religious feeling is any less prevalent than formerly. Many believers feel it all the more intensely and confidently for its having lost the participation of all. But, precisely because all no longer participate, an artist who wants to create a work of religious significance must likewise give up hope of any possible general appreciation through participation. Each hearer is going to consider his composition from a different point of view, and only perhaps among those who may have the same way of looking at religion as himself can he hope to find a real appreciation of his work, in its form as well as in its meaning. It is impossible for one having no faith to react to it otherwise than as to a more or less successful artistic manifestation—unless by an actual miracle a new world should open in his soul on contact with the composition. This would be one chance in thousands and thousands, but it is a chance worth taking. On the other hand, there is always a perfectly normal possibility that, among the faithful, some whose faith is genuine may be shaken out of their devout habits of mind on hearing sacred texts interpreted in some new manner. This is a natural reaction, for usually any faith, however authentic, rests on a complex of intellectual and sensory images that are so solidly fixed as to be practically immutable. These images themselves are not faith, but are only, collectively, a projection of it onto mental and sensory planes. But to the man of faith they present so completely the image of his faith that any other presentation is likely to appear alien, idolatrous, or even almost blasphemous to him.

For all these reasons there cannot be today any living tradition of sacred music; and this is so because such a tradition, if it existed, would be in formal contradiction to the whole present-day concept of art in general. It is our inveterate habit now to take art into our consciousness on the basis of what is most differentiated and most individualized.

Thoughts like these are not likely to encourage a man to start composing any oratorio, least of all a Passion. I thought about all these objections before I undertook my *Golgotha;* and if I did, in spite of all, set to work on it (a task which cost me three years of labor), it was because I could not do otherwise. There was no outside obligation; nobody had asked me to do it, and I did not have anyone in mind to perform it. Quite the contrary: many times I had the feeling that it never would be performed at all, that I was only writing for myself and maybe a few close friends. This idea was a great help to me as I worked; it released me from all aesthetic preoccupations, taking away the obsession that too often paralyzes an artist: what will so-and-so think, what effect may this create? For once I was truly alone, confronting a text and a subject that were far beyond and outside of me in every way.

Utter humility was the only possible approach. I must not think for a minute of trying to be equal to my theme, but simply do my best, at every point and at all times.

I had no worries about what interpreters to have: a mixed chorus, an orchestra, and an organ. I would also need a quartet of vocal soloists to establish contrasts, bring in somewhat more individualized elements, and take the parts of the High Priest and Pilate. Lastly, I would have to have a baritone who could take the role of Christ. As for the musical language, I had already forged it over the years, in such works as my *Vin Herbé* based on the *Romance of Tristan and Yseut* by Joseph Bédier, *Der Cornet,* on a text by Rilke, *Sechs Monologe aus Jedermann,* after Hofmannsthal, as well as in instrumental works such as the *Petite Symphonie Concertante* for harp, harpsichord, piano, and two string orchestras, or *Ballades* that I had written for various instruments; lastly in the oratorio breve *In Terra Pax,* commissioned by Radio-Geneva to be broadcast on the day of the armistice that ended World War II. Even before writing *Vin Herbé* (1938–41), I had done a great deal of studying and experimenting to see what I might do with the so-called twelve-tone technique of Arnold Schönberg, without denying my sense of music, centered on the hierarchical interrelations of notes—systematically refusing, therefore, to go all the way with atonalism.

It was certainly an exciting but a rough crossing, to find a language altogether new for me, one that would satisfy at the same time my sense of tonality, my eagerness for functional dissonance, and my innate and very keen fondness for chromaticism in the manner of Bach. The use of twelve-tone series, as strict as possible but yet keeping my freedom, and likewise a rule I observed to avoid or mask all octaves or unisons, helped me greatly in shaking off many habits which in my opinion are not basic to harmonic music, though they did reign and preside over the whole classic and romantic music. Far be it from me to criticize these; they produced nearly all the masterpieces we live by. No, simply, I felt the need of a language within which I could write with freedom and go forth to discover lands that would be new for me.

I did utilize this language extensively in *Golgotha,* which by its tragic character gave me most of the time a chance to use a rather tormented chromatic style (see Example XVI, 2). However, I did not hesitate to use frankly tonal affirmations wherever the text required. I also got back to a completely diatonic way of writing, if not to tonal writing, strictly speaking (see Example XVI, 3). In some places I used passages of parallel perfect chords. What I tried to do was at each point to find the right expression for my text, without any concern for the application of any one technique, while at the same time seeking to create as solidly grounded a musical form as I possibly could.

When I had finished this piece, without having in mind any possible performance (it had been begun in Geneva and was ended in Holland, 1945–48), I received a letter from Samuel Baud-Bovy, the conductor of the Chant-Sacré, a Geneva choir which specializes in religious music, asking me to let him give the first performance of *Golgotha*. I did not hesitate to grant this, and so it was that the composition was created at Geneva, in Reformation Hall, on Friday, April 29, 1949, with the Orchestra of Suisse Romande. The soloists were H. B. Etcheverry, baritone (Christ); Renée Defraiteur, soprano; Nelly Grétillat, contralto; Ernst Haefliger, tenor; Heinz Rehfuss, bass; and Pierre Second, organist. The Chant-Sacré was conducted by Samuel Baud-Bovy. *Golgotha* was later given by the same artists in Zurich and in Paris.

Written to French words, this oratorio was subsequently translated into German and English, and it has had numerous performances in most countries where choral and symphonic music are cultivated. Thus it happens that a work written for its own sake, with no concern for what anyone might think, say, or write about it, is the very one which most directly brings its message through, not only to the general public but also to musicians and to those whose judgment might have been cause for fear. More than once I have tried this out. The thing is that fear of certain people's opinion is a poor counselor: it keeps the artist from being quite honest with himself and with his own intuition. Many times, teaching composition, I have seen students tremble with worrying about what someone might say of their compositions! I have always urged them to trust their own judgment, because this is the sole and only way of producing a valid, honest, and original piece of work. But it is an attitude of mind exceedingly difficult to maintain, I must admit, unless one is borne up by a subject so vast that all personal considerations and any notion of success or lack of it are, automatically as it were, banished.

This dread of being judged weighs heavily in our days on many young composers, who are held back by their very feeling of what music is, and who should be from flinging themselves into the so-called *avant-garde* movements—let us say, roughly speaking, into atonalism, or, more exactly, into a refusal to admit of any greater or less in tonal relationships, in particular to concede any dominance in the relationship of the fifth. They are many in all, and yet each one feels alone. It is good, no doubt, that this should be, for it forces them, each on his own, to take exact cognizance of what it is that is driving them to such at attitude; it forces them into an act of will and of courage. Indeed it is not agreeable, in one's youth, to be looked upon as a reactionary and to be prevented from taking a leading part in a movement of exceptionally great scope, one which can boast of being the only movement to represent music in our time, the only one, be it especially noted to serve as preparation for tomorrow. To protest "I cannot" almost takes heroism. If one's position in saying this is only negative, assuredly it is worthless; but if dedicated searching and real creative effort go with it, I am not far from thinking that we must look upon it as actually the *avant-garde,* that *avant-garde* which all over the world and at all times keeps fighting with courage and confidence against the passing fashion and the reigning ruts—in a word, against academicism in its own time.

18. *Triptychon*

HERMANN REUTTER
(Translated by Ralph S. Fraser)

HERMANN REUTTER (born in Stuttgart, Germany, on June 17, 1900) was educated at the Academy of Musical Art in Munich between 1920–22. His teachers were Walter Courvoisier (composition) and Franz Dorf-müller (piano). From 1923 until 1932, Reutter was a free-lance composer and pianist. In the early part of the 1920's he belonged to Paul Hinde-mith's circle at Donaueschingen where—besides the festivals for Musical Arts of the Allgemeiner Deutschen Musikverein—his first compositions were performed. The year 1932 saw Reutter accept a post as professor of composition at the Hochschule für Musik in Württemberg. Four years later he was appointed director of the High School for Music at Frankfurt. Reutter remained there until 1945, when he was asked to return to the Hochschule in his native city of Stuttgart. His boundless energy and talents have enabled him to pursue three careers simultaneously—com-poser, pianist, and educator. Despite a busy schedule at the Hochschule, Reutter manages to play numerous concerts accompanying Europe's finest singers. For the past several years, he has been touring colleges and universities in the United States performing his works, lecturing, and coaching singers in German lieder.

FRIEDRICH SCHILLER's three poems comprise this work, which requires a mixed chorus and tenor soloist. The instruments are two piccolos, two flutes, one oboe, one English horn, two clarinets in Bb and A, one alto saxophone in Eb, one bassoon, one contrabassoon, four horns in F, three trumpets in C, three trombones, one tuba, timpani, percussion, and strings. The time of performance is approximately twenty-three minutes.

In the summer of 1959, I put aside all other plans and projects at the urging of Walther Schneider, director of the Liederkranz choral society of Stuttgart, that I write a choral work for the jubilee year celebrating the two-hundredth anniversary of Schiller's birth. The work was to be performed for the first time in November, 1959, in the Beethoven Hall of the Stuttgart organization. My enthusiasm for the new project grew rapidly, especially since I was gratefully indebted to Mr. Schneider's choral group for their very impressive performance of my Hölderlin cantata *Gesang des Deutschen*. In a few weeks the composition was finished. By the end of August the piano reduction was ready, and the score then followed immediately. All in all, the composition took scarcely one and a half months.

Walther Schneider's opinion of the piano reduction that I had sent him was more than flattering. He stated with enthusiasm that in our day my music was the legitimate successor to that of Brahms, and that he could foresee the day when common tribute would be paid me for this great and responsible inheritance. I do not know how much there is to this. As far as I am concerned, I discovered Brahms relatively late, but then, to be sure, with all my heart and with increasing enthusiasm. In this connection I often recall the great violinist Alma Moodie (who died all too soon), whose friend I was and with whom I participated in many concerts. My *Rhapsodie für Violine und Klavier* (Opus 51) is dedicated to her memory. Alma Moodie often said, whenever I found in a Brahms sonata or symphony a passage that was unclear (his lieder, of course, I had admired from early youth): "One must be at least forty to understand the greatness and depth of expression in Brahms' music." And time has proved her right. Scarcely had I "climbed the mountain peak of forty" when all stood revealed to me: his melodic richness, the harmonies which, although almost not equal to Schubert and Beethoven in "modernity" are nevertheless of an absolutely personal stamp, the masterfully balanced architecture of movements in his great sonatas and symphonies, as well as the Rembrandt-like twilight of his orchestral sound.

To return to Walther Schneider: upon a closer study of my work he began to doubt whether the relatively short period of eight weeks would suffice for rehearsals by his chorus, composed as it was by half of singers unable to read music and who, moreover, met for rehearsal only once a week. His feelings grew into certainty, and he asked my permission to postpone the first performance of the work until a later date. So the *première* had a slight delay, but it took place a few months later in a performance which was brilliant, and of which I shall report further below.

In the case of every new work (an artist's creative process is rightfully compared to the act of procreation, its subsequent period of gestation and birth) many influences have a special effect: influences of surroundings, of tradition, of the will that drives us progressively and in which evolutionary tendencies often are more fruitful than a permanent revolution—in short, all those biographical stages of development that form the artist, the poet, the musician and bring him to that maturity of personality that he then represents in life. The external elements, those found in any encyclopedia's few lines, are of far less importance. The "inner" biography is much more essential; and much more meaningful are the encounters, the imponderables of one's childhood home, of the years spent in learning and in travel, of the very landscape, influences of literature, painting, sculpture, and architecture that are scattered throughout one's entire life and that move one deeply over and over again.

As far as I am concerned personally, my so-called career can be told in a few words: from 1907 to 1919, a humanistic education in Stuttgart with musical instruction in piano and cello given by my godfather-uncle, Eugen Uhlig, the outstanding contrabassoonist of the Stuttgart Court Opera; from 1920 to 1923, definitive study in Munich under Walter Courvoisier (composition), Franz Dorfmüller (piano), and Karl Erler (song). From 1924 to 1932, I lived in Stuttgart as an independent composer and pianist, an early member of the Donaueschingen circle of musicians gathered around Paul Hindemith. In 1925, I signed an exclusive contract with the world-famous publishing house of B. Schott's Söhne in Mainz; from 1926 on I appeared almost annually at the Composers' Festivals of the ADM. From 1932 to 1936, I was Ewald Strässer's successor at the Württemberg Musical Academy. In 1936, I was made director of the State Academy of Music in Frankfurt am Main, and this activity continued until the war's end in 1945. From 1952 to 1956, I again taught at the Stuttgart Academy of Music as professor of composition and lieder-interpretation, and since 1956, I have been director of this institute.

This, then, is the external course of my life. But how did I come to music? How did I discover it? How did I find the sounds that exist within me, and the tone that is uniquely mine? Who helped me to bring into the light of day and across the threshold of the unknown this mysterious land, a boundless and endless realm which seemed to my spirit to have been touched magically and powerfully by Polyhymnia's magic wand? The answer to all these questions must be longer and more detailed.

My memory reaches far back into childhood, into my fourth year. I must have been a bit over three, and can yet see myself sitting with my sister playing on the floor of my parents' music room, when my ear first consciously caught a melody. My mother was sitting at the piano playing, and she answered my questions by telling me that the music was the Andante from Mozart's *Sonata in C major.* The arch that rose within and that spun itself forward into endlessness, supported symmetrically and placidly by a counter-voice like a song without words, captivated me completely with a reflective enchantment, a door opened wide and soundlessly within me: I had awakened to music and, as I felt immediately, to my proper calling. I have never lost the memory of this childhood moment, and with an eager curiosity I seized upon everything that I heard from my extremely musical parents, who were performing constantly during the course of the years: the piano music of Mozart, Schubert, and Beethoven; the classic romantic lied through Wolf, Pfitzner, and Strauss; and selections from the operas of Weber, Wagner, and Verdi.

Remarkably enough, although moved by pure music from the very first, I was most drawn to the world of the musical theater, where I was stirred by the masters' structured unity of word, sound, and scene; and I grew most passionately interested in dramatic action as it is transposed into music, the landscape against which it played, and the actors and characters who appeared in it and who carried the action. Thus by the time I was thirteen, fourteen, fifteen, I was familiar with the most significant items of the day's repertoire, and it so happened that the Stuttgart Royal Opera then conducted by Max von Schillings and later by the young Fritz Busch possessed an ensemble of the most magnificent voices, of whom many later attained international fame. (I shall mention here only Sigrid Onegin, Helene Wildbrunn, Karl-Aagard Oestvig, and Carl Erb.) Unique performances of *Norma, Carmen, Aida,*

Walküre, Tristan und Isolde, Meistersinger, Parsifal, Salome, Elektra, and *Rosenkavalier* constitute the unforgettable memories of those days. Then there were the guest performances by great singers and instrumentalists from abroad—Caruso in the forefront, with his tenor that was so inspired in the *mezza voce* and so metallic and darkly radiating in the forte. Then there were Battistini, Baklanoff, Bosetti, Cläre Dux, Maria Ivogün, Teresa Carenno, Vera Schapira, Wilhelm Backhaus, and the manifold impressions from Fritz Busch's symphonic concerts, where even Igor Stravinsky, who had just attained early fame in Paris, got a hearing with a cautious dosage of a short orchestral piece called *Fireworks.*

(With consternation I discovered during this piece for the first time how it is possible to represent in sound a purely visual-acoustic action, namely, the spurt and explosion of rockets and shells [hence, the impression of the effect given by a manufactured object], not in a mere imitative music, but rather in an instrumentation then unknown, rigorously controlled both thematically and rhythmically: a mixture of sobriety and fanciful poetry that was fascinating. It was a most unique experience, different by nature but similar in its effect on me to Reger's *Symphonic Prologue,* which Busch performed for the first time in Stuttgart, and which he, in all seriousness, described to his musicians at the beginning of rehearsals as the most meaningful symphonic work since the *Ninth Symphony*).

At this point the most important experiences of my first Stuttgart period came to an end, and I followed the advice of Fritz Busch, whose assistant, Stefan Temesvary, had introduced me to him. I transferred to Munich, under Walter Courvoisier. Ah, Munich of the twenties! The Munich of Bruno Walter, of Falkenberg's private plays, of the Old and New Pinakothek, of the Odeon concerts, of the theaters: the National, the Residence, the Prince Regent! And the contacts with new music, with the works of Klose, Pfitzner, Mahler, Schoenberg, Schreker (usually with Bruno Walter on the podium); concert experiences with Adolf Busch, Rudolf Serkin, Walter Gieseking, whose meteoric rise was then beginning; the lieder concert evenings of Bender, Brodersen, Erb, Schipper, Ivogün, Onegin, almost all of the "singer-elite" of the Bavarian State Theater!

And I must not forget to mention the lasting impression of Busoni's "new classicism" in his *Improvisation on a Bach Chorale Tune* and in his *Fantasia contrapuntistica,* after my having been already drawn to him as long ago as 1917 by the operas *Turandot* and *Arlecchino* under Busch in Stuttgart. Busoni seems in our day to share the fate of Franz Liszt, in that while his unquestioned and unique mastery as a piano virtuoso is acknowledged, he is underestimated and his significance as a composer and exciting, thought-provoking spirit is almost overlooked. And the masterworks of the naturalistic era of Ibsen, Strindberg, Hauptmann, Wedekind; the guest performances of the great actors, above all Albert Bassermann, then Werner Krauss, Dorsch, Agnes Straub; along with the abundance of young writers like Brecht, Bronnen, Lernet-Holenia, Ernest Penzoldt—how everything came in a rush upon the young musician, usually with the breath-taking joy of a personal encounter, powerfully moving and stirring his wings both within and without under the overpowering sense of creativity!

Munich was, of course, the city of Thomas Mann, who frequently appeared in those days at the lecture desk of the Bavarian Court's Concert Hall, lecturing on political as well as artistic-philosophical themes. And at that time my deep and quiet friendship began with Luise Hohorst, the German Russian from Moscow, the great character-actress and friend of Ricarda Huch. Many years later unforgettably recited poems from Ricarda's *Liebeslyrik* were made music by Luise Hohorst, but in those days the little volumes of *Russischer Lieder* by "Lisa" (Hohorst's name among her friends) were no more than imitatively translated.

But what trace is there today of Franz Schreker, who always had something important and moving to say in each of his somewhat abnormal pieces, who almost attained Shakespeare's heights in the *Schatzgräber* (the scene between the rejected Elis and the fool), and who found such gripping tones and sounds in the farewell duet with Elis? Certainly the comparison with Richard Wagner, as made by Schreker's great apologist Paul Becker, does not hold true in every respect. But how bewitching under Fritz Busch was the *Vorspiel zu einem Drama*—the orchestral introduction to the *Gezeichneten* with those unforgettable scenes of Erb and of Delia Reinhardt—the sound of a gigantic orchestra, shimmering in opalescent brilliance of a magnificence never heard before! Gone and forgotten today is the whole fairy-like palette, unquestionably the palette of a master who perhaps lacked only power and vitality to claim from its *fin-de-siècle* mood an undiscovered and a new land, as Alban Berg was later to do.

But in an even more wondrous way another forgotten name stirs those who are familiar with his work: Friederich Klose, the Bruckner pupil whose writings have disappeared completely from the opera and the concert hall, although at that time his *Eb major Quartet "Dem deutschen Schulmeister gewidmet,"* scarcely surpassed by Reger, was frequently and very successfully played, along with his *Ilsebill,* and although Bruno Walter gave his monumental oratorio *Der Sonne Geist* a great triumph in Munich. But when I met the aged maestro in 1932 at the Composers' Festival in Zurich, he himself disposed of his total work without a trace of resentment, gaily and smilingly, as being "totally without significance." Instead, he showed a complete and unenvying admiration for the music of his Swiss compatriot and colleague, Othmar Schoeck. Few experiences have ever moved me so strongly, so chillingly, and yet so awe-inspiringly, as this self-chosen renunciation of an honored man standing on the summit of a rich and satisfied life, concerning the permanence of his creative moments.

Well: my student years came to a close in 1923, but again and again (and in this fashion each work was composed) I was drawn until 1929 to Munich, concentrating, composing, gathering impressions, and working on them. And then came my years with the great singer Sigrid Onegin, who engaged me as her accompanist (we had had no contact since 1918, when I first performed for her). I definitely owe to Sigrid Onegin the most decisive impressions of my career, owe them to working with this rare artist: she possessed a unique, magnificent voice with a range of more than three octaves and all possibilities of expression, with a brilliant coloratura and all the dynamic shadings ranging from the gently hovering pianissimo to the organ-toned force and richness, a truly dramatic, even demonic voice which could evoke also humorous effects. Not only did she expand my repertoire in a way unimagined before then, but she opened as well the door to the great world of music. Travels throughout all of Europe; unforgettable theatrical impressions

from La Scala, where I heard Verdi and Puccini in most masterful pro-
ductions; in the course of one week with her (this was by no means
unusual) on tour in Berlin, Stockholm, London, and Budapest; not to
mention the seven three-month tours in the United States, Canada, and
Mexico, when she took me along; and the "foreign lands and people"
who received us, brilliant directors, Toscanini in the fore, world-famous
orchestras, the Metropolitan in New York, Carnegie Hall, the countless
dazzling singers and players—it was a glorious time!

Many other moving forces later entered my life: Hindemith's mightily
growing work; the music of Bartok, Stravinsky of the middle period,
Honegger, Dallapiccola; and performing with Martha Fuchs, Lore
Fischer, Henny Wolff, and later (and especially inspiring) with Elisabeth Schwarzkopf and Dietrich Fischer-Dieskau. Great directors and
interpreters like Fricsay, Jochum, Konwitschny, Leitner, Münchinger,
Müller-Kray, Rosbaud, Sieben, Solti, Wand, and Zwissler accepted my
works; Frankfurt and Stuttgart chose me as head of their respective
State Musical Academies; I became increasingly interested in pedagogy
(especially in the fields of composition and song-interpretation); I also
went to Japan for a brief stay; and so, between two world wars, the
ring of years grew slowly but inexorably, stormily or quietly, always
adapted to the flowing currents of the times, in my fourfold career as
composer, pianist, teacher, and academy director.

And if I must confess what has remained unchanged for me during
these decades, immutably and especially dear and admirable, then I
would name these: Bach's *F minor Invention* (that microcosmos in
macrocosmos of the cantor of St. Thomas, a miracle of expression and
construction built in three-voiced counterpoint upon two simple pages
of notes, not one tone without its thematic meaning); the oratorios and
symphonies of Haydn, along with a number of his magnificent solo
scenes; Mozart's *Bb major Piano Concerto* and the overtures to *The
Marriage of Figaro* and *Don Giovanni* (in the latter, primarily the
ballet music with its incomprehensible combination of different dances
and kinds of rhythm), and certainly, all of *The Abduction from the
Seraglio,* by Mozart; Gluck's *Orpheus* (marvelous beyond words, the
flute solo in D minor!); Beethoven's *Fidelio* (especially the canon in
Act I); Schubert's *Unfinished Symphony* and, from his lieder, *An den*

Mond in einer Herbstnacht, as well as the famous cycles; Wagner's *Meistersinger Prelude* and the quintet from the same opera, Act III of *Siegfried,* and a great deal from *Parsifal* (especially the orchestral preludes and interludes and the marvelous oboe melody which begins the "Good Friday Spell"). I would list further the finale from Bruckner's *Fifth Symphony,* the first movement of his *Seventh Symphony* and the secondary theme in the Adagio of the same symphony, the slow movement from the *Eighth Symphony* and the *Te Deum;* Verdi's *Rigoletto, Aida, Othello, Falstaff,* the *Requiem,* and the *Pezzi sacri;* Strauss' symphonic poem *Don Juan* with its stormy onslaught, the terzetto in the *Rosenkavalier,* the Semiseria-technique of *Ariadne,* a great deal in the *Frau ohne Schatten* and the whole masterful *Capriccio;* Mahler's *Kindertotenlieder,* a few songs from the *Wunderhorn,* the *Second* and *Ninth Symphonies,* and the "Farewell" in *Das Lied von der Erde;* Pfitzner's cello sonata, the second act of *Der arme Heinrich, Palestrina*—to my way of thinking, a secularly meaningful work—and many of his songs, of the less familiar the *Leierkastenmann* and *Huttens Kerker* but also *Die Einsame* and *Zum Abschied meiner Tochter,* as well as the song portion of his cantata, *Von deutscher Seele.* Of Schoenberg's work I would mention the *Buch der hängenden Gärten* and the *Orchestral Variations;* Bartok's *Music for Strings, Percussion, and Celesta* and the *Sixth String Quartet;* Milhaud's *Columbus-opera* and the seventh number of *Poêmes Juifs,* with its polytonal control of the theme through C-sharp—a section that does not follow any rule, and that yet sounds magnificent. Finally, I would think of Hindemith's *Marienleben,* some of his chamber music, the *Quartet,* Opus 22, *Trio* (Opus 32), and the preludes to *Mathis der Maler;* of Stravinsky's *Sacre du Printemps* and the earlier ballets, his *Oedipus Rex,* and the *Symphony of Psalms* with its bewildering mixture of Gregorian music, Russian church sounds, Bach, Bruckner, and Verdi. This synthesis of the most heterogeneous elements in style would have to be considered as something snobbish in the case of a weaker composer, but Stravinsky the genius here has achieved one of the most personal of his works.

And as far as the *avant-garde* of today is concerned, I withdraw more and more decisively from its representatives and their efforts, the more they abandon song, which is the origin of all musical writing. By this

I mean "cantabile" in the broadest sense of the word, which can exist completely without reference to text and voice. Think of the allegro movements of Mozart's symphonies, of Schubert's and Verdi's instrumental music, which sound like songs without words. But the balance between vocal and instrumental style has been lost today to a large extent, just as completely as recognition and understanding of the fact that the composer's primary invention must evolve from the music that is sung, wherever song, cantata, or opera is concerned, and no matter how interesting and richly developed the "accompanying" instrumental part may be.

But I am afraid that we are living in a period of over-exaggerated mastery of the instrumental. And as I look around me, I see arithmetic triumphing over the heart, and see that Goethe's demand for an "exact fantasy," a unity of feeling and understanding, is often ignored. In place of it, recently such a once so richly and universally talented, uninhibited musician as Ernst Krenek praised the *number* (Zahl) as the "salvation from the dictatorship of invention." Alongside this there stands the lonely and grandiose effort of Carl Orff to go directly to the sources in things rhythmical, harmonic, and melodic: there is no more moving manifestation of the creative in our time than the coming together of such opposites. But, after so many autobiographical details, aesthetic observations, and stylistic discussions, I have gradually come to my real objective, the analysis of my *Triptychon* as the purpose of my writing:

My reasons for choosing this subject matter came from the impulse that I stated at the beginning. This was the first time that I had considered Friedrich Schiller's works. As the catalogue of my work at the back of this volume will show, my writings as a composer for voice run from the classic ode of Sappho down through the Old and New Testaments to Lorca's romances. Goethe, Hölderlin, Keller, Rückert, Storm, Rilke, André Gide, Ricarda Huch, Thornton Wilder: they are all represented, but never had Schiller been included. This is because his sphere is the drama and at best, the ballad of dramatic intensity, but not the lyric. And as a dramatist—with the revolutionary storm and stress *Die Räuber,* with the bourgeois tragedy *Kabale und Liebe,* with the gigantic themes of *Fiesko* and *Don Carlos,* the fragmentary *Demetrius*—as a dramatist he created a powerfully soaring fantasy within opera composers (think of Verdi, for instance, or, in our own time, the young Giselher Klebe, who has skillfully extracted an unsuspected powerfully musical expression from various scenes of *Die Räuber*). And why, following the examples of Honegger's *Jeanne d'Arc au bucher*, Wagner-Regeny's *Günstling*, and von Klenau's *Elisabeth von England*, should not *The Maid of Orleans, Mary Stuart*, or even the *Wallenstein-Trilogie* be made available to the musical stage? The poems of the *Triptychon*, to be sure, constitute a real expression to Schiller's comparatively sparse lyrical work. Happily, as far as I was aware, they had gone unnoticed until I discovered their immanent musical content. And now that this "three-paneled altarpiece" of varying rhythmical verses has been put into harmonious order, it is time to undertake a closer examination of it:

PROVERB OF CONFUCIUS

Threefold is the form of Space:
Length, with ever restless motion,
Seeks eternity's wide ocean;
Breadth with boundless sway extends;
Depth to unknown realms descends.

All as types to thee are given;
Thou must onward strive for heaven,
Never still or weary be
Wouldst thou perfect glory see;
Far must thy researches go
Wouldst thou learn the world to know;
Thou must tempt the dark abyss
Wouldst thou prove what Being is.
Nought but firmness gains the prize,
Nought but fullness makes us wise,
Buried deep, truth ever lies.

EVENING

Oh! thou bright-beaming God,
the plains are thirsting,
Thirsting for freshening dew,
and man is pining;

216

Wearily move on thy horses—
Let, then, thy chariot descend!
Seest thou her who,
from Ocean's crystal billows,
Lovingly nods and smiles?
Thy heart must know her!
Joyously speed on thy horses,
Tethys, the Goddess, 'tis nods!
Swiftly from out his flaming chariot leaping,
Into her arms he springs, the reins takes Cupid,
Quietly stand the horses,
Drinking the cooling flood.
Now, from the Heavens with gentle step descending,
Balmy Night appears, by sweet Love follow'd;
Mortals, rest ye and love ye,
Phoebus, the loving one, rests!

PUNCH SONG

Four elements join'd in
Harmonious strife,
Shadow the world forth,
And typify life.

Into the goblet
The lemon's juice pour,
Acid is ever
Life's innermost core.

Now, with the sugar's
All-softening juice,
The strength of the acid
So burning reduce.

The bright sparkling water
Now pour in the bowl;
Water, all-gently
Encircles the whole.

Let drops of the spirit
To join them now flow;

217

Life to the living
Nought else can bestow.

Drain it off quickly
Before it exhales;
Save when 'tis glowing,
The draught nought prevails.[1]

Seen from without, the three poems have nothing in common, and yet, an inner relationship can be readily and unmistakably discerned. They unfold like the very course of a day: cool and clear, the stanzas of the *Spruch des Konfuzius (Proverb of Confucius)* rise from the freshness of early morning to the dazzling heat of midday; then the curve sinks, *Abend (Evening)* draws in, a lyricism of Hölderlin-like solemnity is heard; and night enters in the frothy and champagne-like hymn of the *Punschlied (Punch Song)*. I am especially drawn to the glorious poem *Abend*: it moves with classically restricted beauty; the verses rise and fall—for once during his laborius and self-denying life's work, Schiller was moved to flow in soft waves from one stage to the next, like a Roman fountain. The Goethean is there, spontaneously, granted by the gods in an hour of favor. Strangely enough, one is reminded of Goethe's poetry, of him whose lyrical outpouring welled so vigorously and so naturally from heart and mind, but who paid the price of seeing fragile dramatic form break beneath his cautious groping hands. Once only and not to be repeated, so it must seem to us, does Schiller share a calm happiness and joy in the lyrical voice of this "evening fantasy," but this was well and for the best, because here, so to speak, he unexpectedly succeeded with something perfect, he who produced such masterpieces in other spheres, in defiance of a harsh fate.

And the music to the poems? Its thematic material? Its formal expression? The obligato tenor voice? The choral-orchestral tonality? All of these things shall be approached and investigated in detail.

A three-part "painting" stands before us, so to speak, drawn in clear tonal lines: to the left and to the right the key of C, between them the middle section *(Abend)*, which is far removed because of the tritonal

---

[1] The English translation of the *Triptychon* poems is by J. G. Fischer.—H.R.

relationship of F-sharp. The *Spruch des Konfuzius* is recited only by
tenors and basses; the soft female voices are silent throughout; they are
excluded by its cold and masculine philosophical poetry. The form is
rondo-like (following the formula A–B–A–C–A); the choral writing
is basically for two voices, partly with free counterpoint, partly strictly
imitative; and only in a few homophonic places (the inner or outer
highpoints) is there music for three or four voices. To come to specific
details as shown by excerpts: the orchestra at the beginning intones with
fluctuating rhythm (alternately 3/2 and 5/4 time) an easily pentatonally
shaded theme with broad intervals, symbolizing as it were the threefold
measure of space which the poet establishes—restless, endless, bottomless (see Example XVII, 1, at the back of this volume).

The first five lines of text are declaimed diatonically by the chorus,
with a characteristic use of syncopation. At the same time, the orchestra
remains apart and continues rhythmically and thematically with a
motive from the eleventh measure, then from the eighteenth measure
on, reaches back to the melodically sustained quarter-note movement
of the opening.

A mysteriously effective first high point is attained with the recitative
"As all types to Thee are given," which is to be given lento pianissimo.
For the next five lines a subito allegro enters, with sharply scanned
rhythms of the orchestra, immediately taken up fortissimo by the chorus
(see Example XVII, 2). Then just as suddenly, with "Thou must tempt
the dark abyss," it undergoes considerable expansion. The compact and
massive sound of the tutti is reduced; with the measure before Figure
⑤ we have reached Tempo I; the first theme is taken up again in a
rhythmical variant by the orchestra, while at the same time the motive
mentioned above is retained (see Example XVII, 3).

Actually, at this point, the total content of the poem has been expounded. What follows in the closing lines is simply the quintessence
as drawn by the chorus set in intervals of thirds, a sort of free fugue with
a theme that is new and yet is somehow extracted from the introduction
and joined as a further counterpoint by the tenor solo in a last dynamic
intensification, repeating the five beginning lines in the fashion of a
leitmotiv. (Here, too, the art of syncopated declamation plays an important role.) What follows next are, from the più sostenuto, coda-like

cadenzas with a new variant of the orchestral introduction and (summing up in a few words) with a repeating of the text of the five-lined initial verse by the chorus as well, which, with the pedal note held at C throughout the last seven measures, sinks whisperingly and, like a monotoned litany, murmurs away "Depth to unknown realms descends" while the orchestra echoes dissonantly with a long *fermata*.

If one ignores the harmonies which are instrumentally varied and which are to be understood as *campanella* (they appear twice, at the beginning and in the middle), and if one understands the first choral vocalization as it is meant to be, as the echo of the prelude and as the mood-setting basis for the solo voice, then the second movement is penned according to the scheme A–B–A in a great and three-part song form. The individual parts correspond in space of time with a subtle exactness, and I here must point out the cadenza harmonies which lead to F-sharp, G, A, and again to F-sharp. The chorus enters polytonally in a free pursuit of line. The allegretto must not be taken too quickly nor too slowly: hovering eighths are prescribed, not dotted quarters. The male voices are omitted from the mood of this movement; soprano and alto are introduced singing and humming for purely melismatic effects; and with the exception of the nymphlike and urgent call "Rest ye and love ye," the whole text is carried by the tenor solo. Everything is softly colored *sotto voce,* in the soft velvet evening light of violet shades, in which only the *poco vivace* is given an iridescent glitter with the "Ocean's crystal billows."

But the mood that takes shape here (in Example XVII, 4) is a far cry from the giddy gaiety of the usual serenade; a calm and majestic dignity prevails with great serenity, the atmosphere of a complete and placid sensuality. The high point is reached with the adagio (fifth measure after ⑲); the tempo must be clearly distinguished here from the beat of the earlier allegretto. Otherwise, I feel, there is not much left to say: the poem speaks for itself; may the music do the same. Proof of the entrancing scenic power of this poetic vision: the great Delacroix was inspired by it to a glorious painting full of the "sound" of magically glowing colors within an enchanted and mystical landscape.

The *Punschlied* begins with an upward beat; a dithyrambic motive is applied like a refrain, the beat is condensed (8/4=2/4 and twice,

3/4) and, like the *Spruch,* it has a clear rondo character. With the fifth bar there begins an orchestral *fugato* whose theme shows imitatory inclinations even at the third entrance (see Example XVII, 5). Only in this closing portion are all possibilities of the four-part mixed chorus exploited. The first strophe, following the fugue theme, opens the graceful dance of the succeeding verses, couplets with many rhythmic surprises which, in accordance with their poetic content, are characteristically composed completely in 3/4 time with a plastic articulation of the "four elements." Notice here again the use of syncopation and the notation which is in part homophonically compact, polyphonically relaxed in the choral parts, which in the seventh measure after ③④ has interpreted the entire poem in a rapid and concentrated progression for the first time. Now the tenor solo, like a fanfare, begins a sort of modulation of the thematic material by a resumption of the first verse and an ever-rising call to the four elements. Again using techniques of various sorts, the chorus recites the remaining verses and enhances the dancing rhythm in a hymnlike fashion, by using interpolated 2/4 beats while reducing the dynamics to piano and even to pianissimo at the phrase "Let drops of the spirit to join them now flow," giving a reflective, thoughtful effect which, however, is taken up again immediately by the tenor's fanfare. The chorus takes up the interrupted verse fortissimo, alternating with the tenor, who intones the closing strophe lightly, quasi parlando, which then is repeated by the chorus with imitative expressions, in which process the interpolated definite beats are of a uniquely inspiring and electrifying effect. The vocal ensemble maintains a hushed piano sound (as if hovering, withdrawing); only the *stretto*-like orchestral postlude (which is, by the way, a repetitive variation of the fugue theme) vigorously concludes the whole with a full tutti sound, with several recapitulated motifs from the earlier material (see Example XVII, 6).

A few more words concerning instrumentation: as stated, the full sound of the orchestra is employed only in the *Spruch* and in the *Punschlied.* The *Abend* is instrumented like chamber music in a loose tonality with solo effects coming from individual instruments. In general, I pick the individual melody from the innate character of the instrument; the proper theme usually evolves then immediately and with the necessary sound coloration. In this respect, it is worth noting that the style which I represent, and which has evolved and refined itself over the years from one work to the next, aims at graphic and architectonic values more than at purely colorful values. Thus, where style is concerned, I am an expressionist without impressionistic strain; my feelings condense into themes, lines, melodies, from whose counterpoints harmony and total sound develop. But sensitively incorporated color values are not to be denied in my works, just as well-meaning people admit that I have a feeling and sense for rhythmic peculiarities, especially since it has become routine to count me among the "elementary talents" on the basis of some individual movements and scenes. (There is nothing I would rather hear or read!)

Thus, if the sound concept comes about immediately and directly with the thematic inspiration, it can well happen during the development of the score (which begins with the writing of the piano score) that I assign to the wood winds a part originally intended for the strings, or vice versa. These constitute some delightful surprises in the working process; they are certain creative secrets like thematic or formal changes originally not figured in at all.

Here we might be reminded of the vigorous quarrel between Hans Pfitzner and Paul Becker as to which was the more important: inspiration or form, the intuitively discovered detail or the genial concepting of the entire work. Beethoven, said Becker, moved from the total concept down to the detail, while Pfitzner represented the thesis that only from the germ-cell of a unique and precisely conceived inspiration could a composer develop a mightily built structure, the formal arrangement of his creation. It was a quarrel without point: what matters is not *how* something comes about, but *why*. So, too, the technique that a composer uses is of secondary importance, and I refuse the egocentric arrogance and claim of any school that thinks it has all the right answers. Art is like religion: many roads lead to Rome, and many a detour through trial and error brings one to salvation.

Let us thus fear like the plague any shrinking or narrowing of our artistic horizon; let us hold fast to Bach and Mozart for, great encyclopedists that they were, they lost no time in anxious brooding. They drew upon the centuries of their ancestors' creativity, and they boldly opened the door to the centuries lying before them. Bach's *B minor Fugue (Well-*

tempered Clavier I), in its linear expressiveness, its painful tension of intervals, its boldness of diagonal dissonances, has not been equaled up to now by anyone, not even by Reger, let alone surpassed. A short piano piece by Mozart, the *G major Gigue*, could have been written by the classicist Stravinsky. These examples show clearly enough how far we have "progressed," and they show us that many a sensational discovery today does not signify the birth of Western music by any means.

The first performance of the *Triptychon* took place on June 12, 1960, during a concert of the South German Radio Network under Hans Müller-Kray and with the fine tenor Fritz Wunderlich as soloist. The concert was arranged in honor of my sixtieth birthday. Soon afterward, on May 16, 1961, there was the first American performance in Baton Rouge under Peter Paul Fuchs. The work is dedicated to him and to Louisiana State University in appreciation of Fuchs's attempts to promote my music. He called attention to various of my concert and stage works in Louisiana and New York. Here I recall the well-noted first performance of my *Ballade der Landstrasse* which Paul Aron had already performed with a smaller company in a Broadway theater. There were no reviews of this. Everything sounded as it should according to preconceived plan—even the combination of effects as yet untested. This has been the case for several years, during which I have been able to transpose into actual sound effect what my inner ear and my fantasy had first heard. To be sure, I did issue a second edition of several of my stage pieces: *Saul, Doktor Johannes Faust, Der verlorene Sohn,* motivated basically by the wish for a more felicitous dramaturgical interpretation of some individual scenes, in the process of which a different instrument was chosen occasionally. As a matter of course, there is no need for such alterations for a choral cantata like the *Triptychon* with its precise and formal outline.

I do not wish to go quite so far as Hans Pfitzner, to whom the individual tone was almost less important than prescribed tempo. But I do believe that the measures must always be correctly felt and, above all else, correctly performed. (The metronome, no matter how precisely calibrated and indicated its beats may be, is in this respect a quite insufficient aid which merely serves to correctly beat out the beginning measures. It is a purely mechanical and lifeless time indicator, a ticking measurement that rises without life and animation upon the skeletal frame of rhythm and line.) Beats that are held must not be held too long; those that move must not move too quickly. Everything must flow along, even where rest is indicated; nothing must be sacrificed in the way of rhythmical precision and clear enunciation.

At the same time, the dynamic notations of the composer must be followed precisely, not to speak of the importance of those indications of articulation which must be followed conscientiously in performance. Everything that is to be done by the performing artist is indicated in the exactly drawn score of the composer, who is well aware of the "orthography" of the tonal picture in both a physical and artistic sense. It takes a long time to acquire this, of course, and in the learning of it there is no end. By following the indications given in the notes, one has the guarantee of a good beginning to the performance, much like a ship that ventures out upon the open sea equipped with oars, sails, anchor, and cables, trusting to favorable winds and aiming for exotic coasts where, without having been dashed to pieces during a strenuous passage, it is received by the protecting arms of the harbor.

The human singing voice is not a clarinet; it is still less a trumpet, and the fine, elastic and yet so sensitive vocal chords must not be strained in the dizzying zigzag of intervals. In general, as I have already said, the man who has composed a song, a poem, a secular or sacred text for cantata and oratorio in church or in concert hall, or a dramatic piece for the stage, must be convinced of the primacy of the vocal invention in the score and must be capable of placing the main emphasis of the thematic (or melodic) expression on the musically interpreted word. A Schubert song, an aria by Mozart or Verdi, expresses in the melodically inspired vocal line, even set apart from the accompanying instrument or orchestra, the essential nature of a sensation, of a situation, of a scenic or natural impression. The text set to music and centered upon the basic singing voice stands in the center; everything else is mere addition, accessory, ornamentation, detail which is more or less important; and this may be learned again and again from countless examples from the above-named masters, from the simple individual melody to the complicated and artfully intricate ensemble.

The extremities of depth and height should not be surpassed, wherever possible, unless it be that effects of a special dramatic or drastic nature are deliberately intended by the composer. But even then, one must be aware that the singer's recitative is not limited alone to the production of mere sound or to a picture in sound, which is the case of any other instrument, but that the very elements of language, vowels and consonants, must be transposed into sound, brought intimately close to the production of sound. When Anton Webern in his distorted canonical exercises for soprano and two clarinets (and here I am citing only one terrible example from many!) demands for the word "mundo" the interval quoted in Example XVII, 7, then this demand certainly represents proof of a Utopian boldness in invention. But to a similar degree it is a sign of inexperience or, at best, of deliberate disregard in the use of range and an infraction of the limits of the human voice, which does have its natural limitations both in depth and in height. This method should never have found imitators, but it did—unfortunately! In a similar way, false stresses, the trick of giving long note values to short syllables and vice versa, are no less annoying than the fashion of using interval leaps with no consideration of a quickening or lessening of word-rhythm, merely for the sake of satisfying the tyranny of an *ad hoc* train of thought.

All of these things are insults to the poet, deeds of violence not unlike the murderous love act of certain spiders, in which the male partner is killed and eaten by the female after the marriage ceremony. "All this in honor of the twelve-tone system, that it may produce nice music." We might put it this way, something like Hagen's diabolically ironic comment in the second act of *Götterdämmerung*. Just so that I may not be misunderstood: there is no objection to the atmospheric power, the condensed form of some individual chamber music and orchestral works by Webern, nor to dodecaphony as a highly interesting, ingenious discovery of many other technical possibilities. The great Schoenberg undoubtedly developed it from the chromatic harmony of *Tristan;* Dallapiccola, the leading representative of the Italian moderns, has shown what a melodic richness can be extracted from it. But it is a method of composition, no more and no less, and its use alone by no means guarantees a finished artistic result.

In this connection, perhaps an essay by me on the theme "Word and

Tone in Contemporary Music" has attained a certain fame. It has been reprinted frequently in professional journals and newspapers, and I have often given it as a lecture—recently at the International Composers' Congress in Stratford, Ontario, in August, 1960, and again at the opening of the 1961 Contemporary Music Festival in Kassel. Standing in closest intimacy to the thoughts that it contains and the assaults that it makes upon certain prejudices is a considerable part of my pedagogical work, with its growing list of engagements in interpretative courses for singers and pianists both in Germany and abroad, courses that have to do with the formation of the lied from the classic-romantic repertoire down to contemporary times.

That portion of my work that I consider successful and worth-while is available in print, as may be seen from the catalogue published by the Schott Verlag. For purposes of completeness, I may mention the following unpublished works: Opus 1, "Antagonismus" for two pianos; Opus 2, "Sonata for Piano"; Opus 4 to 6 were attempts at song composition; Opus 8 to 15, chamber music of varying instrumentation (among them, as Opus 10, a "Piano Trio" performed for the first time in 1923 at the Donaueschingen Chamber Music Festival); Opus 16 was my first choral attempt, the cantata "Gesang vom Tode" (first performance was at the Donaueschingen Music Festival in 1926); Opus 17 was an "Introduktion, Passacaglia und Fuge" for two pianos; Opus 18 a volume of lieder. Everything from Opus 19 on exists in print, with the exception of a violin concerto (Opus 39) and a few occasional pieces.

For some time now the North German Radio in Hamburg has been presenting so-called "Self-Portraits" of artists and composers, under the direction of Josep Müller-Marein and Hannes Reinhardt. To be sure, these draw upon the total career and work of the subject. In 1961, on the occasion of my birthday, the pleasant task and honor fell to me to contribute to this series of portraits, centering on my works from the years 1923 to 1959, thus not including the *Triptychon*. In this essay, in the spirit suggested to me by Robert Stephan Hines, I have attempted to approach my subject in the opposite way, not so much through general discussion, but rather by more specific points, penetrating into the very heart of my being and extracting the essence, as it were, by self-evaluation and by boldness of personal crystallization.

I have written many choral compositions more expansive than the *Triptychon,* as is shown in my catalogue, among them even an oratorio, *Der grosse Kalender,* which requires an entire evening for its performance. But nowhere else are the insights gained from earlier experiences so concentrated and so united as in the short twenty-three minutes of the Schiller triptych—the imitative technique of two similar voices, diatonic, diagonal, polytonal voice-crossings, finely detailed and madrigal-like vocalizings that chromatically twine about a fixed vocal center, a melodically outpouring lyricism in the solo tenor, powerful polyphonic development derived from the old Netherlands masters, and precise declamation of the text in the rhythmically moving sections—in short, everything that I have been able to discover in the way of worthy and telling effects in previous choral works, be they *a cappella* or accompanied by instruments, is here presented and brought together in concise fashion. In this way, perhaps, the second "portrait" has been successful in satisfying the New World's request in a few well-filled pages, giving the composer's own view, but giving also a modest vision that projects itself from the ego-bound into the realm of the all-embracing, in effect a time portrait of some documentary value. What better thing could have happened, and what more can one ask than this?

PART FOUR

Musical Examples

Example I, 1

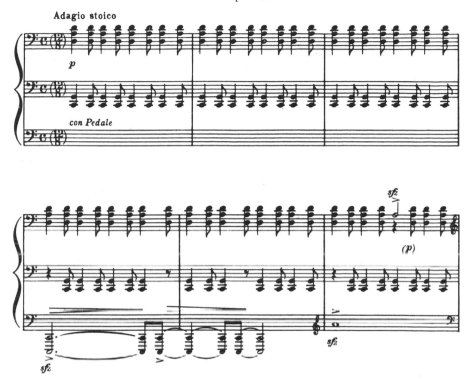

Example I, 2

Example I, 2 (continued)

Example I, 3

Example I, 4

Example I, 4 (continued)

Example I, 5

Example I, 5 (continued)

Example I, 6

ERNST KRENEK

Example II, 1

O=Original   J=Inversion
I=First; II=second half of the basic tone-row
△=Diatonic; ×=chromatic six-tone patterns

Examples II, 1–6, used by permission Bärenreiter Music Publishers, Inc., New York and Kassel.

Example II, 2

A - leph.

Example II, 3

Example II, 4

Example II, 5

Example II, 6

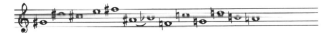

R=Retrograde version of O   RJ=Retrograde version of J
O*=Major third higher   O**=R of first half of O[1]

[1] In these retrograde versions, the melody is reconstructed backwards—the last note of O being the first note of R, and the last note of J being the first note of RJ. For musical variety, the composer does this on different pitch levels. (This is a device dating back to the Renaissance but recently brought into common usage again by the twelve-tone school which includes Krenek and Dallapiccola.) O* is, as Krenek says, a major third higher, exact. O** is a retrograde version of O from the ninth note of O to the first.—R.S.H.

Example III, 1

Examples III, 1–6, copyright 1949 by Carl Fischer, Inc., New York. Used by permission.

Example III, 2

Example III, 3

246

Example III, 4

Example III, 5

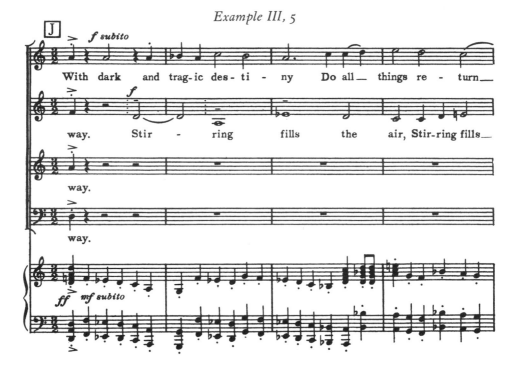

Example III, 6

Example III, 6 (continued)

VINCENT PERSICHETTI

Example IV, 1

Examples IV, 1–3, used by permission Elkan-Vogel Co., Inc., Philadelphia.

Example IV, 3

Example V, 1

Example V, 2

Example V, 3

Example V, 4

Examples V, 1–8, used by permission Elkan-Vogel Co., Inc., Philadelphia.

Example V, 5

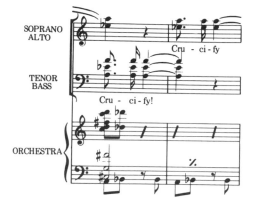

Example V, 6

Example V, 7

Example V, 8

LEO SOWERBY

Example VI, 1

Example VI, 2

Worthy is the Lamb that was slain to re-ceive pow'r, and rich-es, and

wis-dom, and strength,

Wor - thy

255

Example VI, 3

Example VI, 4

Example VI, 5

Example VI, 6

Example VI, 7

Sal-va-tion, and glo-ry, and hon-or, and pow'r, un-to the Lord our God.

Example VI, 8

Example VI, 9

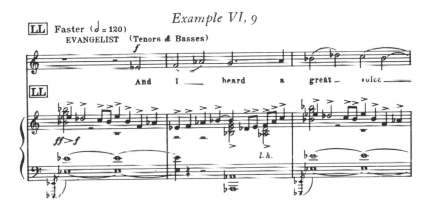

LL Faster (♩ = 120)
EVANGELIST (Tenors & Basses)

And I ___ heard a great ___ voice ___

Example VI, 10

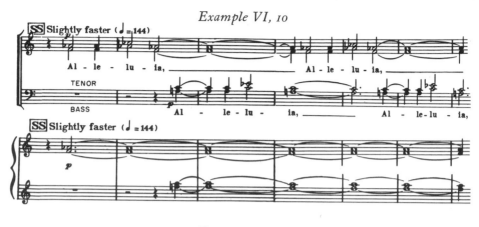

Example VI, 11

Example VI, 12

Example VI, 13

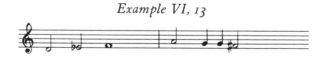

PETER RACINE FRICKER

Example VII, 1

Example VII, 2

Example VII, 3

Example VII, 4

Example VII, 5

Example VII, 5 (continued)

ANTHONY MILNER

Example VIII, 1

By night___ u-pon my bed I sought him whom my soul___ loveth. I sought him, but I found him not; I called him, but he gave no an-swer.

Example VIII, 2

Example VIII, 3

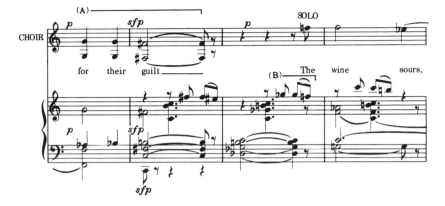

Example VIII, 4

Example VIII, 5

Adagio molto (♩=60)

(Solo) TENOR

I looked on the earth,___ and lo,___ it was waste and void, and to the

Example VIII, 6

Molto lento (♩=50)

(Solo) TENOR

Out of the deep I cry to Thee: Lord, hear my voice. If Thou, O Lord,

wilt mark in - i - qui-ties, Lord, who shall a - bide it?

Example VIII, 7

Example VIII, 8

Example VIII, 9

Example VIII, 10

Example VIII, 11

Example VIII, 12

Example VIII, 13

Let noth-ing dis-turb you, noth-ing af-fright you. All things are passing; God never changes.

Who God pos-ses-es in noth-ing is want-ing; A-lone God suf-fi-ces.

Example VIII, 14

EDMUND RUBBRA

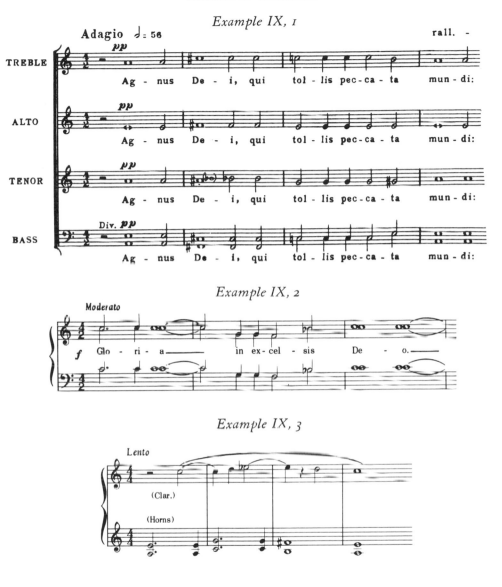

Example IX, 1

Example IX, 2

Example IX, 3

Examples IX, 1–9, used by permission Alfred Lengnick & Co., Ltd., London.

273

Example IX, 4

Example IX, 5

Example IX, 6

Example IX, 7

Example IX, 8

Example IX, 9

Example X, 1

Example X, 2

Example X, 3

CONRAD BECK

Example XI, 1

Example XI, 2

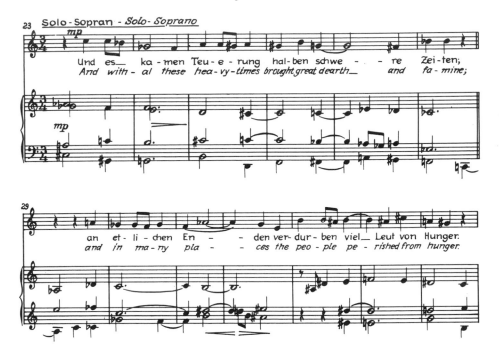

Example XI, 3

Example XI, 4

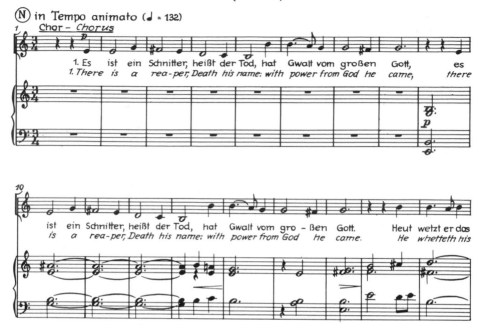

Example XI, 5

KARL-BIRGER BLOMDAHL

Example XII, 1

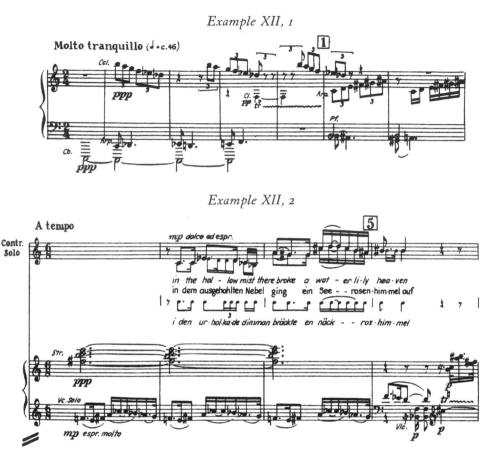

Example XII, 2

Example XII, 3

Example XII, 4

Example XII, 5

Example XII, 6

Example XII, 7

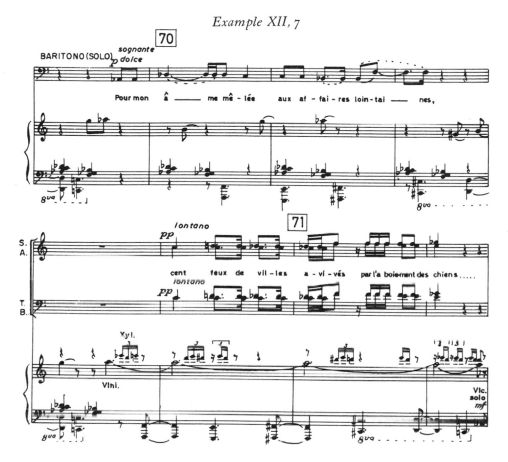

Example XII, 8

Example XII, 9

LUIGI DALLAPICCOLA

Example XIII, 1

Examples XIII, 1–4, used by permission Edizioni Suvini Zerboni, Milan.

Example XIII, 1 (continued)

Example XIII, 2

Example XIII, 3

Example XIII, 4

294

Example XIII, 4 (continued)

295

JEAN FRANÇAIX

Example XIV, 1

Example XIV, 2

Example XIV, 3

Example XIV, 4

Example XIV, 5

Example XIV, 6

Example XIV, 6 (continued)

Example XIV, 7

Example XIV, 8

Example XV, 1

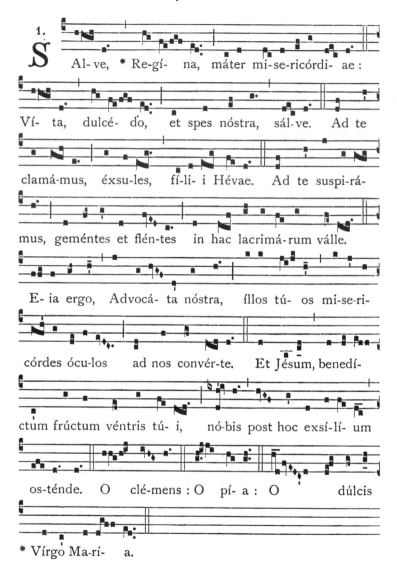

1.
S Al- ve, * Re-gí- na, máter mi-se-ricórdi- ae :

Ví- ta, dulcé- do, et spes nóstra, sál- ve. Ad te

clamá-mus, éxsu-les, fí-li- i Hévae. Ad te suspi-rá-

mus, geméntes et flén-tes in hac lacrimá-rum válle.

E- ia ergo, Advocá- ta nóstra, íllos tú- os mi-se-ri-

córdes ócu-los ad nos convér-te. Et Jésum, benedí-

ctum frúctum véntris tú- i, nó-bis post hoc exsí-lí- um

os-ténde. O clé-mens : O pí- a : O dúlcis

* Vírgo Ma-rí- a.

Example XV, 1 (from page 276 of the *Liber Usualis*), used by special permission of Desclée & Co., Tournai, Belgium; Examples XV, 2a–3b, used by permission Éditions Costallat, Paris.

Ⓔ *Example XV, 2a*

Cum— sanc – to spi – ri – tu   in   glo — ri —

-a — De-i Pa – tris

Example XV, 2b

Example XV, 3a

Example XV, 3b

FRANK MARTIN

Example XVI, 1

Example XVI, 1 (continued)

Example XVI, 2

Example XVI, 3

St. Marc. XIV. 53. 55-65

Example XVI, 3 (continued)

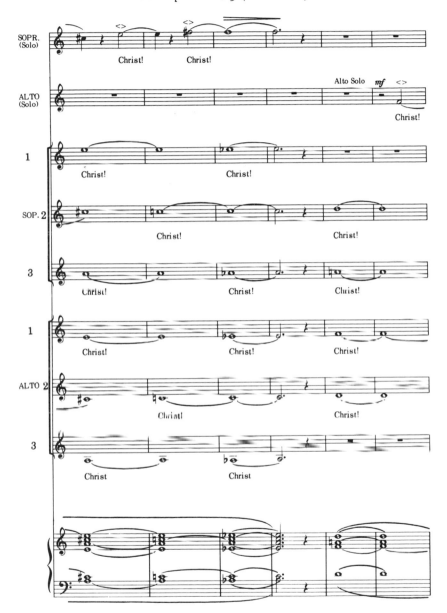

HERMANN REUTTER

Example XVII, 1

Example XVII, 2

Example XVII, 3

Example XVII, 4

Example XVII, 5

Example XVII, 6

Example XVII, 7

mundo

CATALOGUES OF COMPOSERS' WORKS

FOLLOWING is a list of abbreviations used for the publishers in these Catalogues of Composers' Works:

AMP	Associated Music Publishers, Inc., New York
Augener	Augener, Ltd., London
Bibliothèque de la Radio	Bibliothèque de la Radio Paris
Birchard	C.C. Birchard (now Summy-Birchard Publishing Co.), Evanston, Illinois
BMC	Boston Music Co., Boston
Boosey	Boosey and Hawkes, New York, London
Bornemann	S. Bornemann, Paris
BV	Bärenreiter Music Publishers, Inc., New York, Kassel
Carisch	Carisch, Milan
CF	Carl Fischer, Inc., New York
Consortium	Consortium Musical, Paris
Costallat	Éditions Costallat, Paris
Durand	Durand & Cie., Paris
Ernst Vogel	Ernst Vogel, Basel
EV	Elkan-Vogel Co., Inc., Philadelphia
FitzSimons	H. T. FitzSimons Co., Chicago
Gregorian Inst.	Gregorian Institute of America, Toledo, Ohio
Gray	H. W. Gray Co., New York
GS	G. Schirmer, Inc., New York
Hänssler-Verlag	Friedrich Hänssler-Verlag, Stuttgart-Plieningen
Hug	Hug & Co., Zurich
J. Fischer	J. Fischer & Bro., Glen Rock, New Jersey
Lehrmittelverlag	Lehrmittelverlag, Basel
Lemoine	Lemoine, Paris
Lengnick	Alfred Lengnick & Co., Ltd., London
Librairie de l'État	Librairie de l'État, Berne

L'Isle de France	Presse de l'Isle de France, Paris
McLaughlin	McLaughlin & Reilly Co., Boston
Mercury	Mercury Music Corp., New York
Mills	Mills Music, Inc., New York
MP	Music Press, New York (Century Music)
MS	Not published—in manuscript form only
Müller & Schrade	Müller & Schrade, Berne
Novello	Novello & Co., Ltd., London
Oxford	Oxford University Press, London, New York
Philippo	Éditions Philippo, Paris
Revue Améric.	Revue Américaine, Augsburg Publishing House, Minneapolis
Revue Inter.	Revue International de Musique, Paris
Rongwen	Rongwen Music Inc., New York
Schola	Éditions Musicales de la Schola Cantorum, Paris
Schott	Schott and Sons, Mainz, London, New York
Schweiz. Kirchengesangsbund	Schweizer Kirchengesangsbund, Zurich
Schweizerspiegel	Schweizer Spiegelverlag, Zurich
Southern	Southern Music Publishing Co., New York
Stainer	Stainer & Bell, Ltd., London
Summy	Summy-Birchard Publishing Co., Evanston, Illinois
Suvini	Edizioni Suvini Zerboni, Milan
UE	Universal Edition, Vienna, London, New York
Verlag Schweiz.	Verlag Schweizer Musikpädagegisches Verband, Zurich
Williams	Joseph Williams, Ltd., London
World Library	World Library of Sacred Music, Cincinnati, Ohio
Zanibon	Zanibon Edizioni, Padua
Zürcher Liederbuchanstalt	Zürcher Liederbuchanstalt, Zurich

LUKAS FOSS

Choral Music

"Cantata Dramatica" for chorus and orchestra, MS, 1940.

"We Sing," cantata for children plus piano and drums, MS, 1941.

The Prairie, cantata for four solo voices, mixed chorus, and orchestra, GS, 1942.

Adon Olom for tenor solo, mixed chorus, and organ, GS, 1947.

Behold! I Build an House, biblical cantata for mixed chorus and organ, or piano, Mercury, 1950.

A Parable of Death for narrator, tenor, mixed chorus, and orchestra, or chamber group, CF, 1952.

Psalms for mixed chorus and orchestra, or two pianos, CF, 1955–56.

HOWARD HANSON

Choral Music

Opus 25. *The Lament for Beowulf* for mixed chorus and orchestra, Summy, 1925.

Opus 28. "Heroic Elegy" for mixed chorus—without words and orchestra, MS, 1927.

Opus 32. *Songs from "Drum Taps"* (after Walt Whitman) for baritone solo, mixed chorus, and orchestra, J. Fischer, 1935.

Hymn for the Pioneers for male voices, J. Fischer, 1938.

Transcription of Palestrina's *Pope Marcellus Mass* (Kyrie, Gloria, and Credo) for mixed chorus and large orchestra, J. Fischer, 1937.

Opus 39. *The Cherubic Hymn* for mixed chorus and orchestra, CF, 1950.

Opus 41. *How Excellent Thy Name* for mixed chorus and piano, CF, 1952.

Song of Democracy for mixed chorus and orchestra, CF, 1957.

ERNST KRENEK

Choral Music

Opus 14. *Zwingburg (The Tyrant's Castle),* scenic cantata, UE, 1922.

Opus 22. *Three Choruses* (M. Claudius), *a cappella,* UE, 1923.

Opus 32. *Four Small Choruses* (Hölderlin) for men's voices *a cappella* with contralto solo, UE, 1924.

Opus 35. *Die Jahreszeiten (The Seasons)* (Hölderlin), four mixed choruses *a cappella,* UE (German), AMP (English), 1925.

Opus 47. *Four Mixed Choruses* (Goethe), *a cappella,* UE, 1926.

Opus 51. "Little Cantata" (Goethe), mixed chorus *a cappella,* MS, 1927.

Opus 61. *Three Mixed Choruses* (G. Keller), *a cappella,* UE, 1929.

Opus 72. *Kantate von der Vergaenglichkeit des Irdischen (Cantata on the Transitoriness of Earthly Things)* (Poets of the seventeenth century), mixed chorus, soprano solo, and piano, UE, 1932.

321

Opus 74. "Jagd im Winter (Hunt in Wintertime)" (F. Grillparzer), male voices, MS, 1933.

Opus 87. "Two Choruses" (W. Drummond, Sir W. Raleigh) for women's voices *a cappella,* MS, 1939.

Opus 89. *Proprium Missae in Festo SS. Innocentium,* women's voices *a cappella,* Mills, 1941.

Opus 93. *Lamentatio Jeremiae Prophetae,* mixed chorus *a cappella,* BV, 1941–42.

Opus 95. *Cantata for Wartime* (H. Melville), women's voices and orchestra, Schott/UE, 1943.

Opus 97. *Five Prayers* (J. Donne), women's voices *a cappella,* UE, 1944.

Opus 102. "The Santa Fe Timetable," mixed chorus *a cappella,* MS, 1945.

Opus 103. "Aegrotavit Ezechias," motet for women's voices and piano, MS, 1945.

Opus 106. "In Paradisum," motet for women's voices *a cappella,* MS, 1946.

Opus 109. *O Would I Were,* canon for mixed chorus *a cappella,* MP/Mercury, 1946.

Opus 138. *Four Religious Choruses* for mixed chorus, Mills, 1953.

Opus 141. *Veni Sanctificator,* mixed chorus (SAB) *a cappella,* Schott/UE, 1954.

Opus 143. *Proprium Missae in Dom. III in Quard.,* mixed chorus (SAB) *a cappella,* Schott/UE, 1954.

Opus 149. *Psalm Verses,* women's voices, mixed chorus (SAB and SATB) *a cappella,* Schott/UE, 1955.

Opus 151. *I singe wieder, wenn es tagt,* mixed chorus and string orchestra or string quartet, Schott/UE, 1955–56.

Opus 152. "Spiritus intelligentiae, sanctus," oratorio for voices and electronic sounds, MS, 1956.

Opus 159. *Good Morning, America,* mixed chorus *a cappella,* Schott/UE, 1956.

Opus 165. *Missa Duodecim Tonorum,* chorus and organ, Gregorian Inst., 1957.

Opus 169. *Six Motets* (F. Kafka), mixed chorus *a cappella,* BV, 1959.

Opus 174. *Children's Songs* (3 madrigals, 3 motets, 2 rounds), women's voices *a cappella,* Rongwen, 1960.

PETER MENNIN

"Alleluia" for mixed chorus, MS, 1941.

Symphony No. 4, "The Cycle," for mixed chorus and orchestra, CF, 1948.

Four A Cappella *Choruses* for mixed chorus, CF, 1948.

Two Choruses for women's voices (SSA) with piano, CF, 1949.

The Christmas Story, cantata for mixed chorus with soprano and tenor soloists, CF, 1949.

VINCENT PERSICHETTI

Choral Music

Opus 8. "Magnificat" for mixed chorus and piano, MS, 1940.

Opus 31. *Three Canons for voices,* MP, 1947.

Opus 33. *Two Cummings Choruses* for mixed chorus, GS, 1948.

Opus 34. *Proverb* for mixed chorus, EV, 1948.

Opus 46. *Two Cummings Choruses* for women's voices, CF, 1950.

Opus 68. *Hymns and Responses for the Church Year,* EV, 1955.

Opus 78. *Seek the Highest* for mixed chorus (SAB), EV, 1957.

Opus 82. *Song of Peace* for male voices, EV, 1959.

Opus 84. *Mass* for mixed chorus *a cappella,* EV, 1960.

BERNARD ROGERS

Choral Music

The Raising of Lazarus, cantata, Birchard, 1927.

The Exodus, cantata, Birchard, 1932.

The Passion for solo voices, mixed chorus, and orchestra, EV, 1941–42.

A Letter from Pete (Whitman), cantata for soprano and tenor soloists, mixed chorus, and small or large orchestra, Southern, 1943.

"Response to Silent Prayer" for mixed chorus, MS, 1945.

The Prophet Isaiah, cantata for soprano, tenor, and baritone soloists, mixed chorus, and orchestra, Southern, 1954.

LEO SOWERBY

Anthems with Organ

The Lord Bless Thee and Keep Thee, BMC, 1916.

The Risen Lord, BMC, 1919.

I Will Lift up Mine Eyes, BMC, 1919.

The Lord Reigneth, BMC, 1919.

Song of Immortal Hope, BMC, 1920.

Psalm 134 (unaccompanied), BMC, 1923.

Make a Joyful Noise unto the Lord, BMC, 1924.

When the Lord Turned Again (unaccompanied), Gray, 1926.

Motet: O dearest Jesus, FitzSimons, 1926.

The Invitatories (unaccompanied), BMC, 1928.

Agnus Dei in D (unaccompanied), BMC, 1928.

Sentence from the Burial Office, BMC, 1928.

Like the Beams that from the Sun, Gray, 1930.

All They from Saba Shall Come, Gray, 1934.

Now There Lightens upon Us, Gray, 1934.

Love Came Down at Christmas for mixed or women's voices, FitzSimons, 1935.

O Light, from Age to Age (unaccompanied), Gray, 1936.

O Jesus, Thou the Beauty Art (SSA), Gray, 1938.

Blessed Are All They (Psalm 128), Gray, 1939.

Tu es vas electionis (unaccompanied), Gray, 1940.

I Was Glad (Psalm 22), Gray, 1941.

"De Profundis (Psalm 130)" for male voices, MS, 1942.

Good King Wenceslas, Gray, 1943.

Come Holy Ghost (Veni Creator), Gray, 1949.

All Things are Thine, Gray, 1949.

Not unto Us, O Lord (Psalm 115) (unaccompanied), Gray, 1949.

Come Ye and Let Us Go Up, Gray, 1952.

The Snow Lay on the Ground, Gray, 1952.

The Armor of God, Gray, 1953.

Fight the Good Fight of Faith (unaccompanied), Gray, 1953.

Cradle Song, Gray, 1953.

Manger Carol, Gray, 1954.

An Angel Stood by the Altar of the Temple, Gray, 1955.

I Will Love Thee, O Lord, Gray, 1955.

My Heart Is Fixed, O God, Gray, 1955.

I Call with My Whole Heart (unaccompanied), Gray, 1956.

Turn Thou to Thy God, Gray, 1957.

Cradle Hymn, Gray, 1957.

Thou Hallowed Chosen Morn, Gray, 1958.

Eternal Light, Gray, 1958.

Away in a Manger, Gray, 1958.

Motet: Seeing We Also (unaccompanied), FitzSimons, 1958.

Motet: Ad te levai animan meam (Psalm 24), Summy, 1959.

Jesu, Bright and Morning Star, Oxford, 1959.

My Master Hath a Garden, Gray, 1959.

I Sing a Song of the Saints of God (arr.), Gray, 1959.

There Comes a Ship a'Sailing, FitzSimons, 1959.
Little Jesus, Sweetly Sleep, FitzSimons, 1959.
And They Drew Nigh, Gray, 1960.
Come, Holy Ghost, Draw Near Us, Oxford, 1960.
The Lord Ascendeth up on High, Oxford, 1960.
All Hail, Adored Trinity, Oxford, 1960.
The Righteous Live for Evermore, Oxford, 1960.
Martyr of God, Oxford, 1960.

Cantatas with Organ

A Liturgy of Hope for soprano solo and male voices, BMC, 1917.
Great is the Lord (Psalm 48), Gray, 1933.
Forsaken of Man, Gray, 1939.
Christ Reborn, Gray, 1950.

Choral Music with Orchestra

Large work in five parts, unnamed and unperformed, MS, 1923–24.
The Vision of Sir Launfal, Birchard, 1925.
Great is the Lord (Psalm 48) with orchestra and organ, Gray, 1933.
Song for America, Gray, 1942.
Canticle of the Sun, Gray, 1943.
The Throne of God, Gray, 1956.

Services with Organ

Benedictus in B-flat, Gray, 1928.
Jubilate in B-flat, Gray, 1928.
Benedicite in D minor, Gray, 1929.
Te Deum in B-flat, Gray, 1930.
Benedictus in D minor, Gray, 1930.
Magnificat and Nunc Dimittis in D, Gray, 1930.
Office of the Holy Communion in C (unaccompanied), Gray, 1930.
Benedictus in D minor, Gray, 1933.
Te Deum in D minor, FitzSimons, 1933.
Office of the Holy Communion in B minor, Gray, 1934.
Office of the Holy Communion in E (unison), Gray, 1937.
Benedictus es, Domine (Mixolydian Mode) (unison), FitzSimons, 1941.
Benedictus es, Domine, in C (unison), Gray, 1942.
Jubilate in C (unison), Gray, 1942.
Benedictus in C (unison), Gray, 1942.
Office of the Holy Communion in F, Gray, 1954.

Office of the Holy Communion in G, Gray, 1958.
Magnificat and Nunc Dimittis in E minor, Gray, 1959.

PETER RACINE FRICKER

Choral Music

Opus 4. "Two Madrigals," MS, 1947 (withdrawn).
Rollant et Oliver, three fragments from the *Song of Roland* for mixed chorus *a cappella,* Schott, 1949.

Opus 27. *Musick's Empire* for mixed chorus and small orchestra, Schott, 1955.
Two Carols (fourteenth-century texts), Oxford, 1956.

Opus 29. *The Vision of Judgement* for soprano and tenor soloists, mixed chorus, and orchestra, Schott, 1957–58.
"Colet," cantata for school chorus and orchestra, MS, 1959.

ANTHONY MILNER

Choral Music

Opus 1. *Salutatio Angelica,* cantata for contralto, small chorus, and chamber orchestra, UE, 1948.

Opus 3. *Mass* for mixed chorus *a cappella,* UE, 1951.

Opus 6b. *Blessed Are All They,* anthem for mixed chorus *a cappella,* Novello, 1955.

Opus 7. *The City of Desolation,* cantata for soprano, mixed chorus, and orchestra, UE, 1955.

Opus 8. *St. Francis,* cantata for tenor, mixed chorus, and orchestra, Novello, 1956.

Opus 9. *The Harrowing of Hell,* cantata, for tenor and bass solos, and double chorus *a cappella,* MS, 195–.

Opus 10–1. *Benedic Anima Mea Dominum,* motet for double chorus *a cappella,* UE, 1954.

Opus 10–2. *Christus factus est,* motet for eight-part chorus *a cappella,* UE, 1959.

Opus 12. *Cast Wide the Folding Doorways of the East,* part-song for mixed chorus *a cappella,* UE, 1957.

Opus 13–1. *I Have Surely Built Thee,* anthem for mixed chorus and organ, Novello, 1958.

Opus 13–2. *Anthem for St. Cecilia's Day* for mixed chorus and organ, Novello, 1958.

Opus 13–3. *Praise the Lord of Heaven,* anthem for mixed chorus and organ, Novello, 1959.

Opus 15. *The Bee's Song* for three-part women's voices *a cappella,* UE, 1959.

There Was a Ship of Rio for two-part women's voices *a cappella,* UE, 1959.

The Lost Shoe for three-part women's voices *a cappella,* UE, 1959.

The Old House for three-part women's voices *a cappella,* UE, 1959.

Silver for three-part women's voices *a cappella,* UE, 1959.

Dream Song, King Caraway, The Cupboard, songs for children, UE, 1959.

Opus 16. *The Water and the Fire,* oratorio for soprano, tenor, and bass solos, boy's chorus, full chorus, organ, and orchestra, Novello, 1961.

Turbae for the Passion of St. John, Novello, 1958.

Out of Your Sleep, carol for two parts and piano, MS, 19—.

Compline for congregational use, Novello, 1956.

EDMUND RUBBRA

Choral Music

Virgin's Cradle Hymn for mixed chorus *a cappella,* Oxford, 1921.

Opus 1. "The Secret Hymnody, Gnostic Hymn" (translated by G. R. S. Mead), chorus and orchestra, MS, 1921.

Opus 6. *Afton Water,* arranged for mixed chorus *a cappella,* Lengnick, 1922.

Opus 10. *My Tochers the Jewel,* arranged for mixed chorus *a cappella,* Lengnick, 1924.

Opus 12. "La Belle Dame sans Merci" (Keats) for mixed chorus and orchestra, MS, 1925.

Opus 37. *Five Motets* (Vaughan, Herrick, Donne, Crashaw) for mixed chorus *a cappella,* Augener, 1934.

Opus 41–1. *Dark Night of the Soul* (St. John of the Cross) for mixed chorus and orchestra, Williams, 1935.

Opus 41–2. *O Unwithered Eagle Void* (Cecil Collins) for mixed chorus and orchestra, MS, 1935.

Opus 46. *Three Bird Songs* for children's voices, Oxford, 1937.

Opus 51. *Five Madrigals* (Campion) for mixed chorus *a cappella*, Augener, 1940.

Opus 52. *Two Madrigals* (Campion) for mixed chorus *a cappella*, Boosey, 1941.

Opus 55. *The Morning Watch* (Vaughan) for mixed chorus and orchestra, Lengnick, 1941.

Opus 58. *The Revival*, motet for mixed chorus *a cappella*, Boosey, 1945.

Opus 59. *Mass* (Canterbury Mass) for double mixed chorus with organ for Creed only, Lengnick, 1945.

Opus 61. *Three Psalms* for mixed chorus *a cappella*, Lengnick, 1946.

Opus 65. *Magnificat and Nunc Dimitis in A-flat* for mixed chorus and organ, Lengnick, 1948.

Opus 66. *Missa in Honorem Sancti Dominici* for mixed chorus *a cappella*, Lengnick, 1949.

Opus 71. *Festical Te Deum* for soprano solo, mixed chorus, orchestra, and organ (also arranged by C. S. Lang for voices and organ), Lengnick, 1950.

Opus 72. *Three Lamentations* (Tenebrae) for mixed chorus *a cappella*, Lengnick, 1950.

Opus 76. *Three Motets* for mixed chorus *a cappella*, Lengnick, 1952.

Opus 78. *Song of the Soul in Intimate Communication and Union with the Love of God* (St. John of the Cross, translated by Roy Campbell) for mixed chorus, strings, harp, and timpani, Lengnick, 1952.

Opus 81. *Star of the Mystic East* (C. H. O. Daniel), carol for mixed chorus *a cappella*, Lengnick, 1952.

Opus 82. *Salutation* for mixed chorus *a cappella*, Lengnick and Stainer, 1953.

Opus 84. *Dance to your Daddie* for mixed chorus *a cappella*, Lengnick, 1954.

Opus 90. *Portuguese Folk Song*, arranged for mixed chorus *a cappella*, Lengnick, 1956.

Opus 93. *Entrezy tous en surete*, carol for mixed chorus *a cappella*, Lengnick, 1956.

Opus 94. *Festival Gloria* for soprano and baritone soloists and double mixed chorus *a cappella*, Lengnick, 1957.

Opus 95. *Haes est Domus Domini* for mixed chorus *a cappella*, Lengnick, 1957. (Also published in English.)

Opus 96. *The Givers* for mixed chorus *a cappella*, Lengnick, 1957.

Opus 97. *In Honorem Mariae Matris Dei,* cantata for soprano and contralto soloists, mixed chorus, children's voices, and organ, Lengnick, 1957.

Opus 98. *Missa á 3* for mixed chorus (S A or T B) *a cappella,* Lengnick, 1957.

Opus 99. *Autumn* for women's voices and piano, Lengnick, 1958.

Opus 107. *Lord, with What Care* for mixed chorus *a cappella,* Lengnick, 1960.

Opus 108. *Up, O My Soul* for mixed chorus *a cappella,* Lengnick, 1960.

Opus 109. *The Beatitudes* for women's voices *a cappella,* Lengnick, 1960.

Opus 110. *Lauda Sion* for double mixed chorus *a cappella,* Lengnick, 1960.

MICHAEL TIPPETT

Choral Music

A Child of Our Time, oratorio, Schott, 1941.

Plebs Angelica, anthem for double mixed chorus *a cappella,* Schott, 1943.

The Weeping Babe, motet for mixed chorus *a cappella,* Schott, 1944.

The Source for mixed chorus *a cappella,* Schott, 1944.

The Windhover for mixed chorus *a cappella,* Schott, 1944.

Dance, Clarion Air for mixed chorus *a cappella,* Schott, 1956.

Crown of the Year, cantata for girl's school, Schott, 1959.

Four Songs from the British Isles for mixed chorus *a cappella,* Schott, 1959.

Bonny at Morn for unison voices and recorders, Schott, 1959.

Lullaby for six-part small mixed chorus *a cappella,* Schott, 1960.

CONRAD BECK

Choral Music

Lösung (Wolfensberger) for mixed chorus, Zürcher Liederbuchanstalt, 1920.

Der Tod des Oedipus (Morax-Weber), cantata for soprano, tenor, and bass soloists, mixed chorus, two trumpets, two trombones, timpani, and organ, Schott, 1928.

Requiem for mixed chorus *a cappella,* Schott, 1930.

Es geht eine dunkle Wolke ein for mixed chorus *a cappella,* Schott, 1930.

Es kummt ein Schiff geladen for mixed chorus *a cappella,* Schott, 1931.

Der Rover Feldgeschrei (Bolt) for one- and two-part chorus, Schott, 1932.

Vier Frauenchöre for *a cappella* voices, Schott, 1932.

Fünf gemischte Chore for *a cappella* chorus, Schott, 1932.

Lyrische Kantate (Rilke) for soprano and alto soloists, women's voices, and orchestra, Schott, 1932.

"Oratorium nach Sprüchen des Angelus Silesius" for soprano, alto, tenor, and bass soloists, mixed chorus, orchestra, and organ, MS, 1934.

Freude (Unknown) for male voices *a cappella,* Hug, 1938.

Ecce gratum (Carmina Burana) for two-part chorus, solo voice, and piano, Hug, 1938.

Es ist alles ganz eitel (Bible), motet for mixed chorus, Schweiz. Kirchengesangsbund, 1939.

Basler Trummlelied (Knuchel) for three-part children's voices, drum, and piano, Ernst Vogel, 1944.

S'Resslilied (Knuchel) for three-part children's voices and piano, Ernst Vogel, 1944.

Dr rot Fade (Knuchel) for three-part children's voices and piano, Ernst Vogel, 1944.

"Sommerlied" (Gerhardt) for women's voices and orchestra, MS, 1946.

Der Schweizer (Lavater) for male voices *a cappella,* Hug, 1948.

Der Tod zu Basel: Ein grosses Miserere for soprano and bass soloists, three speakers, mixed chorus, and orchestra, Schott, 1952.

Introitus für den Busstag "Aus der Tiefe rufe ich Herr zu Dir" for three-part chorus, Hänssler-Verlag, 1960.

Es ist ein köstlich Ding (Bible), motet for three-part chorus, Hänssler-Verlag, 1960.

Ein Musikus wollt' frölich sein (Unknown) for male voices, Hug, 19—.

Glauben (Haller) for mixed chorus, MS, 19—.

Kharaya (de Rougemont) for women's voices, Librairie l'État, 19—.

Le muezin (Unknown) for three-part children's voices, MS, 19—.

Septämber (Muller), one- and two-part children's voices, Lehrmittelverlag, 19—.

Uff der Fähri (Keller), one- and two-part children's voices, Lehrmittelverlag, 19—.

Wyssi Flocke falle (Keller), one- and two-part children's voices, Lehrmittelverlag, 19—.

Für d'Heimet (Moser), two-part soldiers' song, MS, 19—.

Feu d'automne (De Rougemont) for two-part women's voices, Librairie de l'État, 19—.

Ich hab die Nacht geträumet (Beck) for mixed chorus *a cappella,* Müller & Schade, 19—.

Viel Freuden mit sich bringet (Beck) for mixed chorus *a cappella,* Müller & Schade, 19—.

Mensch, nichts ist unvollkommen (Silesius), two-part canon for medium voices, Verlag Schweiz., 1933.

O Durchbrecher aller Bande (Arnold), unison voices and organ, MS, 19—.

Weihnachtslied: "Gelobet seist du," unison voices, violin, and piano, Schweizerspiegel, 19—.

KARL-BIRGER BLOMDAHL

Choral Music

In the Hall of Mirrors (nine sonnets from *The Man without a Way* by Erik Lindegren) for soprano, alto, tenor, baritone, and bass solos, mixed chorus, and orchestra, Schott, 1951–52.

Anabase for baritone solo, reciter, mixed chorus, and orchestra, Schott, 1956.

LUIGI DALLAPICCOLA

Choral Music

"Due Canzoni di Grado" (Biagio Marin) for chamber women's voices, mezzo-soprano, and chamber orchestra, MS, 1927.

"Due Laudi di Fra Jacopone da Todi" for mixed chorus, soprano, and baritone soloists and chamber orchestra, MS, 1929.

"La canzone del Quarnaro" (Gabriele D'Annunzio) for men's voices, tenor soloist, and orchestra, MS, 1930.

Due Liriche del Kalewala (Translated by P. E. Pavolini) for chamber mixed choir and two soloists, Revue Inter., 1930.

Estate (Alceo) for male voices *a cappella*, Zanibon, 1932.

Sei Cori di Michelangelo Buonarroti il Giovane: First Series for mixed chorus *a cappella*, Second Series for women's chamber voices or two soprano and two alto soloists and seventeen instruments; Third Series for mixed chorus and full orchestra; Carisch, 1933–36.

Canti di Prigionia (Mary Stuart, Boethius, and Savonarola) for mixed chorus and orchestra, Carisch, 1938–41.

Canti di Liberazione (Exodus, St. Augustine) for mixed chorus and orchestra, Suvini, 1952–55.

Requiescant (St. Matthew, Oscar Wilde, James Joyce) for mixed chorus and orchestra, Suvini, 1957–58.

Opera

Volo di Notte (Saint-Exupéry), opera in one act, UE, 1937–39.

Il Ritorno di Ulisse in Patria of Monteverdi (transcription and arrangement for the modern stage), Suvini, 1941–42.

331

Il Prigioniero (Villiers de l'Isle-Adam, Charles de Coster), prologue and opera in one act, Suvini, 1944–48.

Job, sacred stage presentation, Suvini, 1950.

JEAN FRANÇAIX

Choral Music

Cinq Chansons pour les enfants for two-part children's voices and orchestra, Schott, 1932.

"Trois Épigrammes" for mixed chorus and string quintet, MS, 1938.

L'Apocalypse selon Saint Jean, oratorio for soprano, alto, tenor, and bass solos, mixed chorus, and two orchestras, Schott, 1939.

"Deux Motets" for mixed chorus and organ, MS, 1946.

Cantate satirique (Juvenal) for mixed chorus and piano four-hands, Schott, 1947.

Ode à la gastronomie for mixed chorus *a cappella,* Bibliothèque de la Radio, 1953.

JEAN LANGLAIS

Choral Music

Duex chansons (Clément Marot) for mixed chorus *a cappella,* Consortium, 1931.

Cinq motets for two women's voices and organ, Consortium, 1932/42.

"La Voix du Vent" (hymn) for mixed chorus, soprano solo, and orchestra, MS, 1934.

"Duex Psaumes" (in French): CXXIII for soprano and tenor soloists, chorus, organ, and orchestra; LVIII for mixed chorus and organ, MS, 1937.

"Tantum ergo" for eight voices and organ, MS, 1940.

Mystère du Vendrei Saint: Misere Mei for mixed chorus and organ; *O Crux Ave* for mixed chorus, orchestra, and organ, Durand, 1943.

"Cantate à St Vincent" for mixed chorus and string orchestra, MS, 1946.

"Cantate à St Grignion de Montfort" for three-part women's voices, three trumpets (ad lib.), and organ, MS, 1947.

Trois Priéres for voice, unison chorus, and organ, Bornemann, 1949.

Messe solennelle for mixed chorus and two organs (ad lib.), Schola, 1949.

"Musique de scène sur 'Le soleil se leva sur Assise' " (Vidalie) for orchestra, small orchestra, three Ondes Martenot, three-part women's voices, and three-part men's voices, MS, 1950.

"Fuite en Egypte et Massacre des Innocents" (Loys Masson) for soloists, mixed chorus, and orchestra, MS, 1951.

Mass in Ancient Style for mixed chorus and organ (ad lib.), McLaughlin, 1952.

Advent the Promise for mixed chorus *a cappella,* Revue améric, 1952.

Trois chansons populaires bretonnes for three-part women's voices *a cappella,* Lemoine, 1954.

Missa Salve Regina for three-part male voices, unison chorus, two organs, three trumpets, and five trombones, Costallat, 1954.

Lauda Jerusalem Dominum for mixed chorus, congregation, and organ, Consortium, 1954.

"Prélude, Fugue, et Chacone" for mixed chorus *a cappella,* MS, 1956.

"La Passion" (Loys Masson) for mixed chorus, eight soloists, narrator, and orchestra, MS, 1957.

"Regina coeli" for two-part women's voices and organ, MS, 1958.

Cantate: En ovale comme un jet d'eau (Lequien) for mixed chorus and recorder, l'Ile de France, 1958.

Psaume CL (in English) for three-part male voices and organ, McLaughlin, 1958.

Missa misericordia domini for three-part chorus and organ, Gregorian Inst., 1958.

Venite et audite, motet for mixed chorus *a cappella,* Schola, 1958.

Sacerdos & Pontifex (Tu es Petrus) for unison chorus, organ, and two trumpets, World Library, 1959.

"Trois Noels" harmonized for mixed chorus *a cappella,* MS, 1959.

"Trois Noels" harmonized for four-part male voices, MS, 1959.

Noels populaires anciens for mixed chorus *a cappella,* Philippo, 1960.

Neuf chansons folkloriques françaises for unison chorus, soloists (ad lib.) with piano, Philippo, 1960.

"Propre pour le mercredi des Cendres," motet for mixed chorus a cappella, MS, 1960.

"Nouveaux chants français pourla Messe, MS, 1961.

"Ave Maris stella" for three equal voices, MS, 1961.

"O God our Father" for mixed chorus and organ, MS, 1961.

"Praise to the Lord," arrangement for mixed chorus, organ, and brass, MS, 1961.

"Harmonisation à 6 voix mixtes de deux chansons," MS, 1961.

FRANK MARTIN

Choral Music

Le vin herbé (based on *The Romance of Tristan and Yseut,* as done in modern French by Joseph Bédier), secular oratorio, for twelve soloists, two violins, two violas, two cellos, one bass, and piano, UE, 1941.

In terra pax, oratorio breve, for two mixed choruses, children's voices, soprano, alto, tenor, baritone, and bass soloists, and orchestra, UE, 1944.

"Musique de scène et choeurs pour l'Athalie de Racine" for two choruses of young girls, alto solo, and small orchestra, MS, 1946.

Golgotha, oratorio for mixed chorus, soprano, alto, tenor, baritone, and bass soloists, orchestra, and organ, UE, 1948.

Pseaumes for mixed chorus, boy's choir, orchestra, and organ, UE, 1958.

Mystère de la nativité (based on Arnoul Gréban's passion play of the fifteenth century), oratorio or stage presentation for two mixed choruses and a minimum of nine soloists (one soprano, one alto, three tenors, two baritones, and two basses), and orchestra, UE, 1959.

HERMANN REUTTER

Choral Music

Opus 34. *Die Rückkehr des verlorenen Sohnes,* chamber oratorio in five scenes, Schott, 1952. (New version of *Der verlorene Sohn.*)

Opus 37. *Der neue Hiob: ein Lehrstück* (Robert Seitz) for six soloists, two-part chorus of like or mixed voices, violins, cellos, two pianos, and viola, bass (ad lib.), Schott, 1930.

Opus 38a. *Vier Bettellieder* for mixed chorus *a cappella,* Schott, 1930.

Opus 43. *Der grosse Kalender* (Ludwig Andersen) oratorio for soprano and baritone soloists, mixed chorus, children's voices, orchestra, and organ, Schott, 1933.

Opus 44. *Der glückliche Bauer,* a cantata after songs of Matthias Claudius for one or two mixed voices or male voices with instruments, Schott, 1932.

Opus 49. *Gesang des Deutschen* (Hölderlin), cantata for soprano and baritone soloists, mixed chorus, and orchestra, Schott, 1938.

Opus 52. *Chorfantasie* (Goethe) for soprano and baritone soloists, mixed chorus, and orchestra, Schott, 1939.

Opus 53. *Hochzeitslieder* (Herders) for mixed chorus and piano, Schott, 1941.

Opus 71. *Drei Madrigale* for mixed chorus *a cappella,* Schott, 1950.

CATALOGUES OF COMPOSERS' WORKS

Opus 72. *Pandora* (Goethe), cantata for soprano and baritone soloists, mixed chorus, and orchestra, Schott, 1949.
Hymne an Deutschland for female, male, or mixed chorus and piano, large orchestra, small orchestra, or band, Schott, 1950.
"Sechs Chöre" for mixed chorus and large wind ensemble, MS, 1951.
Drei Gleichnisse aus dem Neuen Testament for mixed chorus a cappella, Schott, 1959.
Triptychon for tenor soloist, mixed chorus, and orchestra, Schott, 1959.

THE composers who have contributed to this book are listed in the index only when mention of them appears outside their own essays. The composers' music is listed in the index under the heading musical examples.—R.S.H.

339

THE COMPOSER'S POINT OF VIEW